VOICE IN THE WILDERNESS

VOICE IN THE WILDERNESS

IMRE NAGY and THE HUNGARIAN REVOLUTION

PETER UNWIN

WITH A FOREWORD BY THE
PRESIDENT OF THE HUNGARIAN
REPUBLIC, ÁRPÁD GÖNCZ

Macdonald

A *Macdonald* Book

First published in Great Britain in 1991 by
Macdonald & Co (Publishers) Ltd
London & Sydney

A CIP catalogue record for this book
is available from the British Library.

ISBN 0 356 20316 6

Photoset in North Wales by
Derek Doyle & Associates, Mold, Clwyd
Printed and bound in Great Britain by
BPCC Hazell Books
Aylesbury, Bucks, England
Member of BPCC Ltd.

Macdonald & Co (Publishers) Ltd
165 Great Dover Street
London SE1 4YA
A member of Maxwell Macmillan Publishing Corporation

CONTENTS

The Author

Peter Unwin was the British Ambassador to Hungary from 1983 to 1986, having served there before as a young man. The views expressed in this book are personal and do not necessarily reflect those of the British government.

FOREWORD

There are three reasons why I am particularly glad to
introduce this book.

In the first place, it captures for a non-Hungarian
audience the dramatic, tragic and ultimately hopeful story
of Hungary's twentieth-century history. It shows what
Hungarians have endured and achieved in Hungary's last
tumultuous decades. By doing so it provides a background
to the work of the Hungarian government and people as
they seek to build a better place for Hungary within a wider
European community.

Secondly, the book is a reminder that Hungary has
always had friends in the West as it has today. The author
first came to Hungary in the worst of years, 1958. Imre
Nagy and his companions were executed just before he
arrived. Many other Hungarian patriots, myself among
them, were in prison. The country was prostrate; but it
captured Peter Unwin's imagination. His book shows that
his concern for Hungary, conceived then, has remained
vigorous over more than three decades. He came back to
Budapest as Her Majesty's Ambassador in 1983 when
things in Hungary were better and filled with promise. And

he was with us again in 1989 for Imre Nagy's reburial, when Hungarians threw off the alien authoritarianism which ruled them for more than forty years.

And lastly, the book captures the essence of Imre Nagy himself. A good Communist and a good Hungarian, he was eventually destroyed by the tyranny which Moscow imposed on his country. But in his life, as prime minister between 1953 and 1955 and again in the tumultuous days of the Revolution, he gave Hungary hope and unity. In his death he preserved the pride of a broken nation. And for three decades afterwards his memory prodded the Communist regime in Hungary into more human and patriotic policies.

So I welcome *Voice in the Wilderness* and look forward to the publication before too long of a Hungarian edition.

Árpád Göncz
President of the Republic of Hungary
Budapest
8 March 1991

Prologue

OBSESSION

Puzzles obsess most of us in their different ways. Crosswords have their followers. So do jigsaws. This book tries to solve a different kind of puzzle. It is the enigma of an ambiguous personality who lived his life on a shifting border between two empires of the mind, one called Communism, the other everyday humanity.

Until he was sixty Imre Nagy was an obscure political figure, distinguished only by an unsuccessful attempt to build a more humane Communism in Hungary after Stalin's death. He reappeared suddenly on the political stage in 1956, an improbable hero who nevertheless captured the world's attention for a dramatic and tragic month. Then he vanished into captivity. In 1958 came his secret trial and execution. For a week his name again dominated the headlines. Then came oblivion. For thirty years, Nagy was a man the world forgot.

Only in Europe's year of miracles, thirty-one years after he died, did his story return to the headlines. Hungary broke with the past which had destroyed him. In June 1989, he was rehabilitated and ceremonially reburied. The reburial released demands for freedom, truth and justice. Within the year most of Eastern Europe followed Hungary's lead. Suddenly the questions which Nagy posed so long ago were the issues of the streets. Hungary, Poland, Czechoslovakia, East Germany, even Rumania, prepared to resolve in the nineties the contradictions with which he had struggled in the fifties, a decade before Dubcek, three before Walesa. The forgotten man's legacy became today's agenda.

So Nagy's story is much more than a story which took place in Hungary. It typifies the tragedy which engulfed Central and Eastern Europe under Stalin and long afterwards. More generally, the conflicts of his life, between Party and country, power and people, noble ends and squalid means, these are the conflicts of all politics, in all countries. But it is a story which belongs especially to Hungary and is central to much of its twentieth-century history.

I first became conscious of Hungary in February 1949, seven years before I first heard of Imre Nagy. I was sixteen, an over-serious schoolboy, preoccupied on the one hand with world affairs and on the other with my Catholic faith. The two preoccupations came together with the trial of József Mindszenty, the Primate of Hungary. Mindszenty pleaded guilty to manifestly false charges. He was clearly a broken man, prepared for a show trial by torture. He seemed to stand for faith and people against ruthless authoritarianism. There had been those in the West who had welcomed Communism's coming to Eastern Europe. By the time of the Mindszenty trial few saw it as anything other than a catastrophe, and an irreversible catastrophe at that.

The Hungarian Revolution in 1956 called the second half of that proposition in question. The Hungarians suddenly attempted what twentieth-century experience was supposed to have proved impossible: the overthrow by force of an authoritarian regime. For a few unforgettable days they seemed to be succeeding. Imre Nagy played a central part in their success. Before the Revolution he had seemed to stand for a more gentle, humane kind of Communism. Now the portly middle-aged Communist came to terms with the insurgents and united the Hungarian people. In doing so he accepted that his Party would have to take its chances in a real democracy.

Then the Soviet Union went to war with Hungary. Nagy refused to yield. The Hungarians went down to inevitable defeat, but their courage created a legend. A passing character in a forgettable film a few years later captured the point: 'Funny people, these Hungarians. We thought them a nation of gypsies, and then they astonish the world.'

In 1956 I had just started work in the Foreign Office, in a department concerned with the Middle East. The Suez crisis was growing. But my mind was on Hungary, where the issues seemed infinitely more important than those in the dispute with Nasser. And when, after Suez, my colleagues were preoccupied with the argument about collusion and its impact on our position in the Middle East, I cared more about the bearing of our intervention on the much bloodier Soviet intervention in Hungary.

Eighteen months later, in the spring of 1958, I was told that my first posting was to be to Budapest. In those days one did not ask for appointments with any expectation of getting them; but I was delighted by this one. I started to learn Hungarian, to re-read the story of those tragic thirteen days in 1956. Then, on 17 June, a horrified world heard the news of Imre Nagy's execution. My obsession with the man was born, and I set myself to unravel the enigma which runs through this book. We went ahead with our preparations to uproot ourselves and two small children. A friend wrote that we seemed admirably a for people about to settle in a graveyard. On 6 July we set off for Budapest in a car overloaded with luggage, toys and babies' paraphernalia.

We came to a country heavy with fear. The physical damage of 1944 and 1956 was all round. Terror was palpable. There had been trials and executions before Nagy's, and they continued afterwards. Diplomats lived largely cut off from all except token Hungarians: local employees in the legation, the doctor, the dentist, Foreign

Ministry officials. One sensed that ordinary people were as isolated from one another by fear as they were from us.

Someone took me to the diplomatic petrol pump. It stood in the Fö Utca in Buda, beside the military prison in which Imre Nagy was condemned. I was summoned to the Foreign Ministry, to be told that a Hungarian employee of the legation arrested a year earlier was about to be put on trial. The charge was that after the Revolution he had smuggled Nagy's testament to the West, where it had been published a year later. Just round the corner from the Foreign Ministry stood the statue of General Bem, where the demonstrators in October 1956 had first cut the Communist symbol out of the Hungarian tricolour.

For a year my work in the legation consisted largely of logging rumours: of arrests, trials, sentences and executions. Once a boy took the insane risk of slipping into the legation behind the back of the policeman on duty. He told me that his father in Ujpest, an industrial suburb, had been sentenced to death. What could I do to save him? A story appeared in the Western press, but I never found out whether it stopped a hanging.

Meanwhile I continued to brood on the enigma of Imre Nagy. I studied the regime's White Book about his 'criminal conspiracy'. I read Nagy's own testament, *On Communism*. I read the memoirs of émigrés who had known him and the United Nations special committee's report on the Revolution. I pored over his last broadcast as the Russian tanks closed in on the parliament building. None of my reading helped me resolve what I saw as the central question: was Nagy, when he declared his country's neutrality and condemned the Soviet invasion, and later, when he went to the gallows, the convinced Muscovite Communist he had been all his adult life, or a disillusioned man who was left at the last with only his Hungarian patriotism?

I spent nearly three years in Hungary. At first, János Kádár seemed intent only on fastening an authoritarian yoke back more securely on the nation. To post-revolutionary punishment he added new oppression. Between 1959 and

1961 the peasants were forced back into the cooperatives from which Nagy had released them. The methods used were arbitrary, sometimes violent. Official language about the Revolution was mendacious, about the Soviet Union nauseating, about the West hysterical. The police and the Workers' Guard were to be seen everywhere, the secret police knew everything. Hungary in those years may not have sunk to the depths of the early fifties, but it was a frightened and sick society. When we flew away for the last time in 1961 and saw stretched out below us the Rákoskeresztür cemetery, where we already suspected that Nagy and the other victims of 1956 were buried, it seemed a fitting epitaph on our experiences there.

Yet even before we left Hungary, there were signs that another story was beginning to unfold. I went to Debrecen to call on the Mayor and was astonished at the warmth with which ordinary people greeted him, a good Communist, as we walked down the main street. Once I found myself seated in the opera just behind György Marosán, one of the more hateable of the Communist leaders. He seemed to be unguarded. And there were signs even earlier. Photographs of the May Day celebrations in 1957 show Kádár at ease with what look like very ordinary people.

Throughout the sixties, things continued to improve. Kádár proclaimed that 'he who is not against us is with us', reversing Communist as well as New Testament orthodoxy. In 1963 a major amnesty followed a number of minor ones. Very few political prisoners remained in gaol. As the agricultural cooperatives became established, pressure on the peasants was eased. They were encouraged to work on their private plots, which became miracles of productivity. Preparations for the Economic Reform began. It was intended to decentralize decision-making, encourage initiative, give greater play to market forces. The United Nations dropped its annual examination of 'The Problem of Hungary'. Hungary began to be seen as the most relaxed of Communist states.

In the mid-sixties, I started work on this book. There

was little material: the press and public statements from the Revolution, Nagy's essays, émigré memoirs, a few more scholarly studies of recent Hungarian history. But there were no Hungarian or Soviet documents. I put the draft aside.

The Economic Reform was officially launched on 1 January 1968 after three years' debate and preparation. Within the year, it was overshadowed by the Soviet invasion of Czechoslovakia, so redolent of 1956 in Hungary. Kádár let it be known that just before the attack he had tried to warn Dubcek – 'Do you *really* not know the kind of people you're dealing with?'[1] – and tried to resist pressure for Hungarian involvement in the invasion; but Hungarian troops moved shamefacedly into Slovakia. Thereafter, Kádár went back to his efforts to build a more stable Communist Hungary, reconciled by greater prosperity and a little greater personal freedom to continued Hungarian subservience to Moscow. His kind of Communism began to look like Imre Nagy's.

But Nagy himself remained officially forgotten. When I went back to live in Hungary in 1983 I still had to temper my curiosity about him with discretion. Questions about Nagy probed all the neuralgic points in Hungarian politics, the matters that were never discussed. They were a reminder, for example, that János Kádár, elder statesman that he had become, had deserted his own Prime Minister and come back to take power in a Soviet armoured car. They recalled, too, that Kádár had signed Nagy's safe conduct when he left the Yugoslav Embassy in 1956 and the warrant for his execution two years later. There were still 40,000 Soviet troops in Hungary: it did not do to dwell on the memory of a man who had negotiated their withdrawal and taken Hungary out of the Warsaw Pact when they returned. And Party members did not like to reflect on how little authority their Party would exercise if Soviet troops were ever withdrawn.

There was also a feeling that questions about Nagy were might-have-beens, at the far end of twenty-five years of history. Hungary had to get on with the leadership it had, within the parameters established by the tragedy of 1956. At all costs, Hungary must never again provoke Moscow; and Moscow and the Party must never again provoke the people. When I mentioned Nagy's name to Party members they dismissed him as a dreamer, a waverer, a man given more than his due by Western exploitation of his execution.

All the same, there was in the early eighties a suppressed fascination, particularly among young people, with the Revolution and with Imre Nagy. On the twenty-fifth anniversary, the Party published an analysis of the 'Counter-Revolution'. It condemned Nagy but whetted interest in him. The dissidents took up his case; one of them composed a poem about a lost grave and lost bones, in which the initials I.N. pointedly recur. Two émigré writers asked: 'But in the end, after all of this, who will predict with certainty that there will be no public funeral for Imre Nagy in Budapest?'[2]

I certainly would not. I used to take visitors on a tour of the sights of the Revolution: the Petöfi and Bem statues, the radio building and parliament, Republic Square and the Rajk grave in Kerepesi cemetery. It did not seem entirely fanciful to end at the monument to Lájos Batthyány, another prime minister executed for leading Hungary against an oppressor, and ask how long it would be before Nagy had a similar memorial.

I accompanied János Kádár on his official visit to Britain in 1985. I asked him once how soon after the Revolution he had felt that things were stabilizing. Much earlier than he had expected, he told me; May Day, 1957, had been a revelation to him. I drew his attention to the skill of our police escort and he answered, without irony, that he knew something about police work from his time as Minister of the Interior; but the problem then had not been traffic but rubble. Only once did I hint that there was another view of Hungary than his Party's. As we got into our car I saw my son among the crowd.

'That boy there is my son. He was born in Budapest.'

'He looks like you.'

'I'll let you into a secret. Cardinal Mindszenty baptized him in the American Embassy in 1960.'

'Are you a Catholic or an Anglican?'

'A Catholic.'

'We won't tell them that in Whitehall.'

Thus Kádár turned aside a reference to one of his Party's victims. I did not dare to test him with a reference to Nagy. It was self-evident that as long as Kádár lasted there would be no rehabilitation for the man he had destroyed.

I left Hungary in May 1986. It seemed to me then that I might just live to see the day when the bumptious, brilliant, bloody Hungarians to whom I felt so close achieved something approaching national and personal freedom as we understood it in the West. Six months earlier I had told a schoolboy audience that they might see that day but I would not. At the time I feared that I was falling into the wishful thinking of a diplomat who had stayed too long. In fact, I erred wildly on the side of pessimism.

Three things produced a sudden acceleration in the glacial progress of change in Hungary. Under Gorbachev, the Soviet Union was becoming a dramatically different overlord. In Hungary, economic decline spread the conviction that change was needed to avoid catastrophe. But at seventy-six Kádár was no longer able to cope with change. In 1988 his Party pushed him aside. Out of office he could no longer veto the changes that would lead ineluctably to a re-examination of the past, uncovering so many bones and laying them at his door.

Dissent and opposition had begun to show themselves more boldly in the early eighties. Critics of the system talked about what had happened in 1956 and afterwards, and about necessary change. From the moment Kádár was driven from power, demands for the truth about the past and guarantees for the future were advanced more boldly. The focus of debate shifted. Gradually discussion of the pros and cons of Reform Communism faded away. Discussion of how best to arrange the smooth transfer of power from the Party to parliamentary democracy took its place.

When I visited Budapest in June 1989 for Nagy's reburial the situation had changed more in the three years since I left than in the twenty-two years I had been away before. People felt that pluralist democracy was within reach. The reflective were fearful: of Moscow's impatience, of the neighbours, and of the possibility that demands for change might spiral out of control. There were no doubts that old-style Communism was finished. I asked a Communist veteran of forty years at the top whether power was slipping out of his Party's grasp. 'Not slipping,' he said. 'It has slipped.'[3]

The reburial of Imre Nagy began the European year of miracles. In six months East Germany, Czechoslovakia and Rumania followed Poland and Hungary out of the wasteland of Communism. The Poles and Hungarians had been isolated, tentative, fearful that their search for democracy, national identity and a respect for human beings might yet be reversed. Within six months of the reburial the search had become the East European norm and was spreading into the Soviet Union. As the nineties began the countries of what had once been Stalin's empire buried Communism and embraced the values which Nagy had been the first Communist to articulate in the fifties.

There remain many questions about Imre Nagy. Did he die a Communist or a patriot? Would he stand today for Reform Communism or for democracy? How far did his ideas on a Communism which did not forget man shape the policies of his successor? How central is his role in giving Hungary and what was once the Communist world a chance to build a decent society, more than thirty years after his death? And will Hungarians remember him, as they remember Rákoczi, Zrinyi, Kossuth and Batthyány, as a central figure in their embattled history?

Chapter 1

REBURIAL

On 16 June 1989 the mortal remains of Imre Nagy were reburied in Budapest. Four of his associates were reburied with him. A sixth, empty coffin symbolized the other victims of the repression which followed the defeat of the 1956 Revolution.

By any standards, it was a considerable occasion, the focus of attention for the whole nation. '*Jól temetünk*,' the Hungarians say; 'We lay on a good funeral.' It was also a significant occasion, the latest of a long series of reburials which punctuate Hungarian history. It marked a major step in the process of Imre Nagy's rehabilitation. It had also a contemporary relevance. Justice for the dead of the Revolution asserted the power of their heirs. Reform Communists and the new opposition were building a new Hungary.

So the reburial was a major milestone in the process of political change in Hungary. Change there was part of a broader process. In Poland, Eastern Europe's first free elections for forty years had completed the humiliation of the Communist Party. In Western Europe, the peoples of the Community were electing a new European Parliament. People in West and East were weighing Gorbachev's chances of survival. And in Tiananmen Square the Chinese leadership had just provided a vivid reminder of what authoritarian rulers could do to over-zealous democrats, as the Russians had done in Hungary in 1956.

The exact date of the reburial was significant. It was thirty-one years to the day after the execution of Miklós Gimes, Pál Maléter, and Imre Nagy. With József Szilágyi, executed earlier, and Géza Losonczy, who had died in prison, these three had been the leading Communist members of the government which had tried to keep the Revolution within bounds and, when forced to a choice, had stood with the Revolution and against the Russians. They had been tried in secret and executed at dawn on 16 June 1958. The death sentences were announced only after they had been carried out. Several other defendants were sentenced to long terms of imprisonment.

The executions had shocked Hungary. There had been many executions already after the defeat of the Revolution. But the execution of the leaders, the legal Prime Minister among them, demonstrated that the Soviet leaders would stop at nothing to punish heresy and that János Kádár would go to the very end of the road on which he had set out. A mendacious, unconvincing White Book appeared, describing the 'conspiracy'. The regime's supporters justified the executions, as did official spokesmen throughout the Communist world. The Hungarian people awaited more arrests and trials.

The West denounced the executions. Governments expressed horror, crowds marched on Hungarian legations. Emigrés analysed the regime's announcement and the White Book line by line. The universal conclusion was that the four men were the victims of judicial murder calculated to deter anyone else in the Soviet bloc who thought of resisting Moscow.

The place of the reburial was as significant as the date. It took place in the Rákoskeresztür cemetery in Budapest, away from the centre of the city in the industrial suburbs. Nagy and his colleagues were reburied where they had lain for thirty years in unmarked graves. In the days before the reburial, the macabre story of their original burial had gradually come to light.

Nagy, Maléter, Szilágyi and Gimes were hanged in the

Central Prison of Budapest. It stands across Kozma Utca from the main entrance of the Rákoskeresztür cemetery. Others who had fought in 1956 had been executed there before them. They were buried in Rákoskeresztür, not in the civil plots but far away in a remote corner of the cemetery, in a plot, number 301, reserved for criminals. Graves here were not marked and relatives were given no information about them. Here it was assumed Nagy and his companions had lain since their execution.

When the decision to give them an honourable reburial was taken, it was difficult to identify their graves. When the bodies were exhumed it became apparent that Nagy, Maléter and Gimes had not been buried in Rákoskeresztür in 1958, but two years later. Presumably the regime at the time believed that burial in graves theoretically accessible to the public carried too great a risk of demonstration and disorder. So the bodies were temporarily buried in the Central Prison courtyard, to be dumped secretly in plot 301 with the other criminals of 1956 when feelings had cooled.

There were other macabre stories. The bodies were found wrapped crudely in tar paper, buried face down. It was alleged that their faces had been battered, that police horses had been brought in to trample down the graves. It was a fact that for thirty years plot 301 was abandoned, overgrown, littered with rubble. Families were forbidden to tend the plot in which their husbands and fathers lay. The security police blocked the way to Western journalists who went to look at the criminals' plot in Rákoskeresztür.

But the families remembered their dead and exchanged rumours over the years. The suspicion that they lay in plot 301 became a conviction. Memories of the Revolution remained vivid, in Hungary and among the émigrés. His friends, in prison or in exile, remembered Nagy's own contribution. As times changed and reform succeeded repression, even Kádár's policies started to remind people of Nagy. They seemed to reflect the policies which Nagy had pioneered.

Finally, in 1988, power slipped out of Kádár's hands.

The demand for Nagy's rehabilitation swelled. The man with the greatest interest in suppressing his memory no longer controlled events. At first his successors feared the present day consequences of giving ground, and in June 1988 they broke up a crowd of young people who demonstrated in Nagy's memory. But justice for the dead was inextricably tied up with the movement for reform, towards democracy. You could not build a decent society, it was argued, on the basis of lies about the past. Men and women who had been close to Nagy set up the Committee for Historical Justice. Under pressure, Grósz, Kádár's successor, conceded a reburial, if not yet an official rehabilitation. The bones were identified, and the families and their friends went ahead with plans for a ceremony to honour the dead and at the same time make a clear if discreet political statement.

Perhaps two thousand people gathered around the coffins in Rákoskeresztür cemetery on 16 June. They were relatives, friends, former comrades of the men to be reburied and of all the others buried in plot 301. The arrangements had been firmly retained in the hands of the Committee for Historical Justice, an association of those who had been close to Nagy and other leaders of the Revolution in 1956. The state provided unarmed troops to line the track through the trees to the plot. City buses brought the mourners. But there were no police, no representatives of the state or the Communist Party. Only Hungarian television represented the public interest in the occasion.

The coffins were placed on black catafalques along one side of a stretch of grass among the trees. This was plot 300, next to 301, as yet unused. Since the exhumations both plots had been cleared of rubbish, the undergrowth cut back. Plot 300, had been re-grassed, to create a seemly clearing flanked by trees, the high rear wall of the cemetery, and the crowded plot 301.

Vaguely funereal music played as the congregation gathered. It was a bright June day under a hot sun. A disembodied voice started to recite the names of the men buried or to be reburied there. It provided ages also, and the date of execution. The order was alphabetical. When it came to the name of Miklós Gimes his coffin was brought forward to a grave in the middle of plot 300. Family and friends moved around it with flaming torches. A speech of farewell was delivered. The recital of names continued. Losonczy's turn came and then Maléter's. Their remains too were brought to new graves.

The list came eventually to the name of Imre Nagy. His coffin too was brought forward. But then it was taken in procession from plot 300 to 301, to the same grave where Nagy had lain since 1960. His daughter led the mourners. A long speech followed, part personal, part political. A sudden wind blew up, the sun disappeared behind clouds, there was a flurry of rain. Finally Nagy was reburied in the midst of the ordinary freedom fighters of 1956, a hundred yards from the graves of the men who had gone to the scaffold with him. His grave is closely surrounded by others, some marked with a simple name slab, others only with the traditional wooden grave stakes.

The decision to bury Nagy there, in plot 301 rather than 300 and in suburban Rákoskeresztür rather than the Communist Pantheon of Kerepesi in the heart of the city, was a personal one, taken by Nagy's only daughter, Erzsébet. It denied Nagy and his companions burial among Hungary's great; they were buried instead beside the simple men of the Revolution. Erzsébet Nagy's decision created at a stroke an alternative focus for Hungarian patriotism. It was as if she wanted to draw a clear line between the authoritarianism of the past and Hungary's democratic future. Within days the grave became a place of patriotic pilgrimage. Within a month visiting Western statesmen were including a visit to it in their programmes.

The Hungarian people followed the reburial at Rákoskeresztür on television, but they were present in their thousands at the ceremony in the heart of Budapest which preceded it. From seven in the morning on 16 June, the six coffins were displayed in Heroes' Square. From eight, people came to pay tribute or to demonstrate their commitment to the building of a new Hungary. An unbroken queue snaked around the square, in front of the Fine Arts Museum, behind the massive monument to the founders of Hungary and round to the Art Gallery facing the museum, on the steps of which the coffins were laid. Black and white draperies swathed the façades. A great white banner with a symbolic black-scorched hole jutted out above the coffins, topped only by television gantries. The same funereal music as at the cemetery played over the loudspeakers.

The crowds, thousands at any one time, hundreds of thousands in the course of the long morning, were hushed. As at the cemetery there were no police. Even the hawkers, selling commemorative magazines, patriotic badges, mementoes of Imre Nagy, were subdued. The atmosphere was not tragic but reverent, reflective. There were people of an age to have fought in 1956, parents with young children, young people. An occasional dark suit punctuated the informality. Half the people brought flowers, a single bloom or a small bunch, to lay before the coffins.

As later at the cemetery, a recitation started. Names, occupations, date of execution, age, read slowly and with reverent drama, in strict alphabetical order. There were over three hundred of them, the names of the men recorded as having been executed after the Revolution and buried in plot 301. Most were in their twenties, a few in their teens, a thicker sprinkling in the thirties or forties. At sixty-two, Nagy was the oldest. His closest associates had been much younger, all born in the same year, forty-one when they died. Perhaps ten per cent of the dead had followed middle-class occupations. There was a good number of officers and soldiers. The great majority had been working men. A butcher and a miner were named immediately after Nagy in the long roll-call. As the names rolled out over the loudspeakers the line of people snaked slowly past the coffins. Beside the coffins, tilted high on the steps of the Gallery, a guard of honour of relatives and companions stood rigidly until, on the half hour, they were relieved.

The recital gave way to speeches, prefaced by an appeal that there should be no applause. The first speaker was Miklós Vásárhelyi, tried with Nagy and sentenced to five years' imprisonment, the closest of Nagy's companions to stay on and make a life in Hungary after his release. He spoke gently about what Nagy had stood for and tried to do. Others followed, speaking with increasing passion, less discretion. One had been in the notorious labour camp at Recsk, and had survived only because Nagy, coming to power for the first time in 1953, had ordered the internees set free. Another, Béla Király, had commanded the National Guard in 1956 and returned to Hungary for the first time for the reburial. One speech provoked a short ripple of applause, the next something still subdued but more sustained. Another ended with a call to the crowds to join hands and swear an emotional oath to ensure that Hungary in future respected the things for which Nagy had died.

The last speaker was a young man from a new political party, the Federation of Democratic Youth, born in the sixties long after Nagy and his companions were dead and officially forgotten. He spoke with a passion and a freedom that his elders had avoided, criticizing openly the Communists, even the Reform Communists, whose Party had murdered Nagy and who came now to honour him and claim him for their own. His words cut through the others' caution and discretion. Two sentences in particular reminded his hearers that they still lived in dangerous times, that there were no guarantees that the forces which had destroyed Imre Nagy would not return. He said that they owed the Communist Party no gratitude because it did not now behave like Li Peng in Tiananmen Square. And he reiterated the demand that the Russians should take their troops home, out of Hungary, so that Hungarians could decide their own future. This time the applause was strong, not tumultuous but heartfelt, political, a clear reminder that the whole occasion was as much a statement about the present and the future as about the crimes and tragedies of thirty years ago.

Reminders of the past were all around. On their way to Heroes' Square the crowds swarmed past the Soviet Embassy, where the Soviet Ambassador, Yuri Andropov, had worked during the tense days of the Revolution, perhaps urging intervention in his telephone calls to Moscow, perhaps arguing that Nagy should be given a chance to save what he could from the disaster which had engulfed his Party. On the corner of Heroes' Square itself stood the Yugoslav Embassy, where Nagy and his companions took refuge in 1956. When the funeral procession finally set off towards the cemetery it took the same route as Nagy's party took when the bus that was supposed to carry them to their homes under safe conduct bore them instead into Soviet captivity.

From first to last the reburial was as much about 1989 as about the year of the Revolution or the year of the executions. It was taking place only because events had at last moved beyond the caution and circumspection which had dominated Hungarian policy for over thirty years. That had been a policy of provoking neither Moscow nor the people, giving Moscow political assurance and the people the little freedoms and prosperities which might buy their acquiescence in a hated system. It had been synonymous with the name of János Kádár, the man who had betrayed Nagy, allowed him to go to the gallows, and then tried to build a system under Soviet protection which nevertheless gave Hungarians some of the things Nagy had fought to give them.

The reburial could not have taken place if Kádár had not lost office. And if it represented rehabilitation for Nagy it marked the end of Kádár's reputation. Old and broken, he spent the day of the reburial weeping, endlessly repeating that he had let Nagy hang only because the legal advice he had received had been so mercilessly unambiguous.[1] The funeral was going ahead because the demands for truth about the past, decency towards individuals, democratic guarantees for the future, had become irresistible. The Party had feared the consequences of denying those hopes even more than the dangers of telling the truth and feeding an appetite for more concessions. In rapid succession it had conceded exhumation, a private reburial, the ceremony in Heroes' Square. It asked to be allowed to be represented at this privately organized commemoration. Rationing their favours, the organizers agreed that Party leaders could be present in Heroes' Square, but in a governmental, not a Party, capacity.

The fact that the ceremony was private gave the families and colleagues of the dead and the new political leaders with whom they were associated the chance to demonstrate how little Hungary needed the Party which had battened on it for forty years. The ceremonies in Heroes' Square and Rákoskeresztür cemetery manifested the rebirth of a civil society as the Party's moral and political authority drained away. There were no policemen to control the crowds. No party activist presumed to speak for them. The marshals were civilians, quiet men in 301 armbands. The crowds were simultaneously respectful and demanding, seeing the ceremony as an opportunity both to rebury the dead and record demands for the future.

The battle in Hungary between Reform Communism and democracy did not end on 16 June 1989. As Nagy was reburied the tide seemed to be going democracy's way. Grósz had got rid of Kádár, and was himself about to be displaced by Imre Pozsgay, a Communist who seemed intent on making democratic standpoints his own. But in Hungary as in the Soviet Union, hard men were watching the reformers, reminding them not to provoke Moscow or the neighbours, pointing to the risk of anarchy if power slipped out of the Party's hands. The democratic opposition

seemed frighteningly inexperienced and fragmented, trying
to build organizations in a country where for forty years
only Communists had been allowed political expression.
The economy was menacing, with inflation, unemployment, foreign indebtedness all capable of overwhelming the movement towards democracy. The crowds
on 16 June were moved by hope as well as remembrance;
but there was fear and uneasiness among them too.

All the same, 16 June 1989 was Nagy's day. It recalled
and celebrated what he had done for Hungary. In 1953,
after six years of Communist terror, he had shown the
country that there were Communists who did not forget
man. From 1953 till the spring of 1955, he had tried to
leach terror and manic exaggeration out of Hungarian
politics and economics. Driven from office in 1955, he had
spent the next eighteen months writing and arguing for a
policy of national unity rather than class struggle,
reconciliation rather than oppression. When the 1956
Revolution came he had taken office reluctantly and had
tried to keep popular emotion within bounds. He had
negotiated a Soviet withdrawal. When the Russians
returned, he had declared Hungarian neutrality, withdrawal from the Warsaw Pact, and a multi-party system.
He had fled to the Yugoslav Embassy and resisted pressure
to come to terms with János Kádár. He had resisted the
same pressure in house arrest in Rumania and in prison in
Budapest. At his trial he had refused to recant or ask for
mercy. Stubbornly unbending, he had given Hungary a
dignity in defeat and a national unity which compromise
with Kádár would have destroyed. That record, and its
promise for the future, was what the people of Hungary
were honouring when they gathered in Heroes' Square,
saluted the coffins on the way to the cemetery, or stood in a
nationwide minute's silence to remember the dead.

Chapter 2

YOUTH

In the last eighteen months of his life, Imre Nagy kept a diary. The first thing he recorded in it was that he was born in the year of the millennium. 1896 was a special year in Hungarians' eyes, in which they celebrated the thousandth anniversary of the founding of a Magyar state in the Danube basin. The anniversary was an 'occasion of extraordinary self-congratulation'.[1] It came nearly fifty years after the 1848 rising against the Habsburgs was put down in blood, almost thirty after the Compromise of 1867 gave Hungarians an equal partnership with Austria in the Empire.

Since then they had lorded it over the other nationalities, convinced that they were reasserting a rightful Magyar pre-eminence in the area between Teutons and Slavs. They had seen agriculture flourish, and industry come belatedly to Hungary. Now they celebrated an event which seemed to validate their claim to be one of the historic nations of the Empire, a unique people who had kept their identity and language through a thousand years. Budapest was in the throes of a building boom, which turned it from a small town into a major city in the course of twenty years. The year of the millennium saw the completion of the grandiose Heroes' Square memorial to the Magyar tribal leaders who founded Hungary. The Central Prison was completed in the same year.

In retrospect the 1896 celebrations mark the end of a Hungarian golden age. Disaster was to follow. But there were no forebodings, no sense that the Empire was approaching its end or that Hungarian pre-eminence in the Danube basin was threatened. The social order seemed equally set in adamant. For the possessing, historic classes of Hungary, 1896 was the best of years, an *annus mirabilis*.

The poor joined in the celebrations, as proud as their betters of their Hungarian identity. But objectively they had little to celebrate. Sixteen of the eighteen million people of late nineteenth-century Hungary lived in poverty. The condition of the small urban working class was bad, that of the great legions of the rural poor worse. The landless labourers were at the bottom of the pile. 'It was calculated', wrote Hungary's most objective historian, C.A. Macartney, 'that . . . the labourers got enough to feed themselves and their families adequately only when the harvest had been "exceptionally good" . . . Starvation diseases were common. Hours of work had been lengthened to the extreme limit. The agrarian labour legislation . . . consisted almost exclusively of enactments designed to prevent the labourers from defending their interests against those of the landlords.'[2] Peasants owning small plots of land lived a little better, but with no assurance for the morrow. Even the richer peasants were frustrated by the problems of acquiring land. For Hungary was pre-eminently a country of great estates, in which an Esterhazy told a visiting Englishman that he had as many shepherds as the Englishman had sheep.

There was serious rural over-population, and the situation was not improving. In the early eighteenth century, observers had been astonished by the fertility of the land brought back into cultivation after lying fallow for a century under Turkish occupation. Until the middle years of the nineteenth century, agricultural expansion and work on development projects brought a modest rural prosperity. But the competition from American wheat forced down prices. Estate owners sold out to the banks or to richer, absentee owners. Wages were held down. Emigration could not fully offset the pressure of population. Rural poverty increased. The 1890s saw rural unrest, dealt with firmly by the authorities. In 1891 and 1894 there were disturbances in the towns and villages of the Great Plain. In 1897, the gendarmerie turned out again with fixed bayonets. In the following year strikes by landworkers, hitherto unimaginable, were declared illegal.

The tension which arose from rural poverty was not eased by understanding between the classes. The grandees were infinitely remote. The gentry and the managers thought of the peasantry and labourers as alien beings. The poor went in awe of the gentry. In 1936 the Hungarian poet, Gyula Illyés, recalled his childhood as the son of an agricultural worker: 'How was it then that as far as my eye and imagination could see, the land in all directions belonged to unknown potentates . . .? At very rare intervals their emissaries visited the manor house in a coach-and-four. The common people, stiff with fright, bowed to them and whipped off their hats.'[3]

National and ethnic differences were added to those of class. Each of the minorities – the Slovaks in the north, Rumanians in the east, Slavs, Slovenes and Croats in the south – was subjected to Magyar authority. All were seen by the Hungarians as inferior, non-historic races. In 1896, as before and after, Hungarian politicians were preoccupied with the nationalities question. But there was no concern to accommodate the interests of the nationalities. The object of policy was to bring the non-Magyars to accept their position in a Hungarian state within the Empire and to assimilate them into a Magyar-dominated social and political order.

So Imre Nagy was born in June 1896, into an ordered, complacent Hungary in which social and national injustice was overlaid by sublime Magyar self-confidence. He was born in Kaposvár, the pleasant, sleepy county town of Somogy. Somogy lies in south-west Hungary, between

Lake Balaton and the Yugoslav border. The country is pleasant, gently undulating, fertile, with a soft semi-Mediterranean climate. It has none of the barrenness of upper Hungary or the bleakness of the Great Plain. Its people think of their county as typically Hungarian and yet extraordinary; they call it not Somogy County but Somogy Country.

Nagy was a premature baby, the eldest of four children, the rest of them daughters, in a poor peasant family from Ötvöskónyi, twenty miles from Kaposvár. His father, Jozsef Nagy, was born in the abject poverty of the labourers' barracks on a Somogy estate. He was an enterprising and active man, who escaped from the land to work on the railways. In Kaposvár he improved himself further, getting a job as a handyman and part-time footman in the home of the Sheriff of County Somogy. There he met an upstairs maid. They married, and the Sheriff helped them find a little house in Kaposvár. There the three girls and Imre Nagy were born. The central point is that Nagy was born of poor and simple parents who were nevertheless improving their position in the world.

They were, furthermore, of Calvinist stock. The Calvinists form a substantial minority in predominantly Catholic Hungary. Traditionally they are seen as quintessential Hungarians, untainted by a Catholic Church itself tainted by Habsburg and other non-Magyar influences. There were a few Calvinist magnates, many Calvinist squires in nineteenth-century Hungary. The Calvinists have produced a disproportionate share of Hungary's heroes. They see themselves as the country's backbone, a serious, principled community. Like self-improvement, religion brought a sense of ethical responsibility to the formation of Imre Nagy's personality.

But though he grew up in a town, the strongest influence on Nagy as a child must, to judge from his later development, have been closeness to the family's origins among the rural poor. Concern for the condition of the peasants and landless labourers ran right through his career. In his early manhood he trained as an agronomist. He took this professional skill very seriously. His first achievement as a Minister was to push through a land reform programme. Until his fifties, he presumed to disagree with his Party only on agricultural policy. His Hungarian Communist colleagues in exile in Moscow in the thirties summed him up accurately when they christened him 'the kulak'.

Yet Nagy's parents had bettered themselves, escaped from the farm. They tried to prepare him for a better place in life than a peasant's. They gave him at least the beginnings of a solid education. He went to an elementary school till he was ten and then to the gymnasium. At the gymnasium a teacher encouraged an enduring interest in music and poetry. But in 1908 his school report noted that he showed no outstanding abilities. In view of the family's straitened circumstances, the school recommended that he should not complete the gymnasium course.

The report marked the end of Nagy's formal education. His father apprenticed him to an agricultural machinery manufacturer in Losonc, a hundred miles away in what is now Slovakia. There he picked up German, Russian and Slovak. But a fellow apprentice lost a hand in an industrial accident. His father took Nagy away from the Losonc factory and found him a job in the Mavag foundry in the Angyalföld industrial suburb of Budapest. Somewhere along the way he fitted in a course, perhaps part-time, at commercial college, an education for a boy destined to be a shop assistant or a book-keeper. It was not a preparation for great things, but it was far more than a country boy who had stayed in his village or on an estate would have enjoyed.

Nagy spent four years at the Mavag foundry, one of the biggest industrial establishments in Hungary. He was in his teens, at an impressionable age and far from home. The labour movement was just beginning to assert itself. A Labour Party had been formed in 1880, transforming itself ten years later into the Social Democratic Party. But progress was slow. The vote extended to only eight per cent

of the population and to very few working men. The unions
were debarred from politics, and before 1914 never
achieved a membership of more than 130,000.

There was nevertheless a strong and growing sense of
working-class identity in places like Angyalföld and the
other industrial districts of Budapest, and in one or two
other industrial centres. It was heightened by the sense of
alienation from the well-to-do who dominated political and
social life. In the years before the First World War,
Budapest was fast becoming a great city to rival Vienna or
Prague. But the impact of change was very different in the
industrial squalor of places like Angyalföld and Csepel from
the fashionable heart of Pest. Sir Arthur Nicolson, who
served at the British Consulate General in Budapest in the
nineties, lived in a world scarcely conscious of the different
world of the factories. He cordially disliked the frivolity
and extravagance of the Hungarian society in which he
moved. 'I should be a socialist of the deepest magenta', he
wrote to his wife, 'were I a workman here.'[4]

For the rest of his life, Nagy presented himself as a
countryman, who seemed at times to have wandered into
the Communist Party almost by mistake. His interests,
voice, accent and turn of phrase remained invincibly rural.
Angyalföld left little obvious mark upon him. Yet it seems
likely that he first became involved in socialist politics
there. It was probably a matter of no more than generalized
resentment of poverty and injustice, encouraged by Social
Democrat organizers, without any formal Marxist basis.
But at Mavag Nagy learned a commitment to working-class
solidarity which he retained till the end of his life.

When war broke out in 1914 Nagy was conscripted into
the Hungarian infantry. He was eighteen years of age.
Unlike most of the boys around him, he had some
education, and technical training. His education theoretically qualified him for a temporary commission, but he
stayed in the ranks. His technical training made him a
machine gunner. He fought on the Italian front and was
wounded. From hospital he was sent to the Russian front,

where he was again wounded, and taken prisoner. By the time of the Bolshevik Revolution, he was in a prisoner-of-war camp in Siberia.

The process of political education begun in County Somogy and continued in the Mavag steel works was pressed home by three years' experience in the Hungarian infantry. The First World War was a school for radicals in every army, but the lessons were particularly vivid for the Russians and the Austro-Hungarians. The men of these two armies suffered more than their allies from the particular incompetence and social alienation of their leaders. The Hungarians, junior partners in a predominantly Teutonic alliance, had a further reason for discontent.

In March 1918, the Soviet government bound themselves in the Treaty of Brest-Litovsk 'to refrain from all agitation against the government or the state or military institutions of the other party'. But it was a hollow undertaking. The Bolsheviks believed themselves destined to lead the way to revolution all over Europe. 'I hope we may be able to start a revolution in your country, also,' a Russian negotiator observed at Brest-Litovsk.[5] In April, branches of the Russian Communist Party were set up for each of the nationalities of the Hohenzollern and Habsburg Empires. 'The disintegrated armies of the central powers herded in prison camps proved as fruitful a field as the defeated Russian army for a revolutionary propaganda which relied largely on class discrimination. Work among prisoners-of-war at this time was, as Lenin said later, "the real foundation of what has been done to create a Third International." '[6] Nagy, still only twenty-two, shaped by memories of rural poverty and urban hardship, fresh from experience in the ranks of the Hungarian army, was typically susceptible to Bolshevik influence. In 1918 he became a member of the Bolshevik Party and later of the infant Hungarian Communist Party.

In later life, Imre Nagy cut a quintessentially civilian figure: self-consciously calm, academic, rotund, short-sighted. But in his youth he seems to have been a committed and serious soldier. After three years in the Hungarian infantry he joined the Red Army. In 1955, in an essay intended to convince his Party and the Kremlin of his orthodoxy, he boasted that 'the concept of proletarian internationalism has determined my views and my actions. I gave proof of this during the great trials and bloody battles of the Russian Civil War in which I participated as an internationalist.'[7] This was no exaggeration. Nagy fought in Russia against the Whites in an international unit of the Red Army. He was taken prisoner in Siberia by troops of the Czech Legion, escaped and fought again. It was campaigning in the Russian Civil War that kept him from involvement in the first tragi-comic attempt at Communism in Hungary, Béla Kun's short-lived Soviet Republic.

By the time the Bolsheviks were taking power in Russia, the Austro-Hungarian armies were close to collapse. So was the Habsburg Empire. In October 1918, Count Mihály Károlyi took office in Hungary. He led a well-intentioned but ineffectual liberal government which was to play much the same role as Kerensky's had in Russia. He looked to the Allies to recognize his liberal credentials and give him the support he needed to hold a disintegrating country together.

The Allies, however, were committed to dismembering the Austro-Hungarian Empire. They had promised the Slovaks, Slavs and Rumanians their nationhood. They envisaged a Hungary one third the size of the Kingdom of Saint Stephen, an outcome no Hungarian government could accept and survive. The right in any case saw Károlyi as a traitor to his class, the left as an obstacle to true socialism. While he temporized his supporters drifted away. Béla Kun, a committed Bolshevik fresh from Moscow, replaced him. On 21 March 1919, he declared a Hungarian Soviet Republic, Europe's second Bolshevik state.

Kun and his associates sought instant solutions. They

took power in a deeply traditional society at the end of a long, lost war. They sought to destroy bourgeois society and replace it with an ideal construct of their own. From the first they turned to authoritarian methods. They felt themselves beset by enemies. They even tangled with the Royal Navy, temporarily seizing two motor launches flying the White Ensign of the Danube Flotilla. Even when the advancing Rumanians threatened the capital they persisted with policies which alienated the conservative, property-owning and religious majority. Their fanaticism of ends and means alienated ordinary Hungarians. The Soviet Republic lasted only four months, but in that time Kun and his associates created a model of Communism which haunted the Hungarian imagination until a more enduring model seized power in 1948. Together with the reactionaries who followed them they established a frame of reference which dominated Hungarian politics and within which Imre Nagy and other politicians were obliged to work over the next half century.

The Kun Republic had no chance of outlasting Allied pressure. At the end of July 1919, the leaders slipped away to Vienna and eventually exile in the Soviet Union. Miklós Horthy, Admiral of the Austro-Hungarian Navy, rode up to Budapest from Szeged on a white horse at the head of a small army of reactionary officers. His men disposed of political opponents as brutally as Kun's. They extended their attentions to Jews, turbulent farm labourers and individuals against whom they had personal grudges. A White Terror was carried through to match the Red. It went into the legends of the left as the Red had gone into the legends of the gentry and bourgeoisie. Hungary, already a society of extremes and incomprehension between classes, was further polarized. Even in 1956 the Communists who rallied to János Kádár claimed that they were nipping a new White Terror in the bud.

Installed in power, Miklós Horthy set himself to preside as Regent of Hungary over an attempt, at first partly successful, to put the clock back in most particulars to the world before 1914. But he could not recreate the Kingdom of Saint Stephen. In 1920 the Treaty of Trianon reduced Hungary to a rump of the old kingdom. It lost all the territories hitherto disputed with other nationalities: Transylvania to Romania, upper Hungary to Czechoslovakia, the Délvidék to Yugoslavia, the Burgenland to Austria.

Hungary shrank from a major nation of eighteen million people to a small one of eight. Hungarians would not accept Trianon: in a bitter play on the name, 'No, no, never' became a national rallying cry. Hopes of reversing it became a central theme of politics. If that impossible dream could be realized, the ruling classes believed, Hungary could return, with a regent in place of a king emperor, to the idealized status quo of the golden years before 1914. For twenty years, preoccupation with the wrong done at Trianon crowded out discussion of the political, economic and social evils within the new Hungary. Gradually, it drew the country into association with the only man who seemed able to right its wrongs, Adolf Hitler.

Hungary's economic state in 1920 was in most ways worse than it had been in 1914. The economy had been weakened by four years of war on two fronts. The Soviet Republic and battles with the Rumanians did further damage. Trianon took away much of what had in effect been a hinterland for the industries of Budapest, Miskolc and Györ. From free access to the whole Habsburg Empire, Hungary found itself confined within the frontiers of a small state. It remained heavily dependent on agriculture, which was weakened by American competition and loss of Western European markets.

A much lamented consequence was hardship for the gentry and the middle classes, their numbers reinforced by the return of younger sons who had held administrative positions all over Greater Hungary. The poverty of the city proletariat was of a higher order of seriousness.

As for the rural poor, their situation was desperate. In bad times little stood between the landless labourers and starvation. Hungary's 'three million beggars' were much more than a conceit of socialist propaganda.

Social circumstances brought little relief. 'Hungary', wrote Macartney, 'was emphatically a class state, and in a Europe which believed itself to be advancing towards democracy, it was a conspicuous laggard.'[8] Horthy and the rulers of Hungary were not consciously evil men. But they were profoundly conservative, caught up in the assumptions of a world they saw it as their duty and interest to restore. The official political game was played on a confined pitch, between teams representative only of the possessing classes and with a very heavy bias towards the aristocracy and gentry. The goals scored had little effect on the more fundamental issues in Hungarian life.

In the industrial suburbs and in the countryside, another game was beginning. Its purpose was to engage the political emotions of the mass of the population, in support of opposition parties within the official system and of illegal left-wing parties outside it. This game was about more real issues than those which engaged the official politicians. But its assumptions were if anything even more unreal than those of the game which the Regent refereed. Hungary's political system was shamelessly skewed to protect the interests of the historic classes and the bourgeoisie. Opposition parties such as the Smallholders and Social Democrats had no hope of power as long as that system endured. The illegal parties were playing a game of shadows.

Imre Nagy returned to Hungary in 1921, to play a part in this game of shadows. He was a member of the Hungarian Communist Party, outlawed since the fall of the Kun Republic. He came to promote the Party's interests. But he did so under the cloak of membership of the Social Democrat Party, becoming one of its secretaries in County Somogy. The Social Democrats had reached a concordat of a sort with Horthy. They were legally recognized, tolerated. Membership of the Social Democratic Party gave Nagy, like other Communists at the time, some protection from the attentions of the police.

His role was agitation among the rural poor. It was uphill

work. The peasants and agricultural labourers were as conservative as their masters. The Kun Republic could have wooed them with a policy of land distribution. Instead it had advocated collectivization. Its spokesmen were intellectuals and embittered townsmen, quite remote from the peasantry. The Red Terror alienated the peasantry further. And in the White Terror which followed, they saw the price of attracting the attentions of the established order. They had been cowed from time immemorial. In the twenties they were frightened, suspicious of men like Nagy who professed to help them.

Nagy was twenty-five when he came back to Hungary. He was thirty-one when he left. These six years in the twenties gave him his first practical experience of Hungarian politics. Building on his inherited pre-occupation with farming, he learned at first hand the timeless concerns of the Hungarian peasant. He also got to know something about his opponents: the landowners, their parties, the gendarmerie and the police. Perhaps most significantly, he experienced the contrasts and tensions between his own party and the Social Democrats who gave his work an uneasy legitimacy.

In Hungary and elsewhere, Communists and Social Democrats were very different political animals. The Communists were mostly men of Kun's stamp: townsmen, intellectuals, ideologues, nearly all of them Jewish. Social Democrats had deeper roots in ordinary Hungarian life. Unlike the Communists they sought respectability and self-improvement with an almost bourgeois earnestness, competing for influence with the doctor, the schoolteacher and the priest. Moral seriousness was their mantle. They felt themselves called to lead, not just to criticize.

By background and temperament Nagy was closer to the Social Democrats than to the Communists. He was a man of the people, a countryman, very much a Hungarian. He was no intellectual: his academic formation was to come later. Photographs of Nagy at the time show a Social Democratic leader in the making. He was a plump, schoolmasterly young man in glasses, bow tie and dark suit, handkerchief in breast-pocket.

Yet Nagy had already chosen Bolshevism. As a Red soldier he had fought in the desperate battles of the Russian Civil War. He served now the Hungarian Communist Party. Social Democracy was no more to him than a cloak of respectability. For six years in Hungary in the twenties, Nagy experienced the tensions between two very different schools of politics which can be detected in him till the end of his career.

Even his marriage stretched him between Communism and Social Democracy. On 28 November 1925, he married Mária Egetö, a girl of peasant background whose family were prominent in Social Democratic politics. The marriage introduced Nagy into a kind of working-class aristocracy. Mária's father was treasurer of the Somogy branch of the Social Democratic party. Photographs show a slender young woman apparently more suited to marriage and motherhood than to politics. But her talents, like her father's, were put to the Party's service, and she won some local fame as an actress and singer in Social Democratic pageants. She did not share her husband's commitment to Communism and never joined the Party. But she stayed with him through all his triumphs and vicissitudes, lived to mourn him, and died twenty years after him.

In 1926, the year after Nagy's marriage, tensions between the Social Democrats and the Communists reached breaking point. The Communists and the other illegal parties found Social Democratic cover useful. But for the Social Democrats, legality and respectability were inhibiting. The Communists suffered no such inhibitions. In their attacks on the established order they found it easy to steal the Social Democrats' clothes. Finally, the Social Democrats turned against their fellow travellers. In 1926 they expelled from the Party anyone they suspected of being a Communist. A clandestine Communist, István Vági, formed a party of his own. It was Communist in all but name, but for a time maintained a tenuous legality.

Nagy joined it and took a place among the leadership.
Other Communists still at liberty joined too.

It was a new phase of the game of shadows. In the course
of 1926, the Vági Party made some mark in Hungary. It
recruited several thousand members and organized a few
strikes. It was by the standards of the day a bold attempt to
set up a militant left-wing movement in an authoritarian
and conservative society. But it had little chance of
survival, let alone of political success. 1919 was still a vivid
memory. The authorities were watchful. The Social
Democrats were hostile. The 1929 crisis of capitalism was
still in the future. When, in February 1927, the police
arrested the Party leaders, the organization was snuffed
out. The leaders went on trial in November. Vági got a
heavy sentence. Nagy made a defiant speech in his own
defence and was sentenced to two years imprisonment.

Nagy lived his life in a movement accustomed to political
imprisonment. The character of Mátyás Rákosi, his rival in
the fifties, seems to have been permanently warped by the
long period he spent in prison in Hungary between the
wars. László Rajk and János Kádár experienced both
Horthy's and Communist prisons. So did many other
Communist leaders. Until his final imprisonment, Nagy by
contrast got off lightly. He spent only three years in total in
prison in his youth.

He served his sentence in the Central Prison in Budapest,
built for the millennium the year he was born, finishing
school of Hungarian politicians, in whose courtyard he
finally met his end. He seems to have been psychologically
unmarked by the experience of confinement there, perhaps
because he was fundamentally an unassuming and
uncombative man. He had none of Rákosi's soaring ego and
quick, searching intelligence. He lacked Rajk's passion.
And even the harsh prison regime of Horthy's era was
easygoing by contrast with the horrors which Kádár and so
many others experienced under Rákosi. Legend has it that
Nagy took his bowler hat to prison with him and used it as a
pillow. It saw him through until his release in 1929.

Chapter 3

EXILE

After his release from prison, Nagy was expelled from Hungary. He went to Vienna, leaving behind him a wife and a two-year-old daughter born while he was in prison. The Horthy regime was easygoing by comparison with the Communist system which came after it, but the political police kept an effective eye upon opponents. Nagy could not safely slip over the border into Hungary, and his wife feared the authorities' attentions if they got to know that she had visited her husband in Austria. She therefore enrolled herself and her daughter on a pilgrimage excursion to the shrine at Mariazell in Styria. Safely over the border she left the pilgrimage and went to meet her husband at Schönbrunn.

Her daughter calls it 'the day I met my father'[1]. A photograph shows the little family posed before a Schönbrunn fountain. They look the epitome of bourgeois respectability, a middle-class Middle European family on an outing. But after the outing Maria and her daughter rejoined the pilgrimage and returned to Kaposvár, saying nothing of the meeting with husband and father. It was six months before they heard from him again.

In exile in Vienna, Nagy involved himself with a little group of émigré left-wing figures, members of the Communist Party or close to it. In such circles, agricultural policy was the subject of the hour. The Soviet Party was already split on the subject. Bukharin advocated a policy of gradualism, Stalin headlong collectivization. Other Communist Parties replicated the disagreement, which reached as far as the little Hungarian cell in Vienna. They were discussing the agricultural policy to pursue when once they achieved power in Hungary. Nagy knew the peasantry. He argued in favour of land distribution, not collectivization. The comrades told him that distribution was not the policy of the Comintern. In a lifetime in politics, Nagy coined few striking phrases. But in Vienna he turned on his critics. He did not spring to attention when he heard the Internationale, he told them.

In February 1930 the Second Congress of the Hungarian Communist Party was held in Aprilovka, near Moscow. Nagy went back to Russia for the occasion, his first visit in nine years. He expected to stay only for a couple of weeks before returning to Vienna and, no doubt, to Hungary when the coast there seemed clear.

He naturally spoke in the agricultural debate at the Congress. Once again he advocated the policy which he believed was the only way to win rural support: the break-up of the great estates and the distribution of land to the middle and poor peasants. He was taking his heresy before a larger audience than the group in Vienna. In doing so he compounded his earlier offence and brought Party wrath about his ears.

In the Soviet Communist Party the tide was moving strongly in Stalin's favour. Three years earlier he had seen off attempts to restrain him, when Lenin's letter condemning his dangerous ambition had been put to the Fifteenth Congress. Since then he had increased his drive to destroy the position of his opponents within the Party, notably Bukharin. Now he argued powerfully for agricultural collectivization, not distribution. But for Stalin the agricultural debate was only the beginning of a much broader argument.

It was an argument about the very nature of Communism. In the course of it differences of emphasis which had been present from the beginning hardened into widely divergent trends. Bukharin had wanted to win the consent of the people, carry them forward with the Party. Stalin believed that the Party should set the course and terrorize all those who did not follow it. The movement stood at a crossroads. It had learned conspiracy and paranoia in the underground. It had imposed itself on Russia by force. Lenin had denounced tolerance as weakness, and reserved decisions to the Party. But in the twenties there had been signs of moderation, hopes that the movement, safely installed in power, might mellow.

The adoption of a policy of collectivization dashed such hopes. It could only be carried through quickly by arbitrary means, and in places by terror. But once used in support of agricultural policy, terror would spread throughout Soviet society. The 1930 agricultural debate marked the point at which Lenin's selective use of terror to achieve particular ends yielded to Stalin's choice of terror as a political routine and even, at times, as an end in itself.

So in arguing for land distribution, Nagy was committing himself to the losing side in a wide and dangerous dispute. He expressed deeply held beliefs, which reflected everything his experience as a child and as a rural agitator had taught him. He was also displaying, not for the last time, an academic, almost naive approach to politics. His Hungarian comrades were less simpleminded. They saw which way the Soviet Party was moving and hastened to fall in behind it. They called upon Nagy to recant. Before the end of the Congress he did so. In a speech published many years later he disavowed his 'imprecise and opportunist ideas'. He acknowledged the need for vigilance against 'right-deviationism'. 'It is true that I said in Vienna that I would not spring to attention when I heard the Internationale. I recognize that this is an attitude unworthy of a Bolshevik. I do not want to justify myself but, believe me, I did not want to imply that I would not carry out unquestioningly the decisions of the Internationale.'[2]

This was Nagy's first political recantation. It was typical

of Communist procedure. The language is turgid, the surrender banal. But the incident is important for what it tells us about Nagy and for the light it throws on his future career.

At the Second Party Congress, as on more important occasions later, Nagy faced a contradiction. As a human being who knew and liked other human beings, he believed in a policy which would give the peasants the parcels of land they had always craved. He knew that this was the only way to build rural support for his Party. As a Communist, on the other hand, he believed in the wisdom of the Party and the virtues of discipline. After the outburst of conviction, discipline reasserted itself. Nagy went back to his Party duty.

When Nagy went to Moscow for the Second Congress, he expected to stay a couple of weeks. But after his outburst at Aprilovka, the Party leadership probably wanted to keep a potential heretic under their own eye. He settled in Moscow and after a time his wife and daughter were able to join him from Kaposvár. He found a humble flat in Frunze Square. The Nagys had one room between them, a family of two women and two children the other. There was no bathroom, but the two families shared the luxury of a telephone and a gas cooker.

Having settled in Moscow, Nagy set about underpinning his knowledge of agriculture by enrolling in the International Agrarian Institute, which Bukharin had inspired and built up in the twenties. He studied agricultural economy and sociology, going on to join the Institute's professional staff. Nagy took academic disciplines seriously, and at the Institute he completed his scientific education. By 1932 he had made himself the Hungarian Party's leading agricultural theorist. He drafted a policy paper for the Comintern. He worked too in the Moscow Statistical Office. He started to write for the theoretical journals, mostly about agriculture. In 1934 he published a pamphlet, 'The Situation of the Hungarian Peasantry', which, when circulated in Hungary, had some influence in non-Communist circles.

The Hungarian Communist leaders in exile led intense and introspective lives in Moscow. They suffered the torments of political exiles anywhere, as well as the anxieties common to all Moscow dwellers in the thirties. Until Stalin's terror swept most of them away, they huddled together in the Hotel Lux, suspicious of one another's access to the Soviet leadership, envious of any material advantage such access could bring.

Nagy of course knew the leaders, and they knew him; but he does not seem to have been close to them. György Lukács, the philosopher, who himself lived on the fringes of Hungarian Communist society in Moscow at the time, said of him: 'I thought highly of his personal integrity and intelligence, and also of his expertise in the agrarian question. But I did not regard him as a real politician.'[3] Ironically, perhaps the closest of Nagy's political associates was Ferenc Münnich, who in post-war Hungary earned himself a sinister reputation and who played a major part in Nagy's final destruction: they had fought together in the Red Army in the Civil War and may have been bound together by campaigning memories.

But the Nagys in the Moscow years seem to have been closer to colleagues from the Institute and non-political émigrés than to Party comrades. They involved themselves with a Moscow club for émigré engineers and workers which at weekends solaced their nostalgia for Hungary and which sounds like an expatriates' refuge anywhere. Their daughter remembers Hungarian dancing and her mother making ballet dresses for the children. Someone called her a Bolshevik. 'I'm not a Bolshevik,' the child answered, 'I come from County Somogy.'[4] As the net of Stalin's terror spread wider the club was closed.

Nagy lived this quiet little life right through the destruction of the kulaks, the famine in the Ukraine and the great terror. Bukharin, whose views on agriculture had shaped Nagy's own, much of the Hungarian émigré leadership, half of the intelligentsia of Moscow, went to their deaths. Nagy was untouched. In Moscow in the thirties as later in Budapest in the early fifties, he led a charmed life. One wonders why.

He may have owed his immunity to his unassuming approach, his very insignificance. Perhaps he had learned from the storm that broke about him when he defied the Party in 1930 and consciously confined himself to academic and family concerns. In later life, people remember, he was self-consciously disciplined, determined to listen before he spoke, the very model of discretion. But equally cautious and innocent men went to the camps in their hundreds of thousands. Was there anything else about Nagy to explain his immunity?

It is alleged that during the Terror Nagy acted as an informant for the Soviet secret police. When in 1989 the argument about his rehabilitation grew intense, Károly Grósz, the Party leader who opposed rehabilitation, claimed to hold evidence that Nagy had denounced colleagues who were consigned to the gulag as a result. He has not so far made it public; but it is conceivable that such evidence exists. Even Nagy's friends acknowledge the possibility that he was involved with the secret police. They numbered their informants by the hundred thousand, and if they demanded cooperation it was impossible without supreme heroism to refuse. Foreigners were naturally the subject of even closer attention than native Muscovites. It is perfectly possible that Nagy served the KGB.

It is also possible that he did so not merely to save himself and his family, but out of conviction. Once again we encounter the paradox of Imre Nagy's Communism. We have seen the human being, jovial, easygoing, a family man. We shall see that that side of his nature persisted to the end. But we have seen that he committed himself to Communism in 1918 and served it to the best of his ability for twenty years. We shall see him continue to do so, trying indefatigably to reconcile its demands with gentler qualities. He was a true believer; and convinced Communists accepted that everything might have to be subordinated to the triumph of their faith. It goes against the grain to see such a man, who eventually gave his life to build a Communism which did not forget man, as an informant for the political police. It is not a possibility which we can rule out.

A further question follows. Did his secret police connections dog Nagy's steps when he returned to Hungary in 1944? Did the KGB seek to control him as he played his part in Hungarian political life between 1945 and 1956? Again, the possibility cannot be excluded. The KGB had their placemen, political figures as well as functionaries, all over Eastern Europe. Throughout a long political career in Communist Hungary, Nagy's friend Münnich, for example, was spoken of as a Soviet agent.

But this kind of language tends to obscure the reality of relationships between Moscow and the satellite leaders. The fact is that for at least forty years after the war all Communist leaders in Eastern Europe were in a sense Moscow's agents. In the early years in particular, many may have served Soviet interests out of conviction that they were advancing the cause of Communism and all mankind by doing so. They also knew that there was no survival in office for those who did not. Increasingly, most of them tried to reconcile subservience to Soviet wishes with the service of national interests too. Of course, there were those who made no attempt to balance conflicting interests. Some sought personal advancement by showing particular concern for Moscow's wishes. Some – and Münnich may have been one – had formal links with the KGB.

It is conceivable, but improbable, that Nagy should be counted in this last category. It could explain his immunity from arrest, the fact that the Soviet choice of a prime minister they could trust fell upon him in 1953. But in the forties and fifties Hungarians did not talk or think of Nagy as a Soviet agent. Some saw him as a patriot doing his best for his country, others as a faithful Communist dedicated to his Party and the interests of the homeland of socialism. It is a truism that right up to his fall Nagy tried to serve Soviet interests as well as Hungarian: he believed that he should, and he knew that he had to. But in the end he went all the way to the gallows for his resistance to Moscow's wishes. The belief that he had lived most of his political life as a formal agent of the KGB tortures the facts of even Eastern European politics beyond credibility.

Whatever the reason, Nagy came through Stalin's terror unscathed. In the late thirties he began to emerge from his exclusive preoccupation with agriculture. The advance of Hitler had become the salient fact of European politics. It threatened to destroy democratic and Communist hopes alike. Communism turned to the policy of broad coalition against fascism, the Popular Front.

Just before Munich, Nagy wrote an article in a Hungarian émigré journal advocating Central European cooperation, notably between Hungary and Czechoslovakia. There is something owlish and unrealistic about this first venture into foreign affairs. Cooperation was proposed as a way of checking German expansion in Central Europe. But by the time of Munich the Hungarians had spent almost twenty years resenting the loss of much of Slovakia at Trianon. German claims on Czechoslovakia offered them a chance of recovering what they believed was historically theirs. It was all very well for a Hungarian émigré far from power to advocate cooperation. But if his compatriots at home had taken any notice of the proposition, it could only have reduced still further his Party's chances, slim at any time, of building support in Hungary.

In any event, not even Nagy's article saved Czechoslovakia. The German advance in Central Europe continued. When Hitler prepared to turn against Poland, Stalin came to terms with him. The Soviet-German Treaty of 1939 made a German invasion of Poland and war with the Western powers certain. Stalin may or may not have believed that it bought Hitler's friendship, but it certainly bought time. The price was to add still further to the suspicion in which the Soviet Union was held.

In June 1941 Hitler invaded Russia. For Communists, this swept away any doubts which the pact with Hitler had evoked. The first task was to defend the socialist homeland. Soviet citizens would do so in the Soviet forces. But the East European émigrés in Moscow had particular knowledge and skills. A scheme was devised to train them as partisans to be parachuted into their own countries and wreak havoc there behind German lines. Nagy and Münnich presented themselves for training. Münnich had fought in the Spanish Civil War, but Nagy had been out of uniform for twenty years. Nevertheless, at the age of forty-five, that so obviously civilian, some said slightly ludicrous figure prepared himself for guerrilla warfare and launched himself repeatedly into space.

Before long, this particular project was abandoned. Moscow turned to the power of the spoken word. Nagy was nominated to set up a Hungarian language radio station. With Gyula Háy, the playwright, he started to broadcast for Radio Kossuth. When the German advance threatened the capital, Nagy moved with Radio Kossuth to Tbilisi. His wife and daughter moved with the other émigré families to Tomsk.

Gradually, Nagy's Radio Kossuth broadcasts built up some small following for him personally and for his Party in Hungary. He had a mellifluous voice. He spoke a clear traditional Hungarian. He avoided jargon and appealed to simple people, especially the peasants. And he preached the simple proposition that when Soviet victory had destroyed fascism the Communist Party would give the people land.

Throughout 1941 and most of 1942, the German advance in Russia seemed irresistible. It sharpened the dilemma which the Hungarian government had faced ever since the rise of Hitler. Hungary's dominant passion was to recover what it could of the lands of historic Hungary taken from her at Trianon. The only chance of doing so was as a client of Germany. But the Hungarian government feared Nazi

Germany only marginally less than Communist Russia.

Horthy himself, remembering the dogmas of the old Habsburg navy, believed in sea-power and the eventual victory of the Western powers. He had held back from formal alliance with Hitler. Even so, in two adjustments of frontiers in 1938 and 1940, Hitler had returned to Hungary some of the old Hungarian lands which it had been forced to cede to Czechoslovakia and Rumania at Trianon.

In the spring of 1941, Hitler had turned against Yugoslavia. He pressed the Hungarian government to help, promising them part of the Délvidék in return. They had signed a Treaty of Eternal Friendship with Yugoslavia only months before, but they allowed German troops through Hungary. Horthy's Prime Minister, Pál Teleki, committed suicide. It was, Churchill wrote, 'a sacrifice to absolve himself and his people from guilt in the German attack . . . It clears his name before history. It could not stop the march of the German armies nor the consequences.'[5] Hungary was depicted ever more vividly as Hitler's jackal. And, 'When the time came for Hungary to stand before the bar of judgement . . . no one recalled Pál Teleki's sacrifice.'[6]

Within three months, Hitler turned against Russia. Once again he pressed Hungary for support. Hungary declared war and reluctantly sent token forces into the Soviet campaign. Gradually their numbers increased until by the summer of 1942 the Second Army was holding a hundred-mile front against the Red Army on the Don. That winter the Russians went over to the offensive. In January 1943 they fell upon the Second Army. The Germans on the Hungarians' flanks withdrew, leaving the Second Army without transport. The Russians cut it to pieces where it stood, trapped in snow drifts. Hungary was beginning to pay the human as well as the moral price of going along with the Germans. Fear of the Soviet Union increased.

After the disaster on the Don, the Hungarian government tried to extricate what remained of its armies from Russia. The Germans demanded a continuing commitment, lines of communications troops and forces to fight the Soviet partisans at least. Horthy, and others who dreamed of escaping from the war when the moment came, sought to build up a force at home. But gradually the front line moved south-westwards towards the Carpathians and the Hungarian border. Hungary, tempted and bullied into war on the German side, faced Soviet invasion.

The hopes of the Hungarian émigrés in Russia rose. Most of them had spent ten or even twenty years in Moscow. Béla Kun, their first leader, had vanished during the Terror. Mátyás Rákosi, released by Horthy in return for the historic Hungarian flags captured by the Russians in 1849, took his place. At first he seemed to have exchanged imprisonment for indefinite exile. The war brought hope, but first there was the danger of German victory. The émigrés were caught up in the frantic evacuation of Moscow. By the middle of 1943, however, the war was going the Allies' way. In November, at Teheran, the Russians and Americans rejected the British proposal for a landing in the Balkans, making it more probable than ever that the Red Army rather than the Western Allies would occupy Hungary. Rákosi, Nagy and the other Communist exiles prepared to go home. Nagy's Kossuth radio broadcasts to Hungary steadily attracted more attention.

Horthy and his ministers sought ways to avert a Soviet occupation. There was fanciful talk of holding the Russians on the Carpathians while launching an attack down through Croatia, to open a path into Hungary for the British and Americans from Italy. There were abortive attempts to get agreement that Hungary should surrender to the Western Allies alone. But the Red Army continued its advance. Its first troops entered south-east Hungary in March.

Hitler increased his pressure on Horthy, brutally confronting him with the choice between wholehearted collaboration and occupation. Horthy tried to temporize, but on 19 March German troops entered Hungary, prepared to fight a long bitter battle with the Russians.

Through the summer of 1944, the Red Army advanced across Hungary. By the middle of August it had reached the river Tisza and occupied south-eastern Hungary. The country was devastated, by the fighting and by looting by Germans and Russians in turn. But there was too a sense of relief that the fighting had moved on, and hopes of new life. Political power was waiting to be taken by whoever could organize to seize it.

The Communist Party was scarcely represented in the liberated areas. There was a danger that others would take the lead in re-establishing political and economic life. In the summer of 1944, therefore, Moscow sent a group of Communist émigrés into Hungary. They were led by Ernö Gerö, a hard Communist leader who had fought in Spain. Nagy was a member of the group. After a frightening incident in which they were captured and almost shot by a Soviet patrol, they turned to their political work and set themselves to compete for a hearing with other would-be leaders who came out of the cellars and the woods as the fighting moved westwards.

Meanwhile, units of the Hungarian army continued to fight more or less effectively beside the Wehrmacht. Officials of the Ministry of the Interior and gendarmerie officers helped Eichmann ship the rural Jews of Hungary to their deaths. Then in the late summer, perhaps emboldened by the attempt on Hitler's life, Horthy reasserted himself. He stopped the deportations, and tried yet again to negotiate a way out of the war for Hungary. In October he ordered the Hungarian forces to lay down their arms.

The Germans had friends everywhere in Hungary and had intercepted Horthy's communications with the Allies. As Horthy gave his order, Otto Skorzeny, the Nazi stormtrooper who had rescued Mussolini from his captors in a brilliant *coup de main*, acted as decisively to seize the government district of Buda. Horthy was shipped off into captivity. The Arrow Cross leader Szálasi took power under German protection. His young thugs resumed the persecution of the Jews whom Horthy had rescued from Eichmann in the summer, driving them into the Budapest Ghetto and shooting them out of hand on the banks of the Danube in the fashionable centre of Pest.

One general, Béla Miklós, had succeeded in going over to the Russians when Horthy ordered the surrender on 15 October, taking a few officers and men with him. The Russians brought him to Moscow to discuss the creation of a National Independence Front – a coalition of whatever political forces in Hungary had aligned themselves against the Germans. In November a small group of Communists, with Gerö again in the lead and with Nagy among them, was brought back from Hungary to take part in the talks. It was decided that Miklós should lead a provisional government, with representatives of all elements of Hungarian life except the Horthyites and the Arrow Cross participating.

The disparate group of army officers and exiled Communists returned to Hungary. By now the Red Army had crossed the Danube and advanced into south-west Hungary. They had captured Kaposvár, reached Lake Balaton, entered Pest and begun to surround Buda. The provisional government assembled in Debrecen, a major centre in north-eastern Hungary. At Christmas, 1944, the members of a provisional National Assembly gathered in the Calvinist Great Church there. They endorsed the composition of Miklós' provisional government.

Nagy became Minister of Agriculture. He was back in his own country, representing his Party in an office for which, above all others, he had prepared himself. Hungary was ravaged, divided. But for the man from County Somogy who had given his life to the study of agriculture and to Communism, Christmas 1944 marked the entry into his inheritance. He was forty-eight years of age.

Chapter 4

OFFICE

Between the beginning of 1945 and the middle of 1948, Hungary moved from liberation to subservience and from government by a coalition representative of most Hungarian opinion to Communist dictatorship. In these years the Communist Party destroyed or absorbed all the other political parties. Later, Rákosi boasted that he had destroyed them as one consumes a salami, by slices. In retrospect the events of the salami years seem inevitable, pre-planned. There was much less sense of inevitability at the time, the years in which Nagy first had the opportunity to test his beliefs in action.

The Miklós provisional government in which Nagy was Minister of Agriculture was the creation of the Kremlin. It could operate only with the day-to-day approval of Marshal Voroshilov, the Soviet Commander in Hungary. It depended on the Red Army for things as elementary as transport. From the beginning the Russians gave special support to the Communists within it. But in its composition the provisional government represented a fair cross-section of Hungarian opinion.

Miklós himself was Prime Minister. He was in background a typical officer of the old army, differing from his fellow generals only in his lack of even a residual faith in the Germans and more resolute than they in going over to the Russians when Horthy announced Hungary's withdrawal from the German alliance. Two other army officers were included. The parties of the centre and centre-left, Smallholders, Social Democrats and Peasants, held the majority of portfolios. Only two Communists were included, neither a prominent member of the Party leadership. They occupied the Ministries of Commerce and Agriculture. The most powerful members of the leadership – Rákosi himself and Gerö who had represented the Party in the talks with Miklós in Moscow – remained in the background. So did Révai, Farkas and Vas, who formed with Rákosi and Gerö the inner circle of the Party leadership.

The government faced enormous difficulties. When it took office the battle for Budapest was still raging. North-west Hungary remained in German hands. Forty per cent of the nation's wealth, fifty per cent of its industrial equipment, was lost in the course of the war. Every bridge over the Danube was destroyed. The Germans took with them in their retreat anything movable of value. The Russians, advancing behind them, devoted themselves to looting and rape, and the seizure of what was left of Hungary's productive capacity. A British parliamentary delegation which visited Budapest a year later recorded that 980 of the 1300 public buildings in the capital had been damaged; that 100,000 motor vehicles had been taken away by the Germans; and that only one fire engine remained in Budapest.[1]

But there was reason for encouragement also. The Germans were clearly beaten. Peace was approaching. There was horror at the behaviour of the Red Army and fear of Communism and Soviet occupation. But to most Hungarians anything was better than the Arrow Cross. The Communists were discreet. And there was encouragement above all in the Soviet endorsement of a government representative of all democratic views.

In the spring of 1945, as the Germans and the Arrow Cross were steadily driven out of north-west Hungary, the provisional government limited itself to essentials: communications, food supplies, housing, getting production started again. By comparison, policy issues were of secondary importance and could, if pursued, cause dissension. Only in the field of agricultural policy did the new government commit itself to change. On 14 January it announced a land reform.

The reform envisaged the outright expropriation of all estates of over 1400 acres; the takeover of all but 140 acres of smaller estates; but the exemption from takeover of peasant holdings of up to 280 acres. It was planned to distribute the expropriated land among the peasants and the landless labourers, and to carry out the reform that autumn, after the harvest.

This was Nagy's policy, which he had advocated for twenty years. It would replace the Hungary of great estates with a nation of smallholders and independent peasant farmers. If collectivization, which Nagy had criticized in 1930 and seen so bloodily implemented in the Soviet Union, was considered at all, it was not pursued. Distribution was a policy to which the whole government could commit itself. Collectivization would have divided it.

Nagy prepared the operation carefully, intending to implement it in the autumn after the harvest. But in March Voroshilov intervened. He ordered Nagy to bring the timing forward to the early spring. Nagy acquiesced. The expropriation decrees were promulgated on 15 March, the anniversary of the 1848 uprising against the Habsburgs and a date to conjure with in Hungarian history. The first land was distributed on 29 March, a week before the last Germans were driven out of Hungary.

Nagy's namesake, Ferenc Nagy, a later Smallholder Prime Minister, wrote in exile afterwards that the reform was 'characterised by radicalism and superficiality'.[2] Given the haste, it may have been. But at the time the Smallholders welcomed the strategy of the reform. Observers reported that all liberal opinion in Hungary supported it.

Imre Nagy spoke at the ceremonial first distribution of land. It took place at Pusztaszer near Szeged, celebrated as the place where the invading Magyars under Prince Árpád in the ninth century held their first national assembly. Reformist legend revered Árpád as the man under whose leadership the Magyars had lived in a simple democracy, in contrast with the feudalism which overlaid it. It was therefore an appropriate place at which to take the first step away from the feudal world of the estates. In his speech Nagy gave the Communist Party the credit for a policy which was endorsed by the whole government and which stood Communist orthodoxy on its head.

'Let us begin the land distribution,' he said. 'Let us knock down the fences – and every blow is a blow on the nails of the coffins of the big landowners and, at the same time, a sign of a new world and a new life for the Hungarian serfs . . . I have come here to witness this glorious moment when the people of the Hungarian countryside began the final and definitive liquidation of feudal Hungary . . . I am happy that it was my party, the Communist Party, that brought this about and that I have been able to contribute to this great task.'[3]

The land distribution was enormously popular. The beneficiaries naturally approved of a step that gave them land of their own. But approval went much wider than the rural poor. The problem of agricultural land had been a central issue of Hungarian politics for thirty years and the parties of the centre and the left had long advocated a reform such as this. And it had a wider than agricultural significance. It suggested that the Communists were prepared to put dogma and Soviet practice behind them.

In a memoir written years later, after political imprisonment and disillusion, George Páloczi-Horváth summed up the impression that Nagy's land reform made at the time on him and on people like him. 'It gave me the impression that communism wasn't a rigid set of dogmas . . . I knew that according to Lenin the peasantry was constantly bringing forth small capitalists. Stalin was most insistent on forced collectivization before the war. But now . . . communism seemed to become more flexible. The communists understood the particular situation in Hungary

... For them life came first and dogma afterwards ... No-one could have convinced me that the land reform was just a tactical step, that Imre Nagy was regarded as an "inside-the-party fellow-traveller" and had been entrusted with the land reform just because his "Bukharinite" leanings and peasant origins made him a suitable instrument . . ."[4]

So the land reform brought the Communist Party some cautious approval from people like Páloczi-Horváth. They were eager to be persuaded that Communism had mellowed. The land reform suggested that it had. So did Nagy's style. He seemed gentle, careful and sincere; he looked like an ordinary Hungarian; and it was rumoured that he was prepared to stand up to the occupier when necessary. Suspicion of Communism remained, but Hungarians saw Nagy as representing a more acceptable face of his Party, which they hoped might endure.

But Nagy's popularity, and his very ordinariness, aroused the comrades' suspicions. His daughter Erzsébet recalls that his careful, old-fashioned bourgeois appearance stirred them to resentment. Things like his bowler hat and his nickname, 'the kulak', had been all very well in opposition and exile. Now, close to power, the Party demanded the display of unambiguously working-class virtues. They asked why his wife refused to join the Party. They were suspicious, too, of Nagy's non-political interests: his love of music and poetry, his collection of the works of the nineteenth-century national hero Lajos Kossuth. His irreverent sense of humour aroused his comrades' particular resentment.

So did his daughter's marriage. In 1946, at the age of nineteen, she married Ferenc Jánosi. The bridegroom was a Protestant pastor and the wedding took place in the main Calvinist church of Budapest. A Communist needed Party permission to attend a church service. Nagy asked for it and it was granted; in those early post-war days the presence of a Communist minster at a church wedding added to the Party's reputation for tolerance and broadmindedness. But the comrades held the incident against Nagy, as they did his closeness to a son-in-law who did not share their faith.

Nagy was successful in claiming for his Party some part of the credit for the popular land reform. The vigour which the Communists brought to reconstruction also won them approval. They took as much credit as they could for popular coalition achievements. When the first bridge over the Danube was rebuilt they christened Gerö 'the bridgebuilder', just as later they proclaimed Rákosi 'the father of the forint'. The Russians helped them, putting commandeered offices at their disposal and assigning troops to help with projects for which Communists would get the credit. For their part, the Communists used agitation for the punishment of alleged war criminals as a way of getting at their opponents, and assiduously orchestrated and exploited popular demands.

Nevertheless, there was no escaping the fact that in the early months after the liberation the Communists remained very much a minority in the coalition. They were steadily increasing their Party membership, but from an almost negligibly small base. They were still viewed with intense suspicion. They knew that they must be on their best behaviour. Their problem was to use hard work, Soviet backing and popular measures like the land reform to build up enough support to stand a chance of winning the elections scheduled for the autumn of 1945.

Preparations for the elections started in the early summer. Municipal elections in the capital were to be followed by a general election. The Communists recognized that their chances were slim; and Rákosi revealed long afterwards that in May disagreement had arisen within the Party about how best to maximize them. Those who, like János Kádár, had spent the war years in hiding in Hungary, wanted the Party to commit itself to an attack on its coalition partners. The exiles who had returned from Moscow behind the Red Army argued for a policy of persuasion and gradualness, the sort of policy which Nagy instinctively supported. In August this approach seemed to produce results: the Social Democrats decided, with many of their members dissenting, to campaign on a common list with the Communists. Together they pressed for early Budapest elections, which it was thought would bring them advantage in the general election later.

Instead the results were disastrous for the left. The Smallholders won 51 per cent of the vote, against 43 per cent for the Social Democrats and Communists combined. The Social Democrats decided that association with the Communists had damaged their showing; they would fight the general election alone. Hungary had cleared its first democratic hurdle satisfactorily.

The Communists had led Voroshilov to expect a better result. He allegedly struck Rákosi in his anger. He then took a direct hand in Hungarian politics, calling the party leaders together and demanding the adoption of a single electoral list, with the parties promised predetermined shares of the seats in the National Assembly. He threatened that if he did not get his way he would quintuple the size of the army of occupation.

The Smallholders and their allies defied Voroshilov. Cardinal Mindszenty issued a pastoral letter, putting the authority of the Church behind the Smallholders and abandoning the promotion of specifically Catholic parties. The Western Allies said that they would not recognize a government resulting from a single-list election.

The general election was held on 4 November. Observers judged that it was free, secret and fair, with pressure from the Communists and the Russians held within bounds. A representative if limited range of parties took part. The result was a triumph for the Smallholders, who won 57 per cent of the vote, 245 seats, and an absolute majority. The Communists came second with 70 seats. The Social Democrats won 69 and the Peasants 25. Hungary had stood up to Soviet pressure and, alone in Eastern Europe, had held a genuine and convincing parliamentary election.

There were those in the Smallholders Party who wanted to capitalize on success and take office alone. Prudence and Soviet pressure argued the other way: the Smallholders would do better to lead a coalition. With an absolute majority in parliament they seemed to hold the initiative on the allocation of portfolios. Their leader, Zoltán Tildy, naturally took Miklós' place as Prime Minister. They got Agriculture, Finance and Foreign Affairs without dispute. They also expected to take the Ministry of the Interior.

'The great struggle', wrote Ferenc Nagy, 'was for the Ministry of the Interior. In Hungary as in most European countries, the Minister of the Interior is responsible for the administration and for the public security, and internments are decided at his discretion. His office has exceptional significance in times of turbulence when the police and other authorities are greatly concerned with political issues. He has power to favor certain parties and interfere with others. Even in normal times, when the country has a regular army, the police are a strong armed force. After the collapse, the Hungarian army was weakened by Russian obstruction and by the lack of funds and equipment. In consequence the police were stronger than the army.

'Naturally every party sought the Ministry of the Interior.'[5]

Each of the four parties advanced its claims. The Smallholders pointed to their parliamentary strength. They wanted to appoint Béla Kovács, their Secretary General and the strongest personality in the party. The Peasants claimed that the Interior, which had belonged to them in the provisional government, should remain in their hands. The Social Democrats argued that they could hold the balance between Communists and Smallholders. The Communists asserted that only they could provide the 'strong man' the job required. Finally, the Communists seemed to yield to the Smallholders' claim. Social Democrats and Peasants agreed. It looked like an important victory for the Smallholders and for democratic principles.

The day before the new government was to be

announced, the Communists reneged on their agreement to a Smallholder Minister of the Interior. It was assumed that they did so on Voroshilov's instructions. Faced with this the Smallholders yielded. The Communists obtained the Ministry of the Interior. They had sliced the first piece off the salami.

The Communists moved Imre Nagy from Agriculture to the Ministry of the Interior. There was a strong sense of anticlimax about the appointment. Of all the Communists, Nagy had the most acceptable face. After the land reform he was a familiar, reassuring figure. The Communists had shown their determination to take control of the Ministry of the Interior. The choice of Nagy for the job demonstrated their moderation.

'Nagy was Minister of the Interior in those days,' Ferenc Nagy wrote later. 'Among the Communist ministers, he was most closely Hungarian; for a long time he lived in a little country town. Possessed of an ingratiating manner, he is a politician of small calibre, who blindly follows the instructions of the party chieftains.'[6] He might hold a critical appointment, but he was certainly not the strong man the Communists had claimed it needed. And Communist influence in the government more generally remained limited, with Rákosi as one of two deputy prime ministers and Erik Molnár at Social Welfare. On balance the composition of the government looked as reassuring for parliamentary democracy as the election itself, with democratic principles successfully resisting most of the pressures emanating from the Russians and the left.

So things continued into 1946. Reconstruction went on. On 31 January Hungary was proclaimed a republic, with Tildy as its first President. Ferenc Nagy took his place as Prime Minister. The Republic had a properly democratic constitution, and was recognized by the Western powers.

But East-West tensions were increasing. In a speech in February Stalin argued that capitalism and imperialism were constitutionally hostile to Communism and a threat to the Soviet Union. George Kennan, the United States chargé d'affaires in Moscow, sent his famous 'long telegram', which completed the process of hardening United States attitudes to the Soviet Union. In March Churchill spoke at Fulton, Missouri, of the Iron Curtain being rung down across Europe.

Colder winds blew also inside Hungary. The Communists and the Social Democrats had joined the Smallholder-led coalition, but they announced that they would cooperate only with 'democratic forces' among the Smallholders. The Smallholders yielded, expelling twenty-one deputies whom the left identified as 'reactionaries'. They also acquiesced in a Communist-sponsored bill for the protection of the Republic and of the social order, a catch-all measure which, exploited later by the Communist Minister of the Interior, became known as the 'Executioner's Law'.

That Minister was no longer Imre Nagy. On 23 March, after four months in the job, he was moved aside so that László Rajk could take his place: the 'strong man' whom the Communists had promised in November. Nagy's daughter recalls that he hated the job and looked to ill-health for escape, taking himself off to hospital for an unnecessary operation. She, an enthusiastic teenager, believed that the new order should wreak vengeance on the old: she wanted to move from her job in the Foreign Ministry to the Ministry of the Interior. 'Go anywhere, but not to the Ministry of the Interior,' he told her.[7] 'Nagy, more philosopher than fighter, unsuited for palace intrigue and cloak-and-dagger dealings, did not have the temperament for such a post.'[8]

Rajk was different. He was 'the very personification of the half-educated Communist,' Ferenc Nagy wrote afterwards, 'a resolute and fanatical exponent of the most violent moves precipitated by Communist ideology. If the latent evil in this gentle-seeming schoolteacher had become evident sooner, I would never have accepted him as a member of my cabinet.'[9] It was Rajk more than anyone else who carried through the Communists' destruction of their opponents in the next two years.

When he lost his ministerial office Imre Nagy remained a

member of the Political Committee and of the Central Committee Secretariat. These Party offices were less important than they would become later, when the Communists monopolized all power: the political battle was still being fought in government and parliament. It is hard not to conclude that for his Party Nagy had already served his purpose, first as a Minister of Agriculture who understood the peasants, and then as a reassuring Minister of the Interior until it was safe to unleash Rajk's ferocity. He was left with positions of dignity rather than power.

But at the time there seemed to be no inevitability about the Communists' growing strength in the political game. Coming to Budapest in the late spring of 1946, the British parliamentary delegation noted the 'sense of purpose and political awareness shown by almost the entire population. This is undoubtedly due to the new democratic opportunities provided by the recent Electoral Law . . . and by the fact that the election of last November was clearly established as free and fair . . . there is now established in Hungary the seeds of a new democracy which, given encouragement and understanding . . . may finally establish itself along Western parliamentary lines. Certainly this appears to be the wish of almost all Hungarians.'[10] Even Hungarians, better informed and more anxious than such outsiders, still hoped for a democratic future.

Those hopes, and hopes for a viable Hungary, were now pinned on the peace conference which was convened in Paris in July 1946. Putting aside the question of Germany, it tackled first the problem of peace treaties with Hitler's satellites, including Hungary. Some Hungarians still hoped, quite unrealistically, for a revision of the Trianon frontiers in Hungary's favour. They ignored the fact that the victors saw Czechoslovakia and Yugoslavia as allies, Romania as an enemy which had had the sense to change sides in time. Hungary by contrast had fought almost to the end as Germany's last ally.

It is true that the November election had brought

Hungary credit as an East European state still seeking Western standards of pluralism. But this was not enough to win it favours at the peace conference. When the treaty was signed it brought Hungary 'normalization' but no expansion. It brought no change on the presence of Soviet troops in Hungary; it provided that they should remain in Hungary to guarantee the lines of communication of Soviet forces in Austria.

Political manoeuvring continued through the autumn of 1946. The Communists, supported by Social Democrats and Peasants, forced the Smallholders to expel more 'reactionaries'. The group expelled formed the Freedom Party and began to attract support as a responsible group outside the coalition. When the Communists held their Congress at the end of October they seemed uncertain and divided. Rajk told them menacingly that 'We have stopped halfway, for if we are not merely a bourgeois democracy, neither are we yet a people's democracy.'[11]

The time was approaching for the Communists to take the next slice of salami. In December Rajk claimed that a dangerous plot to seize control of the army had been uncovered. In the New Year he uncovered another, this time to restore the Horthy regime. In February 1947, he turned against the Smallholders.

Béla Kovács, the Smallholder Secretary General and the man they had tried to make Minister of the Interior, was called in for interrogation by the political police. He was accused of espionage against the Red Army and of involvement in a plot said to have been organized by a Masonic-like society concerned to preserve Magyar racial purity.

In attacking Kovács, the Communists were tackling the key personality in the numerically strongest party in the coalition. Perhaps his first interrogation persuaded them that the Smallholders were too big for them. They handed Kovács over to the Soviet military police. The Russians took him away to imprisonment in the Soviet Union. The Western Allies protested, proposed an investigation. But they could do nothing to save Kovács. He emerged from imprisonment only in 1956.

In May 1947, the Communists turned their fire on Ferenc Nagy, the Smallholder Prime Minister. He went to Switzerland on holiday, leaving a four-year-old son in Budapest. In his absence the Communists put it about that he had known about Kovács' conspiracy. His private secretary was arrested. The President, Zoltán Tildy, advised him not to return to Hungary. The Communists offered to send his son to join him in return for his resignation. Nagy agreed, and the child was handed over like a diminutive secret agent on the Swiss-Austrian border. Other Smallholders joined Nagy in exile. Their party had effectively been destroyed.

But the Communists had not yet consumed all the salami. There remained one last chance for pluralism in Hungary. In his speech at Harvard on 5 June 1947, George Marshall offered American strength to rebuild Europe. Ernest Bevin seized on his words. By the end of June the Paris Conference on the Marshall Plan was in session. On 4 July the British representative in Budapest formally invited the Hungarian government to take part. A decision seemed to hang in the balance. But Moscow ordered the East European governments to turn down the invitation. Europe became still more clearly divided on the line which the Red Army had reached in 1945.

The next step was the general election of 31 August 1947. Conditions favoured the Communists far more than they had two years earlier. They had had time to undermine their rivals. A new electoral law disenfranchised anyone accused of support for fascism. Rajk controlled the Ministry of the Interior. The West had proved unable to check Soviet pressure. The Communists were clearly in the ascendant.

Even so, they did not do particularly well in the election. They became the biggest party in the coalition, with 100 seats. But the Smallholders, even without Béla Kovács and Ferenc Nagy, won 68. The Social Democrats, now effectively dragooned into subservience to the Communists, won 67 seats, and the Peasants 36.

And two new parties, formed by men expelled by the Smallholders and Social Democrats under pressure from the Communists, won 109 seats between them. With the support of minor parties they mustered 140 seats, against the coalition's 271: a reasonable basis in orderly times for a constitutional opposition.

But the Communists had broken the nerve of their coalition partners, who supported the Communists in labelling one of the opposition leaders a fascist. His parliamentary immunity was attacked. In November he fled to the West and the opposition disintegrated. The coalition, now dominated by the Communists, ruled unopposed.

At this juncture, just when the parliamentary struggle ceased to matter, Nagy was appointed President of the Assembly. In the eighteen months since he had lost his job as Minister of the Interior he had held only Party office. His new appointment seems to symbolize the contempt in which his Party's leaders held him. He took charge of an already impotent National Assembly. Yet he approached the appointment with his usual outward calm. To some he also appeared to take it seriously. 'It was a decorative position,' Paul Ignotus wrote, 'but no-one took it seriously, as everyone knew that the Party Politbureau decided about policy and not the Government or, for that matter, the nominal legislative body. There was but one man who took Nagy's position seriously, and that was Nagy himself.'[12]

Nagy was still only fifty-one, but seems to have believed that his active political career was over. His heart had started to trouble him and, as a speaker at the reburial thirty-two years later noted, he thought he might not have long to live. Members of parliament noted a sense of fatalism in his first speech as their President. It is recorded that he was more warmly applauded by the other parties than by his own, and it is tempting to speculate that something in his phrasing or manner revealed disquiet with the way his Party was subverting democracy. But the applause was probably no more than a tribute to the man himself. As Speaker Nagy seems to have gone on serving his Party's interests loyally. For example, a report he made on his return from a visit to Western Europe in the spring of 1948 was in routinely Communist language. At a time when the National Assembly's role was being destroyed, Nagy did not effectively defend it. He was already troubled by the way things were going, as later events revealed. But he kept his disquiet to himself and within the Party.

It now remained for the Communists to destroy their demoralized partners in the coalition. The Social Democrats, who had helped the Communists destroy the Smallholders' power, now tried to escape from their embrace. But the Communists pressed them to agree to a merger. In February 1948, the Social Democrats expelled those of their members who opposed fusion and in June formed with the Communists the Hungarian Workers' Party.

Only the Smallholders remained numerically significant. Tildy, the Smallholder President, was got rid of easily. He was replaced by a discredited Social Democrat, Árpád Szakasits. István Dobi, a broken man and a drunkard, became Prime Minister. The only strong personalities left in the government were Communists. Individuals from other parties still clung to office, but the parties themselves were broken.

It was another year before 95.6 per cent of the electorate voted for a single list put forward by the Communist dominated coalition. But for all practical purposes parliamentary democracy was destroyed in June 1948. In 1956, in the middle of the Revolution, Nagy promised to bring it back; but the Soviet intervention swept that promise like so much else aside. It was to be more than forty years until Hungary recovered the parliamentary democracy that had promised so much in 1945 and been so brutally destroyed.

Chapter 5

TERROR

The absorption or destruction of the other political parties was not enough to give Communism absolute power in Hungary. Rákosi needed to complete the seizure of the economy also. He had to break the other centres of civil society, notably the churches. He needed to crush the remnants of the bourgeoisie and the upper classes. And to satisfy Stalin's and his own paranoia he had, finally, to destroy anyone within the Party who might challenge his supremacy. He completed this agenda by 1951 and spent 1952 and the first part of 1953 presiding over the ruins.

Between 1945 and the middle of 1948, Hungary recovered surprisingly quickly from its wartime devastation. Communications were gradually restored, buildings repaired. Casual Soviet looting of industry came to an end. The Hungarians met the onerous conditions of their reparations agreements with the Soviet Union. The great post-war inflation was broken by the introduction of the forint that Rákosi claimed to have fathered. The mines and heavy industry were nationalized. A delegation went to Washington and came back with American credits. On 1 August 1947, the Three Year Plan was launched.

In 1948 the Communists were determined to take matters further. In January they held an activists' conference. It adopted the slogan, 'The country is yours, you build it for yourselves', a slogan which was to mock and haunt

63

Hungarians for years. In March all enterprises with over one hundred employees were nationalized. Centralized control was imposed on every kind of economic activity. And the decision was taken to advance to the collectivization of agriculture.

It was just three years since the break-up of the estates, three short years in which the peasants had at last been able to farm land which they could call their own. There had been no talk in 1945 of moving on from distribution to collectivization. Nagy and his comrades had conveyed the impression then that the Party had abandoned for good its commitment to collective or state ownership. And land distribution justified itself by its success. The peasants' new proprietorial zeal dramatically increased agricultural yields. Agriculture underpinned Hungary's economic recovery. Visitors from victorious England remarked how well-fed the Hungarians were. It was left to theoreticians to pursue the economic arguments for bigger productive units.

The Party's decision to embark on rapid collectivization was therefore bound to arouse resistance. It was dictated in part by an ideological commitment to collective or state ownership, and more urgently by the need to demonstrate zeal in following the Soviet example. In 1945 the Communists had had to walk warily. Now they could afford to impose their will.

The Communists aimed to start collectivization after the 1948 harvest. Party activists would put the case for collectivization to the peasants. In economic terms it was a strong one. Agriculture needed more investment if yields were to be raised further. Only much larger holdings could secure such investment and put it to effective use. Without it the peasants would be doomed to continue on their own land the back-breaking labour which they had known throughout history on the estates. They would remain slaves of the land, unable to produce the cash crop surpluses which the growing urban population needed.

But in human terms the case for collectivization was less seductive. It would take back from the peasants the one thing, land of their own, which they had always longed for. It would force them into large holdings, cooperative or state-owned, not very different from the estates which they had only just escaped. And the Party programme demanded change in the autumn, allowing no time to demonstrate to the peasants the strength of the economic case for change.

While it prepared the collectivization drive in the summer and early autumn of 1948, the Party presented a united front to the outside world. But behind the façade, opinions were sharply divided. In closed Party meetings Nagy argued for a much more deliberate approach to collectivization than Rákosi intended to impose. He claimed to speak with the authority of an expert. 'Among Central Committee members,' he wrote later, 'no one concerned himself so much, so intensively, from a theoretic and practical standpoint, with the development of socialist cooperative, large-scale agriculture, with the problems of its organization and operation, as I did, ahead of all the others, beginning as early as 1946.'[1]

He acknowledged that cooperative farming was desirable and necessary. In a report to the Third Party Congress in September 1946, he had argued that '. . . the transformation of agriculture can only be said to be effective if the agrarian organization of small peasants supplements and surpasses the production of the abolished large landholding system. The small and medium-sized peasant holdings . . . cannot independently achieve such an expanded production. But they are able to do so by joining forces. Mechanization also aids in this direction by fostering the concentration of small holdings in cooperatives.'[2]

But Nagy also believed that the best way ahead lay through a voluntary commitment to cooperation by the peasants. They would be ready for cooperation when the evidence demonstrated its strengths. A gradual approach was necessary. Excess of zeal in urging, forcing the peasants into cooperatives would short-circuit the process. There was nothing capitalist about such gradualism. 'There can be no People's Democracy without a cooperative movement, just as the cooperative movement can only develop and realize its great goals completely in a People's Democracy.'[3] But it would take time to achieve such voluntary cooperation.

This sort of argument would have carried the day in debate inside the Party in 1945, when discretion was necessary. By 1948, Rákosi had no time for it. To him, agriculture was only part of the problem. He was more concerned with his relationship with Stalin, and Stalin had collectivized Soviet agriculture by force. As international tensions increased, so did heresy-hunting inside the Communist camp. Rákosi had to show that Hungary was unambiguously committed to socialism.

To Rákosi, therefore, Nagy's arguments were a tedious irrelevance. He had none of Nagy's interest in agriculture and concern for the peasants. He would have no more hesitation about using terror to transform agriculture than he had shown in breaking political opponents. He was determined that collectivization should start in 1948. The Party backed him. 'In September of 1948,' Nagy wrote later, 'an attitude arose, in the question of the cooperatives, that declared that we would collectivize the whole of Hungarian agriculture in the course of a few years. I do not agree with this . . . This will isolate us from the great masses of the peasantry.'[4]

But the Party decision had been taken. The collectivization campaign was launched immediately after the harvest. Persuasion rapidly became coercion. Early in 1949 Rákosi stepped up the pressure on the peasants. Nagy's arguments were swept aside. In August he was expelled from the Political Committee. In September the Central Committee condemned him as a right-wing opportunist.

Nagy recanted, as he had done in 1930. Our source for this is the same as for the 1930 recantation, an article published in the Party newspaper, *Népszabadság*, in 1957. Its title, 'The Master of Hypocrisy', reveals its purpose. Nagy, by then a prisoner awaiting trial, had to be discredited. So *Népszabadság* unearthed his recantations in 1930 and 1949 as evidence of his hypocrisy.

It recorded that in 1949 Nagy agreed to describe his attitude on agricultural questions as 'my rightist, opportunistic deviation'. He accepted the decision to proceed with the collectivization which he had hitherto opposed. He confessed to ideological error also. He had considered the state of society in Hungary as no more than 'state capitalism'. This had led him to argue for the form of agriculture – individual peasant farming – which corresponded to the capitalist stage of economic development. Yet: 'The individual cultivation of smallholdings . . . as we all know, leads to capitalist farming.'

According to *Népszabadság*, Nagy went on: 'Opportunism became apparent not only in my theoretical work but also in my attitude and style of work. I did not take part in the work of the Party in accordance with my abilities and the tasks that lay ahead of me. I kept in the background, was indifferent, thus giving the impression, outside as inside the Party, that I was in opposition. This entailed great dangers for the Party . . . was bound to isolate me from the Party . . .

'I know very well that it is late to begin to eliminate my mistakes now . . . the self-criticism which I exercise today is only the beginning of the beginning in the correction of my faults; but I have started on the road on which I can and will overcome the faults . . . with the support and assistance of the Party.'[5]

Thus Nagy recanted, as he had in 1930. These must have been weary words when they were uttered and they were even wearier when they were published to discredit Nagy eight years later. They show him abjectly reciting propositions which he had earlier rejected and which flew in the face of his practical experience as well as the agricultural theory in which he believed.

There is no gallantry about this recantation. But there is a kind of gallantry to be detected in the events which led up to it. In 1948, Communism was triumphant. Rákosi was intent on a policy which imitated Soviet practice. Within the Party only Nagy opposed him, fighting hard for the agricultural policy in which he believed. It was a bolder defiance by far than that in 1930. Now he challenged not a band of émigrés but his Party in government. He defied a Party leader who had already demonstrated his ruthlessness. He put his faith in the Hungarian peasantry ahead of loyalty to his comrades. That he then gave way, humiliated himself, is undeniable. The force aligned against him must have seemed invincible. It was not the first such recantation in Nagy's life, but it was the last.

The Party was also preparing a campaign against the churches. It was ideologically committed to atheism. The churches, and especially Cardinal Mindszenty, were thorns in the flesh that it no longer needed to tolerate. Mindszenty had made no secret of his opposition to them. In the elections he had come out openly in support of the Smallholders. He protested when the church lands were expropriated in 1946. In 1947 he campaigned against a proposal to make religious education optional. A year later he urged Catholics in parliament to vote against the nationalization of church schools. As the politicians broke, he became more prominent. 'At a time when all values and belief were discredited and destroyed his total dedication and inflexibility made him a legendary figure. Wherever the Cardinal appeared the roads were blocked by crowds of people who wanted to hear or at least see him.'[6]

At Christmas, 1948, Mindszenty was arrested. He was taken to the political police interrogation centre at 60 Andrássy Ut. The Communists had taken over the torture chambers established there during the war by the Hungarian fascists. Gradually its horrific reputation spread. Nicknamed the 'house of fidelity', it came to symbolize the use of terror to ensure conformity with which Rákosi ruled Hungary. When the torturers went to work on Mindszenty, it took them only a month to prepare the proud and cantankerous prelate for a show trial. He recited a confession which had clearly been drilled into him by torture. He was sentenced to life imprisonment. Other churchmen followed until, in 1950, the churches were reduced to accepting a concordat with the state on the state's terms. The Catholic Church, the Calvinists and the Lutherans had been destroyed as competitors of the Party for public influence.

László Rajk masterminded the campaign against Mindszenty. He similarly prepared the ground for the election of May 1949. A single list of candidates was offered to the electorate. When 95.6 per cent of them voted for the list, the message was as clear as that of Mindszenty's show trial. The Communists had absolute power and would use it ruthlessly against their enemies. The old ways of persuasion and benevolence were no longer needed. Anything that stood in their way would be destroyed. It was the message which Rajk had advocated from the moment he emerged from prison in 1945.

Two weeks after the election, Rajk himself was arrested. The political police prepared him for trial too. Rajk was a hard man to break and the process took four months, right through the summer of 1949. Meanwhile, in the streets of Budapest delegates to the World Youth Festival celebrated the triumph of their progressive cause.

Years later the world learned that János Kádár was involved in the process of breaking Rajk. They were friends; Kádár had been the sponsor at the naming of Rajk's baby son, born during the Mindszenty trial. He visited Rajk in person. He urged him to confess for the Party's sake, promising him that if he did his life would be spared.

By the logic that ruled Eastern Europe in the late forties, there was no particular mystery about the Rajk trial. Stalin was waging a campaign to destroy Tito. Show trials to demonstrate Yugoslav perfidy were required. Each of the East European countries had to produce an example of treachery. Rákosi decided that Rajk should play the role of

Tito's principal accomplice in Hungary. His execution would dispose of a potential rival who was dangerously popular among the Party rank and file.

But the situation mystified Communists who had not yet mastered Stalinist logic. They were torn between admiration for Rajk's work in building Communist power and horror at the crimes of which Rákosi accused him. Most allowed themselves to be persuaded by Rákosi's hysterical campaign against him.

In September Rajk's show trial was held in the hall of the Ironworkers' Union. He pleaded guilty and was condemned to death. Two weeks later he was hanged. The Revolution had started to eat up its own children.

We have seen that Nagy was expelled from the Political Committee as Rajk was being prepared for trial. It might have served Rákosi's convenience to put him on trial for conspiracy with Tito at the same time. There was even something that could have been used as evidence of a sort against him if Rákosi had wished. In the spring of 1947 he had written one of his scholarly, rather unworldly pieces about international affairs. In it he advocated cooperation between the countries of the Danube basin. Others pursued the idea. Such cooperation seemed to make sense as an expression of socialist internationalism. In the summer of 1947 Tito visited Sofia to sign an agreement on cooperation, to make of the Balkan states a 'strong monolithic unity'. But Stalin was suspicious. *Pravda* attacked the idea and it vanished from the agenda. Within a year, Moscow's campaign against Tito was at full pitch. In the summer of 1948 he was expelled from the Comintern and the idea of any Danube grouping was dead. But in 1949 Nagy's earlier advocacy of an idea espoused by Tito could have served as a reason to try and hang him.

Rákosi may have thought Nagy negligible. He had none of Rajk's prestige within the Party. He did not seem to present a threat to Rákosi's authority. But lesser men went to the gallows after Rajk. As in the thirties the question arises why Nagy was spared. It seems likely that he was saved by his links with Moscow. Friends there may have exerted themselves on his behalf, or Kremlin realpolitik may have wanted to keep in play a basically loyal alternative to Rákosi, Gerö, Farkas and Révai. Or the decision to leave Nagy alone may have been Rákosi's, hesitating to touch a comrade with Muscovite connections.

After Rajk's destruction, there existed no one in Hungary who could challenge Rákosi's monopoly of power. He used it to revenge himself on a world which had given him less than he thought his due and which had subjected him to fifteen years in Horthy's gaols. He created in Hungary a terror which, by common consent, exceeded even that in neighbouring East European countries in the terrible early fifties.

Rákosi set unattainable norms in the factories. He pressed collectivization by force. The middle classes were deported from the cities to scrape a pretence of a living in villages where they were alien and suspect. The new class of Party and security police functionaries moved into the flats they left behind. Recalcitrant workers and peasants went into internment camps. Intellectuals, politicians, the prominent, were taken away in the night to interrogation, torture and imprisonment. The fear of the doorbell in the small hours became a new, unmentionable disease. Neighbour betrayed neighbour, friend failed to defend friend.

There were achievements. Industry grew fast. Favourite children of the working classes were pushed forward into prominence. There was a new confidence at first among the workers. But industrialization pre-empted resources. It was wastefully pursued. The shops were empty. Fear ate up all honesty. 'The grimmer conditions became, the merrier the Party's movement marches sounded through loudspeakers in streets and squares. Everybody went to work listening to songs reminding us that we had become "a strong bastion of peace and prosperity", that "victory was in the hands of the people".'[7]

That quotation summarizes in simple terms the hypocrisy which Rákosi's terror imposed on Hungary from 1948 until, in 1953, Imre Nagy began to leach it out of the system. The writer, Gyula Illyés, took a different approach when he set out to describe what tyranny did to his country. In his poem of 183 lines, 'One Sentence on Tyranny', written in 1950 and published during the Revolution on 2 November, 1956, he expressed in one long sentence of poetry some of the terrible realities that Nagy tried to analyse in his tortured prose five years later.

Where there's tyranny,
there's tyranny,
not only in the gun-barrel,
not only in the prison-cell,

not only in the torture-rooms,
not only in the nights,
in the voice of the shouting guard;
there's tyranny

not only in the speech of the
prosecutor, pouring like dark smoke,
in the confessions,
in the wall-tapping of prisoners,

not only in the judge's passionless
sentence: 'Guilty!'
there's tyranny
not only in the martially

curt 'Attention!' and
'Fire!' and in the drum rolls,
and in the way the corpse
is thrust into a hole,

not only in the secretly
half-opened door,

in fearfully
whispered news,

in the finger, dropping
in front of the lips, cautioning 'Hush!'
there is tyranny
not only in the facial expression

firmly set like iron bars,
and in the stillborn
tormented cry of pain within these bars,
in the shower

of silent tears
adding to this silence,
in a glazed eyeball,

there is tyranny
not only in the cheers
of men upstanding
who cry 'Hurrah!' and sing,

where there's tyranny
there's tyranny
not only in the tirelessly
clapping palms,

in orchestras, in operas,
in the braggart statues of tyrants
just as mendaciously loud,
in colours, in picture galleries,

in each embracing frame,
even in the painters' brush,
not only in the sound of the car
gliding softly in the night

and in the way
it stops at the doorway;

where there's tyranny, it's there
in actual presence
in everything,
in the way not even your god was in olden times;

there's tyranny
in the nursery schools,
in paternal advice,
in the mother's smile,

in the way a child
replies to a stranger;

not only in the barbed wire,
not only on the booksellers' stands,
more than barbed wire
in the hypnotic slogans;

it is there
in the goodbye kiss,
in the way the wife says:
'when will you be home, dear?'

in the 'how are you's?'
repeated so automatically in the street,
in the loosening of the grip
to give a nonchalant handshake,

in the way suddenly
your lover's face becomes frozen,
because tyranny is there
in the amorous trysts,

not only in the questioning,
it is there in the declaration of love,
in the sweet drunkenness of words,
like a fly in the wine,

for not even in your dreams
are you alone,
it is there in the bridal bed,
and before it, in the dawning desire,

because you only believe beautiful what
once has already belonged to the tyrant;
you have slept with him
when you thought you were making love to another;

in plate and in glass,
it is there, in your nose, your mouth,
in coldness and dimness,
out of doors and in your room,

as if the windows were open
and the stink of corruption flooded in,
as if in the house
there was a smell of leaking gas;

if you talk to yourself,
it is tyranny that questions you,
even in your imagination
you are not free of it,

above you the Milky Way's different, too:
a frontier zone where the light seeps,
a minefield; and the star
is a spy-hole;

the crowded heavenly tent
is a single forced-labour camp,
for tyranny speaks
out of fever, out of the sound of bells,

out of the priest in the confessional,
from the sermon,
church, parliament, torture-chamber
are all only a stage;

you open and close your eyes,
only this looks at you;
like an illness,
it accompanies you like memory,

in the train's wheels you can hear it,
you're prisoner, you're prisoner, that's what it repeats;
on a mountain or beside the ocean,
this is what you breathe;

the lightning flashes, it is this
that's present in every unexpected
noise and light,
in the missing heart-beat;

in tranquillity,
in the boredom of the shackles,
in the whisper of the rain,
in the bars that reach to the sky;

in the falling of the snow
white like the prison wall;
it looks at you
out of your dog's eyes,

and because it's there in every ambition,
it is in your to-morrow,
in your thought,
in every one of your gestures;

like a river in its bed
you follow it and you create it;
you spy out of this circle,
it looks at you from the mirror,

it watches you, you would run in vain,
you're prisoner and warder at the same time;
into the tang of your tobacco,
into the fabric of your clothes,

it seeps in, etches like acid
down to your marrow,
you would like to think yet no idea
but it comes into your mind

you would like to look but you see only
what it creates like magic in front of you,
and already there is a circle of fire,
a forest-fire made out of match-sticks,

because when you dropped one,
you didn't crush it;
and thus it guards you now,
in the factory, in the field, in the house;

and you no longer feel the meaning of life,
what is meat and bread,
what it is to love, to desire
with wide-open arms,

thus the slave himself
forges and bears his own shackles;
when you eat you nourish it,
you beget your child for it,

where there's tyranny
everyone is a link in the chain;
it stinks and pours out of you,
you are tyranny itself;

like moles in the sunshine,
we walk in the dark,
we fidget in our chamber
as if it were the Sahara;

because where there's tyranny
all is in vain,
even the song, however faithful,
whatever the work you achieve,

for it stands,
in advance at your grave,
it tells you who you have been –
even your dust serves tyranny.[8]

Thus Illyés described, in his lovely sibilant Hungarian, the country's experience between 1949 and 1953. No one escaped the experience of tyranny, and few were untouched by the terror. It struck down Communists and churchmen, workers and intellectuals, rogues and honest men. Those close to Rákosi felt it as much as the peasant illegally slaughtering a pig or the clumsy working man accused of industrial sabotage. Even today, forty years afterwards, it will be difficult for democracy to exorcize the moral corruption which it bred.

But Nagy came through Rákosi's terror, as he had come through Stalin's, apparently unscarred. When he was driven from Party office in 1949 over agricultural policy he had no political occupation. He was however allowed to put his academic expertise to work, teaching quietly at Karl Marx University in Budapest and at the School of Agronomy at Gödöllö a few miles away. His daughter, by then in her early twenties, recalls how contented he seemed at that time. He appeared satisfied with an academic career. Having made his Party recantation he avoided, with whatever difficulty, showing in his teaching too obvious a clash between his own beliefs and his Party's agricultural policies.

But however contented he may have seemed out of politics, Nagy was back in political office by the end of 1950. Rákosi appointed him Minister of Food and later of Crop Collection. Neither was a senior post. The first involved responsibility for living standards, the second for ensuring that the farms met their delivery quotas. The balance between town and country was changing fast, as workers from the countryside poured into the new factories that the Five Year Plan required. The towns had to be fed, but collectivization had devastated Hungarian agriculture. Production on the collective farms fell. The peasants looked for black-market outlets for the food they grew on their private pocket-handkerchiefs of land.

The risk of failure in both jobs was great. Neither offered any chance of popularity. In appointing Nagy to the two ministries in turn, Rákosi was imposing the old Party discipline that required a critic to implement the policy he had attacked. At the same time he hoped to rob Nagy of what was left of the popularity he had won with the land reform in 1945. But in these thankless positions Nagy acquired experience of collectivized agriculture that he put to good use when he finally obtained power.

The Second Congress of the Hungarian Workers' Party was held in the early spring of 1951. The Korean War had broken out eight months earlier and East-West tension was at its height. Rákosi was using terror to create a matching tension in Hungary, imposing servitude on what was left of the church leadership and consigning one political figure after another to death or imprisonment. The new industrial and agricultural policies were breaking down: bread and meat rationing had just been re-introduced. The Party had lost any moral authority it had once enjoyed and depended for its authority on fear. Its isolation from the people was complete. Yet at this worst of times Nagy, who had argued for tolerance, for policies which would breed trust between Party and people, continued his climb back to influence. The Congress re-elected him to the Political Committee. He was appointed a member of the Party Secretariat. Only Rákosi and the three men closest to him held real power, but Nagy had become again one of the dozen most prominent Communists in Hungary.

For another two years, Nagy sat with Rákosi on the Political Committee and worked with him in the Secretariat while the Party imposed the tyrant's policies and whims on the country. They were almost as bad as the worst of years, 1951. Their hallmarks were continuing terror, increasing adulation of Rákosi and a subservience to the Soviet Union which grew ever more absolute as Stalin, in his dotage, increased his demands upon his creatures.

Years afterwards, Nagy summed up in his essays what happened in the years of terror. His language is clumsy, but it provides a counterpoint to Illyés' poetic description of the effects of tyranny: 'The "left-wing" deviationists, primarily Rákosi and Gerö, in the years 1949 to 1953 brought the socialist reorganization of agriculture to a dead end, bankrupted agricultural production, destroyed the worker-peasant alliance, undermined the power of the People's Democracy, trampled upon the rule of law, debased the people's living standards, established a rift between the masses and the Party and government – in other words swept the country towards catastrophe.'[9]

It is a damning retrospective indictment. At the time Nagy could do nothing to moderate Rákosi's excesses. He had made his protest in 1948. Now he lent his name to a regime which he could not affect, made himself useful to Rákosi and to Moscow, gradually re-established some of the influence with his comrades which he had lost when he spoke out against forced collectivization, and waited for better times.

Chapter 6

POWER

The terror which Rákosi inflicted on his country between 1948 and 1953 was dictated by many things. Prominent among them was his desire to please and emulate Stalin. He wanted to show even greater zeal than his East European rivals for the master's favour. The destruction of rival political parties, the attack on the churches, collectivization, extravagant production norms, all these were part of his tribute to Stalin, a tribute as complete as any barbarian ever gave to Rome.

From first to last, Rákosi was as proud to be called Stalin's best pupil as the wise father of his own people. But by early 1953 Stalin was nearing his end. There was a last outburst of paranoia, in which Moscow was convulsed by his belief that the doctors were plotting his destruction. It led to arrests in Budapest and other East European capitals as well as Moscow. But then, on 5 March, Stalin died. In the next few days the Soviet Union and Eastern Europe stumbled into a new world.

The news broke in Budapest on 6 March. The official reaction was lamentation: 'The greatest man of our era has left us.' Those who were there describe a very different reaction on the streets and buses – relief, hope and private joy. On 7 March Rákosi left for the funeral in Moscow. On the following day, parliament adopted a bill to commemorate Stalin. It was moved by Nagy, in a decent if fulsome

panegyric. With Lenin, he said, Stalin had created the
Soviet system. The hopes and happiness of all mankind
depended on it. It had liberated Hungary and was helping
her to build socialism. The whole people had been shocked
by Stalin's death. By completing his work in Hungary they
would build his true memorial.

Stalin's successors made a more realistic assessment.
They seem to have feared insurrection, and they deployed
security troops with tanks and flamethrowers around the
Kremlin before they announced that the great man was
dead. They were united in a sense of relief; all Stalin's
intimates had lived near to disaster in the old man's last
mad months. Now that he was gone they probably
recognized too the most compelling of reasons for hanging
together. Beyond that they differed. There were personal
rivalries, and differences on policy. Malenkov argued from
the start for a more liberal approach, with concessions to
the consumer and to ordinary human nature. His rivals
talked of discipline, of the priority of heavy industry and
of Western threats. But they agreed that reassessment was
necessary. There were at the time various interpretations of
the Soviet leaders' actions in the first weeks after Stalin's
death. But in retrospect they were clearly the actions of
frightened men who wanted above all to avoid trouble while
they analysed their situation.

If there were stirrings of discontent in the Soviet Union
in the months after Stalin's death, the security system was
able to suppress all news of them. In the Eastern European
countries things were different, and the world soon learned
of unrest there: discontent in Czechoslovakia, then protests
in the towns of northern Hungary and peasant demonstrations in the Great Plain. Each of these was
symptomatic, but none was particularly important in itself.
It was only in June that the uprising in East Berlin showed
the world the vulnerability of the system Stalin had left
behind him.

But well before the East Berlin rising, the Soviet leaders
seem to have recognized the need to reduce the pressure on

their East European satellites. They were receiving
troubled reports from their representatives there. But in
Hungary Rákosi showed no sign of reading the portents.
He saw no need for change. A general election was due, and
in his campaign speeches he produced one unqualified
justification after another of existing policy.

Nagy made three major campaign speeches of his own, in
which Western analysts claimed to detect a softer tone on
the collectives. But if he was challenging Rákosi at all it was
with infinite discretion. On 17 May, the election produced
an old-style result, with 98.2 per cent of the electorate
loyally recording their vote in favour of the candidates of
the single list. In County Somogy, where Nagy headed the
list, the result was as clear-cut as elsewhere: of 257,624
persons entitled to vote, 254,469 voted for the single list.

The Soviet leadership were less satisfied about the
situation in Hungary. At the end of May they summoned
Rákosi to Moscow and warned him that he could no longer
remain prime minister as well as general secretary. They
asked him to nominate someone who might replace him as
prime minister. He found fault with every name put
forward. And when he conceded the possibility that
someone else should head the government, he gave the
Russians the impression that he envisaged a prime minister
without effective powers.

This encounter between Rákosi and the Soviet leadership
seems to have produced no conclusion, but in early June
the Russians determined on more effective action. They
pressed Rákosi to recognize the need for policy as well as
personnel changes. He proposed that he should return to
Moscow to discuss the matter, accompanied by his two
closest associates, Gerö and Farkas. But the Russians
insisted on seeing a delegation representative of the whole
Hungarian leadership. So Rákosi took a bigger team to
Moscow. It included Dobi, the President of the Republic;
several younger men; and Nagy. The Hungarians were
received by the whole Soviet leadership on 13 June.

The meeting in the Kremlin was, so far as we know,

Nagy's first encounter with many of the Soviet leaders. He
knew Malenkov; and over the next twenty months their
stars rose and fell together. The others he had met, if at all,
only on formal occasions. He may have thought his
inclusion in the delegation surprising. Rákosi was of course
a regular visitor. The inclusion of Dobi, a non-Communist,
in this Party meeting was surprising but unimportant. The
younger men were bag carriers. But Nagy had been around
for decades, without ever previously breaking into the
charmed circle at the centre.

The Russians made much of unity and of collective
leadership. But they were already at odds. Beria's
elimination was imminent, and the Hungarians were among
the last outsiders to see him. The others were suspicious of
one another. But Nagy's impressions of the talks, which
can be pieced together from what he told associates and
from the essays he wrote later, give no indication of
disagreement between the Soviet participants. No doubt
they had made their own diagnosis of what was wrong in
Hungary and had agreed the line to take in detail
beforehand.

The Russians put the blame squarely on Rákosi. He had
forced industry and agriculture so hard as to make nonsense
of the Plan and destroy all hope of popular support. The
industrialization programme had been ill-considered. 'The
matter of economic planning,' Nagy records Mikoyan as
saying, 'shows a certain adventurous spirit, particularly the
excessive development of your own smelting industry.
Hungary has no iron, no coke. All this must be imported.
No one in Hungary has figured out yet exactly the price of a
ton of iron ore and steel in Hungary. Hungary is building
foundries for which no one has yet promised to supply the
ore. In 1952, for instance, there was a shortage of 700,000
tons of coke. There is also extravagance in the field of
certain investments.'[1]

Rákosi had become mesmerized by the cult of
personality, believing that only he was fit to govern. On this
point Soviet venom overflowed. Tibor Méray, who

probably had an account of the meeting from Nagy, claims that Beria said to Rákosi, 'We know that there have been in Hungary, apart from its own rulers, Turkish sultans, Austrian emperors, Tartar khans, and Polish princes. But, as far as we know, Hungary has never had a Jewish king. Apparently this is what you have become. Well, you can be sure that we won't allow it.'[2]

The Russian remedy was simple. Rákosi would remain First Secretary. Nagy would become Prime Minister. They would work in double harness. The Russians also laid down policy. There must be no continuation of the old methods; if there were, Krushchev said, the people would drive them out with pitchforks. Industrialization must be slowed down, targets made more realistic, the idea of industrial autarchy abandoned. Pressure for the collectives was to be relaxed.

'At the June 1953 Moscow Conference,' Nagy wrote later, 'Comrade Molotov . . . reassured us as follows: "The farm cooperatives must not be disbanded by fiat; but, should they choose to disband voluntarily, they shouldn't be hindered. No harm will come of it." '[3] The cult of personality was to be cut back. Révai and Farkas must be dropped from the Political Committee. Simple legality was to be reasserted.

There, largely on the strength of Nagy's own account, we have the evidence of the Soviet origins of what was to become Nagy's New Course. He describes them straightforwardly, showing no surprise that the Kremlin should dictate even the details of Hungarian policy. He passed as a typical Hungarian countryman, and at the end he showed himself a great patriot. But he had learned Communist discipline in his years in Moscow. Like the other Hungarian leaders, he had become accustomed to the absolute subordination of policy to Moscow's wishes. He accepted almost instinctively that the Kremlin's instructions were there to be followed, not questioned.

This was part of Nagy's attraction to the Russians, who had clearly made up their minds before he arrived in

Moscow that he should become Prime Minister. He was a man they believed they could rely on. He spoke Russian and had lived in Moscow. He was a disciplined Marxist. Yet he seemed to stand a chance of winning support in Hungary, where some at least would remember his role in the 1945 land reform and his resistance to collectivization in 1948.

On their return to Budapest, the Hungarian leaders prepared a Party resolution. On 27 June, Nagy presented it to a special meeting of the Central Committee. It confronted this elite audience with a sweeping indictment of Rákosi's use of power. It recorded that he and his associates had violated Marxist-Leninist principles. They had replaced collective leadership with the cult of personality. They had used arbitrary methods to force their policies through, ignoring and by-passing the legal system. And those policies had brought the country to the verge of collapse.

The Central Committee adopted the 'June Resolution'. It should have been enough to reduce Rákosi to the same subordination to Nagy which Nagy had hitherto shown to him. But in the fortnight since the Kremlin meeting, the Berlin uprising, although swiftly crushed by Soviet tanks, had frightened the Soviet leaders. In Moscow Malenkov's opponents had asserted themselves. In Budapest Rákosi saw his opportunity. The Party, he asserted, could not allow the general public to know of disagreement among the leadership. The Resolution must be kept secret – as it was for thirty years.

Nevertheless, the 'June Resolution' attained fame at once in Communist circles. All subsequent argument between dogmatists and reformers turned on interpretation of it. Today their arguments – Nagy's as much as his opponents' – read as turgidly as most documents of the old Communist school. But it has its significance as the first blueprint in any Communist country to document the turn away from Stalinism.

The first hint the general public got of this ferment

within the Party came on 30 June, when the composition of a new Political Committee was announced. In the list Nagy displaced Gerö from his usual position just below Rákosi. Then, on 3 July, the press announced the government's resignation and the appointment, 'on the recommendation of the Central Committee', of a new government, with Imre Nagy at its head.

On the afternoon of 4 July, Nagy spoke for the first time as Prime Minister. Excitement had risen in parliament when Rákosi left the seat allotted to the prime minister and retired to a back row. Now parliament listened to Nagy as he spoke in terms very different from those that had become standard over the last five years, and outlined a very different programme.

The speech marked a peak of Nagy's career. It seems likely that then, if ever, he tasted fulfilment. He was Prime Minister of his country, the nominee of the Party to which he had devoted his life. He knew that he had Soviet backing. He described a policy in which he believed, which he thought could avert collision between Party and people. He was not yet disillusioned. He had twice quarrelled with his Party, seen in the Soviet Union and Hungary the damage that could be done by dogmatism. But he had maintained self-discipline as a Communist, which he thought of as the height of Marxist seriousness. Now he had the chance to present a policy which could bring things back from the edge of the abyss. He knew the people would welcome what he had to say.

He may also have hoped that he would get the backing of the Party. But Rákosi was already making difficulties. In Moscow he had seemed to defer to Nagy as soon as the Russians had made their position clear. Now he clearly did not intend to cede authority without a fight to a man he despised. His supporters put it about that there were doubts about Nagy in Moscow – as there were among Malenkov's enemies. It was suggested that he was propounding government policies distinct from those of the Party. Party members held back until it was clearer that Nagy would succeed in forcing his policy through. They would not help him formulate his plans for the New Course. He wrote them, as he wrote his speech in the Assembly, almost unaided.

The speech itself was comparatively short and to the point. After preliminaries about the support for the government demonstrated at the May elections, Nagy emphasized that his policy was based on the 'realistic objectives and proposals of the new directives of the Central Committee' of the Party. It was almost the last reference to the Party in the speech. At once Nagy launched into criticism of the past. The economic planners had over-reached themselves: it was obvious that a revision of targets was necessary. The government would therefore carry out a substantial all-round reduction, in accordance with the capacity of the country, of the pace of development. Moreover, 'there is no reason whatever for any excessive industrialization or any efforts to achieve industrial autarchy, especially if the necessary sources of basic materials are wanting.' The country could meet some needs from imports from its East European neighbours, the Soviet Union and China, even the capitalist countries. They must lay stress on the food industry and light industry, slow the pace of heavy industrial development.

In agriculture too there had been misjudgements: because of excessive emphasis on collectivization, 'agricultural production was held up in its advance and just marked time during recent years.' To put things right the government would encourage individual farming. This year the usual autumn campaign to promote cooperatives would be omitted. Individual cooperative members would be allowed to leave and, if enough members so wished, cooperatives would be dissolved. The first task was to 'make agricultural production secure', not to pursue collectivization.

'The basic principle of our new economic policy is

continuously to raise the living standard of the population.' After the harvest prices would be cut. They would enforce the labour code and reduce overtime, improve utilities and housing, and simplify the system of compulsory food deliveries. Small-scale private enterprise would be licensed more freely.

Nagy called for respect for the intelligentsia. The way they were often treated was 'not worthy of the People's Democracy'. He called for greater tolerance of religion and for more spending on primary education. He came to the question of 'socialist legality'. He admitted that legality had not always been observed. Groundless and ill-considered prosecutions had 'loosened the ties between the working people on the one hand and the state authorities and local councils on the other.' Minor offenders would be released, internment camps closed, deportees returned to their homes. All discrimination against kulaks would cease.

If this new policy were to succeed, Nagy concluded, the active participation of the masses was needed. The government's choice of objectives should secure this: 'They are objectives suited to rally our working people more closely than ever behind their government.' On this basis they would open a new chapter in the history of the building of socialism.[4]

The 4 July speech left unsaid much of what Nagy had told the Central Committee a week earlier. It condemned past abuses and mistakes only by implication. It minimized the change which the New Course represented. It perpetuated the myth that the nation supported the Party. There was no reference to political liberties. There was no mention of the secret police, of the show trials, or of the hundreds executed since 1948. But Hungarians recognized how much further it went than would have been imaginable in Stalin's time. It reminded many of them of Nagy's role in the 1945 land reform.

The speech was broadcast live. It carried a great wave of relief over Hungary. It was cautious, and in places it paid lip service to things in which only the Party faithful believed. But it suddenly showed that on the broad issues the official world recognized reality. Even the language was straightforward, the official jargon limited. Nagy's calm and homely voice added to the effect. The fact that new policies were announced by the Prime Minister in the National Assembly rather than by the General Secretary in the Party newspaper was seen as symptomatic.

One simple memory, recalled by a woman in her forties who had lost everything under Communism, captures the moment: 'We were walking along the shore at Balatonfüred when loudspeakers began to transmit Nagy's speech . . . soon we noticed that Nagy's speech and style were entirely different and so we began to pay all our attention to what he said . . . and when we heard . . . that the evictees would be allowed to return home and the grave errors in the country's agricultural policy put right we felt sure that a miracle had happened.'[5]

The broadcast reached prisoners as well as holiday-makers. Páloczi-Horváth describes its reception in the punishment wing of the Central Prison in Budapest: 'I was lying on the palliasse in the afternoon of the 4th of June 1953' – an error: July is intended – 'when the miracle happened: I heard the wireless! Down below, on the ground floor, was the guard's duty room in our wing. The wireless grew louder, so loud that all the convicts could hear it. The guards had never done such a thing before.

'We all heard the speech in which the new Prime Minister, Imre Nagy, announced his "new course". He spoke against all the evil aspects of the regime. He promised a new, democratic way of life.

'I listened with feverish attention. This was salvation! Next morning when I woke up I thought that the whole thing must have been one of my hallucinations. Surely, surely it could not have happened?

'At noon the punitive section was disbanded. A very courteous young S.P. officer took me back to the intellectual section . . . Our "small hotel" of intellectual convicts was in turmoil. Everybody was talking about Imre

Nagy's speech and its consequences.'[6]

There was suspicion as well as relief. For many the story was simple. Communism was responsible for the evils which Imre Nagy described. He was a Communist who had put a good face on his Party's policy in the past. He seemed to be working in double harness with Rákosi, who had boasted of the Party's ability to deceive. For these people the New Course was nothing more than a tactical device. Others who were prepared to give Nagy the benefit of the doubt and put faith in his proposals were nevertheless sceptical of his ability to carry them through. It was only later in his period as Prime Minister, as the New Course started to produce results and the tensions between him and Rákosi became more manifest, that Nagy began to win personal popularity on any scale. It became a serious political factor only in 1956, by which time Rákosi had driven him temporarily out of politics altogether.

Yet for all the doubts and scepticism, Nagy's speech in parliament on 4 July deserves its place in history. It was the first public expression, not just in Hungary but throughout the Communist world, of a new kind of Communism. What Nagy said was crabbed and cautious, silent on many points of importance. Others soon followed where Nagy led. And of course he spoke to Soviet instructions, by Kremlin licence. Nevertheless, to Nagy goes the credit of being the first Communist after Stalin's death to talk in terms of the rights and aspirations of ordinary people and of a Communism which did not forget man.

In July 1953, Nagy was just fifty-seven. He had become the solid, comfortable figure whom we know from the 1956 photographs. He had the 'appearance of a country schoolteacher, stocky, round-faced, bespectacled and moustached.'[7] The moustache drooped over a kindly mouth. Thick glasses contributed to an owl-like, professorial expression. He was not a charismatic figure.

The Nagys lived in a comfortable but unpretentious villa

in a quiet road in Buda: two ground-floor rooms with a big conservatory along the side, a big study and cramped bedrooms above. Their daughter and son-in-law lived next door with their two children, six and two years old in 1953, who became the apples of their grandfather's eye. Three years later the little boy and girl assumed a political significance of their own when Nagy, by then out of office but the rising hope of the people, took them into Pest on the bus to buy ice cream and attracted the notice of half the population by doing so.

But in July 1953, Nagy had work to do. He had the levers of governmental power in his hands. He set about turning the New Course, as yet no more than a Central Committee Resolution and a speech in parliament, into reality. He was by nature slow to decide and slow to act. His approach was laborious, and he had none of the drive and appetite for paper which kept Gerö, for example, at his desk for seventeen hours a day. But in 1953 Nagy had a vision and the determination to implement it. He wanted to save his country, improve her politics and society, give her back a modicum of sincerity, decency and trust between individuals. He thought that if he could do so he might save his Party also. To achieve all this required unremitting pressure to force changes through against obstruction. So a man who was naturally reflective and academic was committed to an administrative grind.

Shortly after the speech on 4 July the first measures to begin implementing Nagy's programme were introduced. On 15 July the press reported the trial of a local official who, in his cups, had illegally searched the flat of a harmless citizen – the first suggestion for years of a check on small-town tyrants. On 23 July came a resolution on welfare and accident prevention in the factories. Three days later a minor amnesty was announced. On 1 August came a decree cancelling arrears in crop deliveries. On 23 August taxes on the peasants were reduced; a week later the police lost their discretion to deal with petty offences as they thought fit. On 2 September there was news of government credits for craftsmen, on 6 September of price reductions. On 16 September a reduction in agricultural delivery quotas was announced. The first summer of the New Course had yielded something for everyone.

This quick start must have demanded all the political will and attention to detail that Nagy could muster. He made no major public appearance all summer, but he broke his silence with a major speech at Kecskemét on 29 September. The tone was cautious and may have disappointed those who had begun to pin their hopes on the New Course. Nagy took the opportunity to remind his audience of the superiority of cooperative over individual farming. He warned peasants who were considering withdrawing from the cooperatives that they might regret the move: given more capital, which would come from the government in time, cooperatives could give their members a better living than they could earn by farming on their own.

Thereafter Nagy went back to his calm, office-bound approach. He made careful, unemotional speeches, mostly about agriculture: to a conference of agricultural experts in October, to county council officials in November. The physical and emotional pressures must have been great, and they told on Nagy later. But in 1953 he still had the physical toughness to carry him through. He had a peasant's constitution and as we have seen he, almost alone among Communist leaders, had not suffered the physical and emotional strain of a long period of imprisonment.

Nagy was a lonely figure in 1953. If he was to give the Kremlin and the Hungarian people what they expected of him, he needed, above all, Party support. But this Rákosi did his best to withhold. Within a week of Nagy's speech in parliament a speech by Rákosi to a Party audience was interpreted as a thinly veiled hint that Nagy's new policies were not to be taken too seriously: 'The experience of these last few days has shown that it would have been better to announce these tasks on behalf of the Party first, because several comrades were not sure whether the proposals submitted to the National Assembly by Comrade Nagy had been worked out on a basis of the decisions of the Party Central Executive.'[8]

Very soon a comparison of Nagy's speech with Rákosi's led Western observers to talk of dualism. They did not know what had happened at the June meeting in the Kremlin, but they concluded that although Nagy seemed to have the initiative Rákosi, with his command of the Party machine, could put effective obstacles in the way of action. And if action was delayed it would be Nagy's credit which would be destroyed. It was he who had raised hopes with his speech in the National Assembly.

By October Rákosi was attacking again, in the Central Committee. The Committee stayed loyal to Nagy. He later recorded the terms of their resolution: 'The attitude . . . the "left-wing" sect are taking . . . is extremely dangerous . . . These comrades fail to realize that their behaviour is . . . hindering . . . resolutions aimed at increasing the welfare . . . of the working people and particularly the industrial workers . . . Unless such behaviour is vigorously dealt with, there is the danger that the Party will become isolated from the workers, peasants and intellectuals alike.'[9]

Nagy clearly felt vindicated by this resolution. But more significant than his victory is the fact that Rákosi felt safe in pursuing his vendetta with Nagy, and that not even language like this caused him to desist. He could not overthrow Nagy as long as Moscow supported him, but he knew that he had more support within the Party than Nagy. Throughout the New Course, Nagy had to rely on the government machine alone to put through changes precisely because Rákosi had such a firm grip on the Party. And Party influence penetrated everywhere in government while the government was sedulously shut out of Party channels.

Nagy would have been less isolated in 1953 if Rákosi's Communist victims like János Kádár had been at liberty. But while it was relatively easy to close the internment camps it was much more difficult to get political prisoners out of gaol. Rákosi's Communist enemies had been formally sentenced; formal measures were needed if their sentences were to be rescinded. Once at liberty they would threaten Rákosi's position, and he used every device to obstruct the process of legal review.

Nagy made efforts to reduce this isolation. His son-in-law Jánosi was with him from the beginning, but he was a lightweight, whose standing was damaged by the very fact of their relationship. In March 1954 he recalled Zoltán Szántó from Paris and put him in charge of information: he was a friend from the old days who seemed a loyal supporter. Others joined him: Zoltán Vas, Lajos Fehér, even Mihály Farkas, who had been among the most vicious of Rákosi's supporters. But Nagy began to get supporters within the Party in serious numbers only when the political prisoners started to come home in the autumn of 1954. By the time they had found their political bearings, he was out of office. For most of his time as Prime Minister he had very few close supporters, none of them in important positions. His strengths were far from the Central Committee. He depended on Soviet benevolence on the one hand and cautious but growing popular support for the New Course on the other.

The balance of success and failure of the New Course, like most things associated with Nagy, has not attracted much cool analysis. For years it was traduced or ignored inside Hungary and over-praised abroad. And objectivity is not easy. The experiment was too short-lived – the whole thing came and went inside twenty months – to produce conclusive evidence either way. But it is possible to draw a rough and ready balance sheet.

The best starting point is the economy. It is generally accepted that between 1949 and 1953 Rákosi and Gerö imposed far greater strains on the economy than it could bear. Before the war it was a simple, predominantly agricultural, economy. It had been ravaged in the war and immediately afterwards. It was ill-equipped to stand new strains. The Communists' unrealistic schemes of industrial expansion exacted a high political price. They alienated the country, which could be kept in check only by terror. But these schemes also took a purely economic toll, and this too was disastrously high. They doubled Hungary's industrial output and forced productivity up by sixty-three per cent. But it was impossible to keep up that pace. As we have seen, by 1953 the economy, as much as society, was at breaking point. A change of economic policy was essential, and Nagy provided it.

He gave priority to raising living standards, which had fallen between 1949 and 1953 by a quarter. The consequence was that in 1953 and 1954 the rate of growth declined. Nagy argued that the decline was the result of the crisis Rákosi had provoked, not the measures he had introduced to tackle it. But it remains a fact that Nagy had to cut back capital investment if he was to improve living standards. He had to relax the ferocious industrial discipline of the Rákosi years if he was to heal social wounds and convince Hungarians that the country they were building was at last truly theirs. He had to raise wages if he was to correct the fall in the standard of living which had made such a mockery of the promises of socialism.

In making these shifts he was calling a halt to a process which had begun to change Hungary, however wastefully, into a potentially more productive society. There is the charge to answer that by doing this he threw away the economic rewards which four years of extreme economic self-sacrifice would in due course have brought. His answer would be that in the absence of the changes he introduced society and the economy would have collapsed. The New Course averted such a collapse. But the tragedy is that he was unable to keep the country on the New Course long enough to reap the benefits which better morale and better motivation in the factories might eventually have brought.

The effect of the New Course in industry was therefore marginal: a shift from heavy to light industry, from investment to consumption, a breathing space after the

gigantic efforts to create a heavy industrial base. The effect
on the worker was also marginal: he took what relief he got
but remained suspicious of the Party's intentions and
fearful of a reversal of course. Nagy did not face the
ingrained apathy generated by seventy years of Communism with which Gorbachev is faced today. But apathy and
suspicion there were. And unlike Gorbachev, Nagy could
not publicly blame his predecessor. He was committed to
partnership with Rákosi and to Party loyalty.

Things went better in agriculture. Here Nagy hoped that
freedom – to leave the collective farm, to wind up the
cooperative, to keep profits for oneself – would bring higher
production in return. He presented his new policies in
practical, not ideological terms. Individual farmers grew
most of the nation's food. They complained of discriminat-
ory taxes and delivery norms purposely set high to
persuade them to join the cooperatives. To persuade them
to make the effort needed to raise production, these
complaints must be dealt with. The cooperative drive must
be abandoned for the time being. Cooperative farming
would have to demonstrate its superiority in practice.

The decrees permitting the dissolution of the cooperatives went through in October 1953. A quarter of a million
members left them, reducing the collectivized sector from
almost forty to about twenty-five per cent of arable land.
The political pressures were taken off in other ways also.
The prosecutions of the kulaks for illegal slaughter and
threshing, for withholding goods and black marketeering,
for agitating against the cooperatives fell away.

The peasant went back to farming in the way he had done
between 1945 and 1948: on a smallholding of his own, with
his own labour and his family's, with inadequate plant and
fertilizers. The result was somewhat better levels of
production, continuing difficulties in meeting the needs of
the towns, a persistent black market, inadequate investment. Some cooperatives continued, deprived on the whole
of their most vigorous members. The ambitious ideas of
transforming Hungarian agriculture and rural life were set

aside. Agriculture under Nagy did better than under Rákosi, at a lower price in human happiness. It fell short of what Rákosi had promised.

In January 1954, Nagy went again to Moscow. He discussed with the Soviet leaders the difficulties Rákosi was putting in his way. According to Nagy, they were outspoken in condemning Rákosi. 'Comrade Malenkov said, "The faults we noted in June are being remedied very slowly. Rákosi has not taken the lead in remedying the faults." Comrade Khrushchev also noted, "Gerö has no words of self-criticism or feeling of responsibility for the serious mistakes of the economic policy; at best he admits, 'It is possible that Comrade Nagy is right in feeling that I am held back by the old economic policy.' " '[10]

Nagy quotes another outburst from Khrushchev: 'In June, 1953, we correctly passed judgement on the Hungarian Party's leadership and that judgement is still entirely correct today. They can't hide behind Beria as Rákosi is trying to do. We were there, too, when these errors were ascertained, every one of us. We were right, and what we decided then is also right today. This should have been acted on already.'[11]

To Nagy, these quotations demonstrated the Soviet leaders' support for his policy and its rightness. But they demonstrate yet again how far Rákosi had felt able to go in resisting the will of some at least of the Soviet leaders. The reason is, of course, that the Kremlin was divided. There were those who wanted to destroy Malenkov and who therefore encouraged Rákosi's opposition to Nagy, whom they rightly saw as Malenkov's disciple in Budapest.

For the time being, however, the Kremlin continued to back the New Course. Nagy was in the ascendant. On his return to Budapest he reported to the National Assembly on the past six months and the plans for 1954. His speech was complacent, but it was well received. 'The joy and enthusiasm with which people everywhere have received the news of the new government programme show how timely and necessary the far-reaching changes . . . have been. We may state that on the whole we have tackled without major hitches the tasks set forth for 1953 . . .' In agriculture, 'the government set as the main task a development of agricultural production which will . . . lay a solid material basis for a steady rise in the living standard. As is known, this great, I may say historic, task has . . . been successfully solved.'[12] Of course Nagy exaggerated, but there had been real progress in 1953 and there were real hopes for 1954.

The first test in the New Year came at a meeting of the Political Committee. The subject was cultural policy, and on this as on all else Rákosi deployed his opposition. His hardliners came forward with criticisms of what they saw as dangerous consequences of Nagy's policies. Writers had started to express themselves rather than Party orthodoxy. A young poet had described life in the countryside as it was, not as the Party line asserted it was. A young playwright had gone further. *The Cucumber Tree* described the adventures of a careerist who put his own advancement before all else. His task in life was to manage an enterprise charged with the collection of surplus animal fur. Singlemindedly, he took furs where he could find them, even off the backs of living animals. The allegory was obvious. And the Party faithful were even angrier when Hungary's greatest living poet joined in. Gyula Illyés published an article about the poet's right to describe sadness as well as joy. His 'One Sentence on Tyranny' was still a secret in his desk drawer; but this article lent his reputation to what the faithful construed as criticism of the Party.

Nagy fought off this attack, but the hardliners soon attacked again. The Third Congress of the Party was scheduled for the late spring. Resolutions adopted there would become the ideological basis for policy, reinforcing or correcting the Resolution of June 1953. Manoeuvring started early. One of Rákosi's associates, István Kovács, wrote a letter purporting to seek advice on a point of Party policy. Not for the last time, Nagy was ill at a moment of crisis. In his absence another of Rákosi's satraps circulated a reply implicitly but clearly critical of Nagy.

When Nagy returned to his office he organized a counter-attack. The position was restored. But the incident, like the cultural policy dispute, demonstrates the freedom with which Rákosi mounted his attacks, and the extent of Nagy's isolation within the Party. He later called the Kovács letter 'the first crude attempt by Mátyás Rákosi to place the blame for the troubles arising from opposition to correcting old faults on the New Course and on me personally . . . to achieve what he did achieve in the spring of 1955.'[13] It was not the last.

Rákosi tried to use the opportunity presented by Nagy's illness to make trouble for him with the Soviet leadership also. He proposed that he should visit Moscow to discuss the Congress. But the Soviet leaders were wary. They ruled that the whole Hungarian leadership should come to Moscow when Nagy was fit to travel. The Congress should be postponed to the end of May.

During May, therefore, the Hungarians made their way to Moscow. Like schoolboys who could not agree, Nagy and Rákosi laid their disagreements before the Soviet leadership. It is possible, even in Nagy's own account of what happened, to detect some attempt by the Russians to save Rákosi from humiliation. In January, when Nagy had been in Moscow alone, Khrushchev had said to him: 'The detainees are being released slowly. This is Rákosi's fault . . . Rákosi alludes to the fact that his nerves are bad. Nerves don't count. He has lost confidence in the correction of errors.'[14] In May, to Nagy and Rákosi, he said: 'It is not permissible to denounce men and to throw suspicion on them.' But he added: 'The rehabilitations should be carried out so as not to destroy Rákosi's authority . . . We will protect Rákosi's authority only in so far as it is not prejudicial to Party authority.'[15] The Kremlin, in short, continued to back the New Course. But their support for

Nagy was cooling. Rákosi's opposition to the New Course could yet serve Soviet interests.

The Hungarians went home to hold their postponed Party Congress in the last week of May 1954. Thirty-seven years later two things about it stand out. One was yet another challenge to Nagy's position, the other an initiative of his own to create a basis of popular support. Together they tell us something about Nagy's position as he fought off criticism and simultaneously tried to mould the Party and nation to support the New Course.

The first was yet another coded attack on Nagy and the New Course from Rákosi. While Nagy opened the Congress in uncontroversial terms, the General Secretary followed with a five-hour speech. He had been warned off overt criticism of the New Course in Moscow, and Voroshilov was present as a Soviet fraternal delegate to ensure that he did as he had been told. So he stressed his concern at things like kulak hostility to the Party and the danger of stagnating industrial production. His audience knew how to read between the lines.

The second salient feature of the Congress was a proposal from Nagy to revive the Patriotic People's Front. Communists in power and out have got such Fronts a bad name, as organizations in which Lenin's 'useful idiots' can be manipulated to Party ends by harder-headed men. But they can serve a more constructive purpose, tempering Party excess, communicating between Party and people. And they can, as some would argue the Hungarian Patriotic People's Front did in the eighties, offer a wider view than the Party and strike deeper roots.

There is no certainty about how Nagy saw the Patriotic People's Front when he talked of reviving it in 1954. As a Communist he may have seen it as a way of binding the country to Party policy. As a Hungarian he thought that through the Front he could bring national and popular influence to bear on his opponents in the Party. He did not see the Front as a mere sounding board. He wanted it to have a life and vitality of its own. He wanted it to include people who might, for whatever reason, take a view that was not the Party's. And he seems to have envisaged the Front giving life to the interest groups that the Communist Party had uprooted – precisely the institutions of civil society that are so essential and yet so difficult to re-establish.

Party stalwarts criticized the very concept of the Front. They argued that the idea of universality contradicted Party tenets of irreconcilable class differences. They suspected any organization outside the Party. Rákosi alleged later that Nagy hoped to make the Front a rival power centre. That overstates Nagy's aim; but he did see the Front as a useful focus of influence in a country where the Party, having monopolized all influence, misused the power which it brought. We know from his essays that he was obsessed by the Party's isolation from the people. In a pragmatic, step-by-step sort of way he may have hoped that the Front would help to bridge that dangerous gap.

The Third Congress accepted Nagy's proposal, and work was put in hand to launch the Front in the autumn. It was the start of a concept which was to survive, often against the odds, for the next thirty-five years. For much of that time the Patriotic People's Front was nothing more than a belt to transmit Party wishes to other organizations. But it provided some representation for those organizations. In recent years it has played a real if cautious part in bringing Hungary back to decency. Whether it might have played such a part in the fifties if the New Course had survived is a might-have-been of history.

So the May Congress broke up with Nagy under pressure but still to all appearances in command of events. Two months later came an opportunity for a dramatic expression of national unity. The Danube overflowed and the floods reached the level of national disaster. The whole nation united in response. The press was full of reports of people working spontaneously together, 'Like a Big Family'. It would have been an unprintable concept when Rákosi was demanding unremitting struggle against the class enemy. It

seemed a natural expression as the country worked together
to fight the floods. For a week in July 1954, Hungarians
showed how they could work together. It was a precious
experience for a people who had for years been cut off from
one another by propaganda and fear. They recaptured the
experience in even more extreme circumstances two years
later.

In the summer and autumn of 1954, most of the
Communists who had gone to prison at the height of
Rákosi's terror were released. Kádár came out in July. Like
the others, he was broken by prison, temporarily fit for
nothing. But unlike the deportees and the people who came
back from the internment camps in 1953, these
Communists were political animals. As Party members,
they came back to play a political role. As they gradually
resumed their places in the Party, they began to speak
about the injustice that had been done to them.

All these men were Rákosi's enemies. Their freedom
depended on keeping Rákosi at bay. They were natural
allies for Nagy. In the Uprising many of them were with
him. Some went to gaol, even the gallows with him. Others,
like Kádár, changed sides before the heavens fell. But all
that was for the future. For the moment they were welcome
reinforcement for Nagy.

At the beginning of October came a meeting of the
Central Committee to review the New Course. Once again,
Nagy fought off a demand, advanced by Rákosi and Gerö,
for a reversion to the old economics. He based himself on
the classic arguments of expansionists in any age: 'I
emphasized, with the complete agreement of the Central
Committee, that socialism cannot be built by narrowing the
basis of production but only by broadening it; not by
restricting or neglecting the material interest of the
producer but by augmenting it; not by discouraging the
buyers but by increasing the stock of merchandise.'[16]

Nagy won a famous victory at that October Central

Committee meeting. Allies were beginning to join him. He
convinced some of the waverers that he had the essential
thing, the confidence of Moscow. The Patriotic People's
Front promised to mobilize support outside the Party.
Nagy felt new confidence. A shrewder man might have
sought Party organizational changes to reinforce his
position. But as Ferenc Váli puts it, Nagy 'was no plotter –
and only in conspiring, as his opponents did, could he have
attained an ascendancy within the Party over his enemies.
He had neither the inclination nor the aptitude to organize
his camp, to surround himself with disciples, recruit
others, and intimidate the foe. He was rather a teacher than
a statesman, an apostle of his ideas, and not a revolutionary
conspirator.'[17]

Nagy's interest in getting his arguments published
illustrates his preference for a pedagogue's approach rather
than a conspirator's. In preparation for the Central
Committee meeting, he had published a collection of his
speeches and articles since the liberation, under the title
One Decade. It received favourable reviews, which recorded
openly his disagreements with ,the leadership in 1948-49
and stated clearly that he, not Rákosi, had been right. For
Nagy, this was welcome validation of his record and a
tribute from the Party to the author of the New Course. But
it meant little. It would blow away in the wind if
circumstances changed. And the reviews laid him open to
the charge of indiscipline in exposing Party disagreement to
the public.

On 23 October 1954, two years to the day before the
Uprising broke out, the inaugural meeting of the Patriotic
People's Front was held. Elderly Hungarians still vividly
remember Nagy's speech there. He spoke like a Hungarian
traditionalist and the historical resonance of a reference to
'little Hungarians' appealed directly to national sentiment.
The speech reminded Hungarians of how much Nagy had
moved them in his first speech as Prime Minister eighteen
months before.

Newsreels show us the party that was held in parliament

to mark the event that evening. They show an old-fashioned occasion, less self-consciously proletarian, more representative of the whole nation than had become the form on Party occasions. Nagy greets the guests with stately courtesy. He dances a graceful *csardas* with a girl in peasant costume. Looking around his party in parliament that evening, Nagy could have believed without too much self-delusion that he had brought together the Party he served and the country he loved. It was the high tide of the New Course.

But in that same month of October Rákosi went to the Soviet Union on holiday. He stayed almost two months. While he was there, Khrushchev, Bulganin and Mikoyan visited Peking. Their talks with the Chinese seem to have convinced them that Malenkov must be turned out of office. His revisionist policies threatened Communist solidarity. At the end of his holiday, Rákosi went to Moscow to represent Hungary at the conference which prepared the way for the Warsaw Pact. He talked to his friends in the Soviet leadership and he learned what was in store for Malenkov, Nagy's patron. On 3 December he came back to Budapest, ready to launch yet another attack on Nagy.

Nagy's last success was the council election on 28 November 1954. In his essays he claimed that 'The Party's connection with the workers was strengthened, and the prestige of the executive branches grew. An impressive and intimate political atmosphere developed, where the great majority of the citizens expressed their faith in the basic aims of building socialism.'[18] True or false – and there is a ring of self-delusion about Nagy's words – all this was beside the point. What mattered was that opinion in Moscow had turned against Malenkov and the New Course in Hungary was doomed.

Rákosi became bolder, more outspoken. Nagy's Party support withered away. The last act was played out at Debrecen, the town in north-eastern Hungary where the provisional government was formed and Nagy prepared the land reform of 1945. Just before Christmas, government and Party representatives assembled in the Great Calvinist church there to mark the tenth anniversary of the first meeting of the provisional National Assembly. Rákosi spoke confidently, to applause. Nagy followed, with a faltering speech. 'One could not have deduced from one word of Nagy's speech that the Prime Minister had noticed the conspiracy against him,' wrote Tamás Aczél and Tibor Méray, two of his supporters among the writers.[19]

A meal was served afterwards in the Golden Bull, 'the biggest village inn in the biggest village in Europe'. At the head table was Rákosi and the Party leadership, at the bottom of the room a group of writers. A short flight of steps led down into the dining room. 'A short, portly man with a moustache and a pince-nez was now walking down those steps, looking about him with interest. He was not followed by a suite or by a circle of courtiers. He came alone, apparently enjoying the cheerful atmosphere as if he were someone who was at home in the town and in the hotel.'[20]

Nagy was putting a bold face on his discomfiture. The writers invited him to their table. One or two political figures who were still committed to Nagy's policies joined them. To the writers, the Party leaders at the top table, the Prime Minister who sought to bind Party to people at the bottom, represented different worlds. As Nagy rose to leave a non-Communist said to a Communist: 'Friend, if they would only let him, this man would lead the Hungarian people straight to socialism!'[21] But they would not let him. A few days later Nagy and the rest of the Hungarian leaders were summoned once again to Moscow. The Kremlin wanted to put an end to the New Course.

Chapter 7

OPPOSITION

The Hungarian leaders travelled to Moscow early in January 1955, for what was to be Nagy's last meeting in the Kremlin. He has left no written description of what passed there, but the substance if not the tone of Tibor Méray's account probably accurately reflects what Nagy told him on his return to Budapest. From this account, and from subsequent developments, the Soviet leaders' purpose is clear. In June 1953 they had turned to Nagy to introduce the New Course; in May 1954 they had checked Rákosi's attempts to obstruct him; but in January 1955 they turned their criticism on Nagy. They blamed him for mistakes in the direction and excesses in his advocacy of the New Course. They ordered him to act and speak more prudently in future. And they told both Nagy and Rákosi to work together from now on.

The 1955 Kremlin meeting illustrates once again how Soviet concerns predominated when it came to deciding Eastern European policies. Malenkov's colleagues in the Soviet leadership were growing restless. They wanted at the very least to trim his power and check his policies. They had heard that the Chinese leadership shared their doubts about where Malenkov's policies were leading. If the Soviet Union were to alter course, so must the satellites. Nagy's New Course in Hungary was a direct consequence of Malenkov's pre-eminence in Moscow; it had gone further than reforms elsewhere in Eastern Europe; now it was particularly vulnerable. And Rákosi was on hand to confirm that the very faults which the Kremlin leaders now found with Malenkov's polices were quite as valid when applied to Nagy's.

At the Kremlin meeting it was left to Malenkov to open the criticism of the Hungarian New Course. From a heavy dossier he quoted from Nagy's speeches and articles to illustrate charges of ideological error and insubordination. He quoted evidence of economic failure also, stressing particularly the foreign exchange crisis which had followed the decision to increase imports to help satisfy consumer demand. Méray asserts that Nagy was scandalized by the crudeness with which the Russians presumed to dictate on Hungarian affairs, an odd sentiment for a man who had reported their criticisms with unquestioning approval when they were directed at Rákosi.[1]

More important, Nagy seems to have shocked the Russians by the vigour with which he answered back. Breaking for once his own iron discipline, he told a friend in Budapest afterwards that Khrushchev snarled at him: 'Who do you think you are? I have had better men than you hanged.'[2] But Nagy and Khrushchev were of course arguing past one another. Nagy was defending a policy which he believed was starting to show results and which was based on the careful academic analysis by which he set such store. The Russians were playing power politics for far bigger stakes than the well-being of one unimportant country; they expected disciplined compliance, not academic wrangling.

But at this stage the Russians did not want personnel changes, either at home or in Hungary. The immediate aim was to discipline Malenkov, not drive him from office. And just as they had kept Rákosi in Party office when they put Nagy in government office in 1953, now they wanted Nagy to continue in double harness with Rákosi. The Hungarians were told, therefore, to work together as a team, while implementing tougher policies, giving priority to heavy industry, and watching their ideological Ps and Qs.

Nagy must have left Moscow troubled and angry, but he put as good a face as he could on the situation. With Malenkov still in office, he may have had hopes of salvaging the essentials of the New Course. He may have decided to hang on and bide his time, as Rákosi had done since 1953. Having privately challenged the Soviet leadership he went back to his political work in Hungary. By 25 January he was publicly propagating the new and harder line at a conference on crop collection. It began to look as if, despite his rebellion in the Kremlin, he would play a dutiful part in the undoing of the New Course.

But everything turned on events in Moscow. And in early February the Soviet leaders pressed the attack on Malenkov further. He was replaced as prime minister by Bulganin. The time had come for Rákosi to destroy Nagy's position. Things were made easier for him by Nagy's absence from office. Once again he was ill at a critical juncture, this time with a minor thrombosis. Rákosi laid his case against Nagy before the Political Committee.

Nagy's only hope was to get matters out of the hands of the Political Committee which, the more particularly in his own absence, Rákosi dominated. Nagy had more friends in the Central Committee. In his essays he says that during February he twice wrote to complain that Rákosi was forcing issues through the Political Committee, without reference to the government or to the wider Party machine. But at the beginning of March the Central Committee itself endorsed an attack on Nagy, condemning his 'right deviation' and 'anti-Marxist conceptions'.

Rákosi made sure that this resolution, unlike that of June 1953, was widely publicized. It showed the Party which way the wind was blowing and rallied the activists behind him. A few days later the rumour went round Budapest that Rákosi had had Nagy arrested and then, on reflection or on Soviet orders, released him. The rumour was unfounded but it illustrates how vulnerable Nagy seemed at the time. And through the early spring of 1955 things continued to go Rákosi's way.

The tenth anniversary of the liberation was approaching. April 4, the date on which the last German troops had been driven from Hungary in 1945, had become the National Day. The tenth anniversary was to be an occasion of particular rejoicing. President Voroshilov himself was to attend. He was a well-known figure in Hungary, having commanded the Soviet forces at the end of the war and presided over the establishment of the provisional government. He had put his weight behind Nagy's land distribution and taken in his stride a protest Nagy sent him when his troops stripped the orchards in Kecskemét. He once told a visitor that Nagy was the only honest man in the Hungarian Party leadership[3] and even after the execution he said some benevolently tactless things about him. As the 4 April celebrations approached, Hungarians watched for any indication through Voroshilov of Soviet intentions towards Nagy.

But the signals when Voroshilov came were ambiguous. One story had it that he expressed surprise when he arrived in Budapest and saw no portraits of Nagy beside those of Rákosi. Hundreds were quickly put on display. But according to another story, Voroshilov brought orders for an all-out attack on Nagy, which was delayed until after he had left so as to give an impression of Hungarian spontaneity. A third version suggests that Rákosi simply put it about that Voroshilov had ordered an attack on Nagy. What is clear is that an all-out attack started the day after Voroshilov left for Moscow.

It came to a head at a Central Committee meeting on 14 April. By now Nagy's supporters were too cowed to speak for him there. A resolution condemning his policies was adopted. He was expelled from the Political and Central Committees. Four days later he resigned and was replaced as Prime Minister by András Hegedüs, a man in his thirties who had made his way in the Party as private secretary to the leaders. Personal attacks on Nagy continued, and on 18 May he was forced out of his remaining offices: the Patriotic People's Front, the National Assembly, the University and the Academy of Sciences. He tried to hold on to the last position, arguing pedantically that it was a scholarly, not a political appointment. But he was faced with the choice of losing this academic distinction or a pension on which he would be dependent. He chose to keep the pension.

Nagy's political eclipse was almost complete. Rákosi had destroyed him far more completely than in 1949. But he could not drive him to self-abasement as he had then. Nagy went on arguing his case. He addressed a series of letters of complaint to the Central Committee. He said that he accepted the validity of the March resolution which had committed the Party to the new line of policy which Moscow had laid down. But he argued that its predecessor, the resolution of June 1953 which Rákosi had suppressed, should be published too. He had based all his policies in the New Course on that resolution. Its publication would show the whole Party how gravely Rákosi had distorted its significance.

Nagy's letters sound plaintive and futile even today. Rákosi had won the hand and seemed close to winning the game. He had got Moscow's approval, the backing of the Political and Central Committees, and control of the levers of power. Nagy had lost office and had no power base. His letters to the Central Committee were those of a beaten politician trying to make what he could out of academic Party issues and the retailing of old wrongs.

At the time, the essays on which Nagy now started work were just as futile. In 1955 and the very early months of 1956, he composed twenty-five essays on political and economic questions. He wrote them to justify himself and attack his opponents. He was writing for his own satisfaction, for a Party readership, and for anyone in the Kremlin who would pay attention. The essays were his only weapon. He was out of office. His academic posts had been taken from him. He was ill. He was under close surveillance. Until things started to go his way in 1956, friends kept away from him. Circumstances, and his obsession with the injustice that had been done to him, drove him to a painstaking, academic restatement of his policies and views. He poured himself into what he called his 'dissertation', 'a justification of my principles and . . . a detailed reply to the accusations made in public against me since March of 1955.'[4]

In the course of 1955 and 1956, Nagy's essays circulated in typescript quite widely among senior Party members and intellectuals in Hungary. After the Revolution they were smuggled to the West where they were published in 1957 in English as *Imre Nagy on Communism* and in French under the more expressive title *Un Communisme qui n'oublie pas l'Homme*.

By that time Nagy had become a world figure, a national hero in prison awaiting trial. The essays created a stir when they were published, which was revived when Nagy was executed a year later. They gave what was then a unique insight into the closed world of the Communist leadership. They documented how arrogantly the Kremlin dictated policy to the satellites. And Nagy's accusations against Rákosi seemed the more telling, coming as they did from a man who had served Communism for thirty-five years and still expressed himself in the language of a convinced Communist.

But even at the time the essays were a nine-day wonder. They read very turgidly today. Nagy was engaged in self-justification. He wrote from within a Communist tradition which over decades had narrowed his thinking and blunted his style. He was seeking to persuade a prejudiced audience. He had to accommodate those prejudices. His logic and language are often tortured in consequence. And all but two of the essays are concerned with points which, vital as they may have been to Party in-fighting then, seem petty and inconsequential thirty-five years afterwards.

Yet even in such long retrospect, there is a value to these essays. They come from inside a system which has only very recently brought itself to conceive the possibility of error. Their revelations of stupidity, error, gross abuse of power, are all the more telling for that. They also reveal what was happening at the heart of the most secretive of all political systems, illuminating relations between the Kremlin and a satellite in a way which was hardly equalled for thirty years.

If we make allowances for the context in which Nagy was writing and the audience which he had in mind, they also tell us a good deal about the man: conformist and conventional Marxist on the one hand, passionate and courageous individualist on the other. And two of the essays in particular show us an author prepared to follow the evidence of experience where it led, moving far beyond the assumptions which had governed his actions in office, only a year before. These two essays at least show us a Nagy increased in stature by adversity. They deserve detailed analysis.

For his part, Nagy attached a naive significance to all his essays. He believed that they were politically and scientifically important. If the authorities in Moscow and Budapest would only read them, they would find the true path. He never attempted to conceal the essays. He expected his friends to study them, debate them. Once a recipient who thought he was about to be arrested stuffed his copy in the stove. The essays, Nagy reproached him, were to be defended, not burned.

Knowing what we do of Nagy's later career, it is tempting to think that he wrote with tongue in cheek. At some points perhaps he did. In defending his gradualist agricultural policies, for example, he quotes from Stalin's words and writings in the twenties, before the great change of 1929. But of course he knew that Stalin backed that change and made the policy of collectivization his own; that he never expressed a word of regret at the results, even when they drove his wife to suicide; and that Soviet doctrine still insisted that the course Russian agriculture had taken in the thirties was the right one. But a Marxist-Leninist could not argue for amendment of policy in the light of national circumstance. He had to cite Soviet texts. Those texts Nagy found in Stalin's early writings.

Nagy may also have been insincere in giving the impression that he rejected all salvation outside the Party. It would have been fatal to give his Party audience the impression that he saw merit in non-Communist views. He could go no further than arguing, as he had done so often before, that Communism must not lose contact with the people, and especially the peasants. He was in fact better disposed to non-Communists than the essays suggest: he had friends outside the Party and in the Revolution he collaborated easily with non-Communist politicians who joined his government.

But by and large, it is clear that Nagy wrote in 1955 as a convinced Communist; that he still believed that Marxist-Leninism held the key to the future; and that when he urged reform he did not anticipate that the logic of his own argument might lead to a destination outside the Party.

The two most important of Nagy's essays, referred to above, were written later than the rest, in December 1955 and January 1956. They show us a different Nagy from the author of the earlier ones. He has moved beyond the process of rehashing old arguments to prove himself right and embarked on something grander and more dangerous. These two essays show us a man in his late fifties who is becoming intellectually adventurous. Yet he has not cast off all his old assumptions. And he seems too naive to see where his argument is taking him. The two essays deal with international relations and with morals and ethics. They are far more ambitious than the others, more lucid and far-reaching; and they are much easier to follow than Nagy's involuted acerbities about productivity and agricultural policy.

The thesis for the first of these two essays – 'The Five Basic Principles of International Relations and the Question of our Foreign Policy' – is a simple one. It is also profoundly shocking: to the Communist because it cuts unwittingly through a tangle of double-think; to the non-Communist because it reveals such blindness towards Communism's limitations.

Writing in January 1956, Nagy started with the five principles of Bandung (national independence, sovereignty, equality, self-determination and non-interference) which the Russians, Chinese, Yugoslavs and most of the Third World had endorsed in the summer of 1955. The Bandung Conference made a great impact at the time. The Communists seemed to be succeeding in allying themselves with emerging nationalist forces in Asia and Africa and replacing colonialism there with a non-alignment which in practice inclined towards Moscow and Peking. The Third World welcomed new and powerful friends. The West feared the loss of political and economic influence.

In his essays Nagy took these five basic principles of Bandung as applying not just to the Third World but also to relationships between East European states. He argued that they imposed on Hungary the obligation to rethink her international position. The new Soviet leadership, Nagy argued, had accepted the five principles and recognized that they did not conflict with Marxist-Leninism. Hungary must advance towards socialism by adherence to them. Her geographical position and her new membership of the United Nations would make this easy, and she would have Soviet backing.

The essay is perfectly coherent. International and Hungarian considerations are blended effectively. But there is not a word to suggest that Nagy recognized that for Moscow the five principles of Bandung were political and propaganda tools to be put to work in advancing Communist interests in the Third World. He did not seem to realize what dynamite for the Soviet bloc was hidden in his argument. There is in the essay no expression of deference to Soviet strategic requirements, no recognition of the danger of a chain-reaction if Hungary tried to go down the path he advocated. He did not seem to understand that what Soviet propaganda could welcome in the Third World, Soviet policy and Russian imperial interests must reject in Eastern Europe.

Nagy was in effect proclaiming that for the Eastern

European countries too there was a national way to socialism. He was declaring obsolete the Brezhnev Doctrine on the relationship between the Soviet Union and the satellites more than ten years before it was propounded. The real world had to wait thirty years before Gorbachev came to validate Nagy's theories. Nagy was by implication calling in question all the assumptions about the relationship which were taken for granted in Moscow and every East European capital. He was turning a blind eye to the Kremlin's interference in Hungarian affairs which he documents elsewhere so clearly. In this essay he set out with astonishing frankness an argument which could have been used in earnest when, nine months later, he declared Hungary neutral and tried to take her out of the Warsaw Pact.

The second outstanding essay was 'Ethics and Morals in Hungarian Public Life', written a month before 'Five Basic Principles', in December 1955. In it Nagy analysed with boldness and precision the abuses inflicted on Hungary by Rákosi's arbitrary rule. Passages in it are in their solemn way as powerful an indictment of dictatorship as Illyés' 'One Sentence on Tyranny':

'One of the causes of the ethical and moral crisis . . . is the attitude of the leading organs of government, of society, and of the Party . . . Under their leadership, the building of socialism was reduced to the socialization of the instruments of production, the establishment of the economic basis of socialism, the transformation of the economy and the class relationships dependent thereon, and the acquisition and consolidation of political power. They completely forgot about living society, about man with his manifold, complicated, individual and social relations, at the crux of which are ethical and moral problems.'[5]

This is generalization, but Nagy goes on: 'The degeneration of power – the appearance of Bonapartism – is not new in Hungary. It dates back to those times when the clique headed by Rákosi, which came to power in the Party on the basis of charges that have since been proved false and through intrigues and crimes . . . crushed the basis of Hungary's young democracy and liquidated our people's democratic forces and the democratic partnerships of socialism . . . It was then that power began to slip away from the people. The isolation of power and its use against its own supporters led to the dissolution of that pillar of strength, the worker-peasant alliance. Political guidance, the persuasion and winning of the masses, was increasingly replaced by the use of force . . . Rákosi made himself independent of the will and opinion of the Party membership and of the decisions of the Party. He subjugated the Party . . . and . . . forced it to execute his wishes.'[6]

In 'Morals and Ethics' Nagy displayed a sense of urgency which he seemed to lose as 1956 approached its climax. In 1955, he asserted, 'the abuse of power exceeded even the malpractices of the period from 1950 to 1952.' The Party was destroying its own standing. 'Whatever has become of Communist morality, human respect, and honour, if there are Communist leaders according to whom the unjustly executed Comrade László Rajk was a coward because he admitted to false charges in order to deceive the Party leaders, leaders who act as if it were not they themselves who contrived the mendacious charges and the means of getting the confession?'[7]

The Party talked about unity. 'What kind of unity is it that is held together by knowledge of and participation in crime?' They had a clear choice. 'We have two ways to extricate ourselves from the disastrous situation brought upon the country by the Rákosi regime: we can either liquidate Stalinist policy ourselves and lead the country back to the June road . . . or we can refrain from changing the course of events with the result that the increasing tension may bring the country to the verge of a grave crisis. In either case, the Hungarian Communists must become masters of the situation.'[8] 'Today, probably, a return to the policy of the New Course . . . could . . . avert catastrophe.

But it is doubtful whether a return to the June principles would suffice . . . tomorrow . . . there is a danger that the masses, having lost their faith, will reject both the June way and the Communist Party.'[9]

Nagy's essay on ethics and morals is an impressive indictment of the corruption wrought by Stalinism, Rákosi and the cult of personality. It is particularly impressive that it was written before the Twentieth Party Congress. But reflection demonstrates that Nagy's view of politics was still blinkered. He was describing how a whole society had been crippled by Communist rule. He had been a member of the cabinet and Political Committee which Rákosi dominated. He had left office because Rákosi threw him out; and he had deluged the monster with requests for reinstatement. It is true that Rákosi was to blame for the worst of what Communism did to Hungary. But the arrogance of a Party which systematically crippled all rivals and then could do no more with absolute power than surrender it to Rákosi, this seemed to escape Nagy's notice. The unfounded charges against Rajk were condemned, but Rajk's equally unfounded charges against non-Communists were ignored. Even in this, the boldest of his essays, Nagy seems wilful as well as naive in his faith that Communism could rise above the crimes committed in its name.

There is also a tragic irony about this essay. 'A Communism which does not forget Man' summarizes exactly what Nagy wanted. The things he condemned in Rákosi's system stem from its inhuman disregard of everything except personal power and tactical advantage. What Nagy wanted to put in its place was a Communism which would serve man. Where Rákosi wanted a monolith, in which only he would exercise the rights of personality, Nagy wanted a free society of individuals. The best individuals, he believed, would devote themselves to the service of the guiding force, the Party; but all of them would participate in decisions. The irony is that Nagy thought that this was what Communism was really about. After half a century in a movement which in Hungary as well as Russia had used bloodshed to enthrone tyranny, he still believed that the good in Communism was permanent and the Rákosis, the Stalins, temporary. He did not yet see that once the alignment with Moscow and the Party's monopoly of power were abandoned, Communism would not survive long enough even to begin to pursue the better policies in which he still believed.

George Páloczi-Horváth was one of the political prisoners released from imprisonment under the New Course. He knew that he owed his freedom to Nagy, but his experiences had destroyed his faith in Communism. He wrote of Nagy: 'I knew that he wanted . . . communism without terrorism, but I was firmly convinced, as I still am, that this was the most impossible of all impossible propositions. The party is dictatorship, the party is the Security Police, the party is terrorism.'[10]

When he was writing his essays, Nagy would not have accepted this. Most of them express the limited view of the politician, the last two the vision and naïveté of the academic in his study. For all his human warmth, Nagy at the beginning of 1956 was out of touch with the forces that were beginning to stir men to action. In the Revolution it took him days to reach the understanding that he could not serve both Communism and man and to decide that he must give man priority.

Chapter 8

CROSS-CURRENTS

A s we have seen, 1955 was a bad year for Imre Nagy. In January he lost the Kremlin's backing. In April he was expelled from office. In May he was driven out of the Patriotic People's Front. Rákosi ignored his letters and essays. He was isolated, unemployed and ill. On the surface, his career was over. And Rákosi seemed intent on taking the country back to the old dreadful certainties of the early fifties.

But there were cross-currents. The Soviet leadership had not got rid of Malenkov to replace him with a new Stalin. Khrushchev and Bulganin presided over an uneasy collective leadership. They wanted a tougher economic policy than Malenkov's, but saw the need to balance it with some concern for the consumer. They wanted to put an end to the old debilitating feud with Yugoslavia, and in May Khrushchev and Bulganin took the road to Canossa and made their grudging peace with Tito. They feared and distrusted the West, but they wanted better relations if they could get them. They signed the Austrian State Treaty and a neutral Western country was established on Hungary's border. In July Khrushchev went to Geneva for talks with Eisenhower.

In circumstances like these there was no question of letting Eastern European Stalinists off the leash. Rákosi would have liked to gaol Nagy, but he no longer had a free hand. Right through the summer of 1955 there were rumours that he intended to put Nagy on trial, but they came to nothing. Nagy lived out his quiet retirement not in the Central Prison but in his comfortable house in Buda. We have seen that Voroshilov asked after him at the liberation anniversary. Envoys from the Kremlin came to his sick bed, suggesting reconciliation. Rákosi had led the satellite pack against Tito; the Kremlin might still have a role for Nagy if it decided to sacrifice Rákosi to win Tito's friendship.

Domestic factors were changing also. The released prisoners were gradually finding their place in Hungarian life. Some were broken, all fearful. But as they asserted themselves even in little ways, they chipped away at Rákosi's strength. Accounts of false charges, torture, betrayals, predetermined trials and prison conditions far worse than under Horthy spread guilt and self-doubt within the Party.

These stories added to the disquiet which more and more of the intellectuals were already discreetly expressing to one another. Men like Illyés who had condemned the evils of the Horthy era had nevertheless hated what Communism did to Hungary from the very beginning. Others had justified it, praised it, benefited from it. They were slowly changing their minds. 'The authors of this book were worse than Communists,' wrote Tamás Aczél and Tibor Méray later. 'They not only believed in the system, but they also fanatically supported it. And the system treated them generously . . . Their eyes were not yet opened even in the summer of 1953, when Imre Nagy announced his program to their country. It took another year – and the revelation of the unprecedented crimes committed in the Rajk affair – to make them at last realize the kind of system they were supporting.'[1]

Yet Rákosi seemed determined to ignore these cross-currents as far as he could. Sitting at home, alone with his frustration, Nagy saw the policies of the New Course eroded. In June the Central Committee reiterated that collectivization was the way forward for Hungarian agriculture. In August Rákosi demanded administrative measures to enforce it. The new emphasis on industrialization reversed Nagy's concern for the consumer. He was blamed for the increase in the country's debts. In November 1955 he was expelled even from the Party. The rumours of a trial started again. Reporting them at the beginning of 1956 the British legation concluded: 'For all practical purposes Nagy must now be written off as a factor in the political situation of this country.'[2]

Even before the Revolution broke out, events in 1956 were to prove this judgement dramatically wrong. Rákosi still seemed to monopolize all power, subject only to Moscow's supervision. But beneath the surface the tide was running against him. As ex-prisoners, writers, journalists, Party members and private citizens started to speak more frankly, it gradually became apparent that Rákosi had no support outside the Party and the security police. The mass rallies were as disciplined and apparently as enthusiastic as ever; but a quarter of the working population had been touched by Rákosi's terror. Its unexpressed hatred of the system was at least as great as the intellectuals'. Gradually 1956 proved Nagy right when he wrote at the end of the previous year that a change today might avert catastrophe but that a return to his own principles tomorrow might be too late.

But still Nagy stood apart from others who like him hated what Rákosi was doing to Hungary. The returning political prisoners took their places in a Party from which he was excluded. The more prominent among them had little natural sympathy with Nagy. Most were of a younger generation; he had been in office when they went to gaol; he had not shared their sufferings; to them he was, for all his human face, a Muscovite Communist. Among the men coming out of prison were a few, such as Losonczy and Ujhelyi, who were in time to form Nagy's circle and his staff during the Revolution. But they were a small minority.

Yet in a more general sense, Nagy's influence was growing, with Party members, the intellectuals and the people. He was remembered for the gentleness of his advocacy, his everyday calm, which contrasted so vividly with Rákosi's stridency. He had shown his capacity in office in 1953 and 1954. And as Rákosi's command of the situation waned, so the influence of Nagy increased. There was a feeling too that he had matured into something more than just a Communist politician.

Remembering Nagy's time as prime minister and hearing perhaps of his continued defiance of Rákosi in his essays, people began to recognize more confidently that he stood for national values. 'Where did this old Bolshevik, this experienced Comintern worker, find the courage to resist the leaders?' wrote Aczél and Méray. 'True, he had a stubborn streak in his nature. But there was more to it than that. During his career . . . he had always been ready to "confess his errors" without visible resistance. The fact was that now, however, both the situation and, even more, the man had changed. In all his career it was only during the years of Nagy's premiership that he had met with mass sympathy. And Imre Nagy, who had always yearned for such sympathy, would . . . not forget his strong ties with the people who had given him such sympathy. His faith had become stronger than his fear. His confidence in his calling had become stronger than his Party discipline.'[3] All this may have been clearer with hindsight after the Revolution, when Aczél and Méray wrote, than it was in the early months of 1956. But there was a sense even then that Nagy had changed, and the beginning of a tacit understanding between Nagy and the very disparate groups of people who within the year were to make the Revolution.

But as these groups and Nagy found their separate ways to express their opposition to Rákosi, the danger of a violent counter-stroke increased. In the autumn of 1955, a group of Communist intellectuals submitted a memorandum to the Central Committee criticizing the Party's cultural policies. Rákosi either sensed collusion between

them and Nagy, or decided to exploit the memorandum as
an occasion to attack them both. He took the opportunity to
order the Central Committee to expel Nagy from the Party.
It also rejected the memorandum. Then Rákosi took things
further, determined to terrorize the intellectuals. On 6
December, they were summoned to a mass meeting in the
great hall of the Ironworkers' Union. Rákosi presided and
turned the proceedings into a savage attack upon dissent.
Party stalwarts joined in. When Rákosi's critics attempted
to defend themselves they were shouted down. The
atmosphere of hysteria reminded people of that at the Rajk
trial, held in the same hall six years before.

Rákosi pressed home his attack on the intellectuals. They
were summoned to appear before Party representatives
individually and confess their error. Some did, but others
refused to recant. They expected imprisonment. Instead
the ringleaders were expelled from the Party, others
reprimanded. The sense spread that Rákosi could still
threaten but no longer destroy. Events were drifting, under
a leader whom the Russians would not allow to eliminate
his critics but who was still unwilling to listen to them, let
alone share power with anyone.

The attacks on Rákosi, and his counter-attacks, convulsed
Hungary and preoccupied political attention there. But an
event was in the making which would overshadow any
excitements which the satellites could generate. The Soviet
leaders had decided on a step as fundamental at the time as
Gorbachev's commitment to *perestroika* thirty years later.
At the end of January they summoned the East European
leaders to Moscow to warn them of the attack on Stalin
which Khrushchev intended to deliver at the Twentieth
Congress.

In February the East Europeans assembled again for the
Congress itself. Rákosi represented Hungary. On the night
of 24-25 February, Khruhschev delivered his 'secret
speech'. He declared that war was no longer inevitable. He

envisaged different roads to socialism. And he denounced Stalin's crimes, in a move that changed the face of Communism for good.

The speech was secret only in form. It leaked, as no doubt it was intended to, and was soon published in the West in full. By the second week in March, Rákosi was giving an account of it to the Central Committee. However he presented it, the speech clearly threatened his own position; no one had forgotten the pride he had taken in his reputation as Stalin's most faithful disciple. By the end of the month he was reduced to blaming Rajk's execution on the secret police, and promising rehabilitation. The release of the political prisoners continued. Rákosi's threats in December seemed hollower than ever.

The Soviet leadership continued their efforts to break with the past. The Cominform was wound up; each Communist Party would decide for itself on its links with other parties. They tried to stand back from events in the East European countries. Khrushchev and Bulganin visited London. Molotov was sacked in a gesture of appeasement to Tito. But the efforts were partial. The Soviet leaders continued to believe that they had a right to control every development in their Eastern European empire. They were particularly troubled by developments in Poland, where government and Party were trying to respond to popular dissatisfaction. On May Day, 1956, Khrushchev said to the Polish Ambassador at the Kremlin reception, 'You have your sovereignty, but what you are doing today in Poland is against your sovereignty and against socialism . . . They need to have their knuckles rapped.'[4]

Yet Khrushchev's speech two months earlier might have been calculated to arouse in Eastern Europe just the hopes of change which caused him such concern when they were expressed in Poland. In Hungary its effect had been to undermine what little was left of Rákosi's authority. Attacks on him rose to a crescendo. He was called a Judas. The playwright Gyula Háy spoke passionately against the cult of personality. And at the Central Committee in May

Kádár, now moving back into the mainstream of Party activity, demanded that Farkas should be tried for his part in the Rajk trial.

To deflect the attack, Rákosi played to the Central Committee the famous tape of Kádár's last conversation with Rajk in prison, in which he urged him to go along with the farce for the Party's sake and promised that if he did he would not be executed. But Kádár, forewarned, produced the uncut tape, which made it clear that he was speaking on Rákosi's instructions. Two reputations were critically damaged: that of the falling leader and that of the man back from the living death of prison. Rákosi held a meeting of Party militants and delivered himself of self-criticism, confessing to a personality cult and legal violations. He attended a meeting with the leadership of the security police. Even they attacked him, telling him that he had reached the lowest point to which political morality could sink. In an attempt to ease the pressures by buying Tito's approval, he concluded a very generous trade agreement with Yugoslavia. But Tito continued to ask for his head.

In the summer of 1956, Tito visited Moscow. His rapprochement with the Russians continued, but the relationship was still uneasy and wary. Rákosi's position was a major issue between them. The Soviet leadership seem to have done their best to defend Rákosi and as late as 13 July Khrushchev told the Yugoslav Ambassador that they were giving him their full support. He had always acted on Stalin's instructions. Admittedly, he had made a mistake in expelling Nagy from the Party: 'Nagy should have been left in the Party, where he would now have been very useful.' Khrushchev added that they were sending Mikoyan to Budapest to discuss the situation. But if things got worse, 'We here have decided to use all means at our disposal to bring the crisis to an end.'[5]

In fact the Soviet leadership had already sent Suslov to Budapest to consider the situation with the Hungarian leaders. He saw Nagy privately. Nagy was still in theory no more than a private citizen living in quiet retirement in his villa in Buda. But his political influence was growing by the day and he did nothing to discourage attention. In June, a minister attended his sixtieth party which, in the words of a critic of Nagy writing long after the event, became 'a demonstration against Party policy and in support of Imre Nagy'.[6] A friend recalls that in these summer months of 1956 he used to say: 'I am going out to draw attention to myself'[7] and his expeditions with his grandchildren did just that. By the time Rákosi's position became critical in July many observers saw Nagy as a natural successor.

The fact was that by the early summer the situation in Hungary was rapidly moving beyond the power of the Communist Party to control. Gatherings of intellectuals, writers, Party members and journalists were all increasing the pressure on Rákosi. In June they were formalized into a series of meetings of the Petöfi Circle, named after the revolutionary poet who in 1848 had helped set all Hungary ablaze against the Habsburgs. The meetings became the focus of all political activity. For the first time since 1948 the Party had lost the political initiative. Its need for someone who could bridge the gap between Party and opposition was manifest to all except the inner circle of the leadership.

But Rákosi was still unyielding on substance. He summoned the Central Committee to condemn these meetings, which he saw as conspiratorial gatherings to challenge his authority. Events however continued to confound him. The Soviet press published the Party decree 'On overcoming the Cult of Personality and its Consequences'. Imre Nagy's essays were now circulating widely. Finally Rákosi in angry desperation put to the Political Committee a plan to arrest four hundred people, including Nagy. If it could have been carried through it would have destroyed his critics at a stroke. But inevitably the news of it leaked. Friends made plans to spirit Nagy away if necessary into concealment in northern Hungary until the danger was over.[8]

The Political Committee gave Rákosi's plan some sort of

endorsement. He prepared to put it to the Central Committee, but like everyone else the Soviet leadership knew what was in the wind. On 18 July Mikoyan flew to Budapest and appeared unannounced at the Central Committee session. In a brutal intervention he turned on Rákosi, reversing at a stroke the policy of support for him which Khrushchev had described to the Yugoslav Ambassador. He called for Rákosi's dismissal.

The Central Committee obediently expelled Rákosi from the Political Committee and from his office as General Secretary. He was shipped off that night to Moscow. The long career of the wise father of the Hungarian people was finished. For eleven years he had dominated Hungarian life. Moved by fear or awe or admiration he had given absolute priority to Soviet interests. Yet he had fought back savagely when the Kremlin appointed Nagy to share power with him. His departure marked the end of an era. Gerö, his loyal lieutenant, took Rákosi's place. The butchery done, Mikoyan went on to Belgrade for talks with Tito. On his way home he passed through Budapest. Like Suslov he went to talk to Imre Nagy.

For Moscow, the Hungarian situation was disturbing. But that in Poland seemed much more threatening. On 28 June rioting had broken out in Poznan. Micunovic, the Yugoslav Ambassador in Moscow, describes in his diary how much this frightened the Soviet leadership, and how their obsessive belief in hostile conspiracy led them to exaggerate the problem. 'They see in this the beginning of the counter revolution which, as they put it here, the West, led by the United States, has organized with the objective of splitting the "camp" and separating Poland and the other socialist states from the Soviet Union.' The United States, Khrushchev told Micunovic, had concluded that the Soviet Union was weak: 'We shall show them that they've made a great mistake.'[9]

The elements that were to make up the tragedy of 1956

were fitting into place. The Poles were asserting themselves. The Hungarians, elated by their success in getting rid of Rákosi, were determined to follow where the Poles led. Moscow was torn between its desire for détente with the West and fear that the Americans would exploit Soviet weakness. Inside Eastern Europe, which it saw as its own back yard, it was trying to reconcile its insistence on Communist order with a crude understanding of the East Europeans' desire to cleanse themselves of Stalinism. And the Soviet leaders were still not at ease in their new relationship with Belgrade. For them, the nationalization of the Suez Canal on 26 July came as a godsend. With trouble of its own, the West would have less opportunity to feed the flames which threatened to consume Eastern Europe.

Chapter 9

REVOLUTION

When Mikoyan deposed Rákosi on 17 July and sent him into exile in the Soviet Union, he was removing from the scene the strongest personality in Hungarian political life. Rákosi was hated, discredited. His judgement had failed, he was on the run. But there was no one else in the Party with anything like his experience of power and office. Even in 1953-55, he had never been eclipsed by Nagy. Only Nagy had any prospect of replacing him successfully. But although by July Nagy was once again becoming a figure of influence, he was still out of office, out of the Party. Having deposed Rákosi, Mikoyan appointed not Nagy but Ernö Gerö in Ràkosi's place.

In retrospect it is clear that in doing so Mikoyan made revolution inevitable. He missed the chance of making a clean break with Rákosi's hated regime. Gerö was an experienced, compulsively hard-working apparatchik. He had been close to Rákosi since the liberation. He was less hated than Rákosi, but only marginally less discredited. He lacked Rákosi's flexibility and skill. If Mikoyan had chosen Nagy in July he would have given him the chance to create a position like Gomulka's, strong enough to resist both popular and Soviet pressure and so to save his country. But we have seen how suspicious the Kremlin was of the Polish Party's efforts to come to terms with the people. Mikoyan did not want to replicate those circumstances in Hungary.

So Nagy's return to power was postponed for three vital months in the late summer and early autumn of 1956, which Gerö wasted.

Many Hungarians concluded from Mikoyan's choice of Gerö that nothing of real importance had changed. They even feared a reappearance of Rákosi from the wings. In those summer months it was still unthinkable that anyone other than a Communist should become prime minister. But by now all the old regime's critics were convinced that if real change was to be achieved Nagy would once again have to take charge.

But Rákosi had been so dominant, so widely hated, that Mikoyan can be forgiven for hoping that the very fact of his removal would restore the situation. Gerö was a tested subordinate. If he could establish his authority by firmness and some concessions, well and good. Nagy, by contrast, had shown himself insubordinate in 1955 and unrepentant ever since. And Mikoyan kept in touch with Nagy, visiting him on his return from Yugoslavia. He calculated that if Gerö failed he could still turn to Nagy.

Of course, Mikoyan misjudged the strength of Hungarian feeling. For this Nagy is partly to blame. Throughout 1955 and 1956 he had stubbornly insisted on the rightness of his views. But he had done so privately, in his essays and in letters to the Central Committee. He had refused to join openly with the writers and journalists in their campaign for reform. He declined to take his views to the people. He still insisted on respecting the discipline he had learned in the Party from which he had been expelled. He may have given the Russians the impression that he saw the public expressions of dissatisfaction which convulsed Budapest in the summer months as emotional and insubstantial. If this were so, firmness on essentials and a show of concession on peripheral matters would restore the situation.

This was the policy Gerö doggedly pursued through August and September. Power was as closely held as ever. But the rehabilitation of political prisoners continued. Economic concessions were promised. Mass outings to

Vienna were organized, the first opportunity for people to go to the West since the Communists seized power. There was no attempt to silence the rebels as they clamoured for liberalization, freedom of the press and reform.

The success of this policy depended on the leaders of the reform movement being able to keep it within bounds, winning informal popular control of peripheral spheres of national life but stopping short of any attempt on the central issue of political power. If the reformist leaders or their followers chose to press for political guarantees of their new peripheral freedoms, conflict was inevitable.

This was why Gerö was so reluctant to readmit Nagy to the Party and give him a forum for renewed political activity. Throughout the second half of the summer, Nagy's status remained unchanged: private citizen, former Party member, without any formal links with the Party, yet a Bolshevik of nearly forty years' standing, a former prime minister and the one individual to whom the nation and most of the Party looked for a lead. Gerö took no action when it was rumoured that Nagy's associates planned to launch a magazine in the autumn. He did nothing when Géza Losonczy published what everyone took to be an authoritative statement of Nagy's views. He was silent when he heard that Nagy had sent an associate to investigate peasant complaints. He turned a deaf ear to tumultuous applause for Nagy at the Writers' Association General Meeting. He even ignored rumours that Nagy's friends were talking to old Social Democratic leaders.

But on 4 October Nagy applied in writing for readmission to the Party. His language was much more moderate than in his essays. He argued that his expulsion had violated Party statutes, but reaffirmed his agreement with the main stream of Party thinking. He specifically accepted 'democratic centralism' and a socialist economy. And he recognized as binding on him if he returned to the Party the July 1956 Central Committee Resolution, in which Gerö had summarized his intentions when he took over from Rákosi. This moderation incensed Nagy's friends, who felt he should at last assert his strength.

Even so, Gerö took nine days to respond to the application. Nagy's friends thought the delay a deliberate insult. He took it calmly, once more demonstrating loyalty to the Party, caution bordering on timidity, and a conviction that events were going his way. Gerö and Kádár summoned Nagy to discuss his readmission. They urged him to dissociate himself from his circle of advisers, and he halfheartedly agreed. Finally, after discussing the matter with Moscow, Gerö agreed that Nagy should be readmitted to the Communist Party.

But while Gerö weighed his response to Nagy, popular exploitation of an earlier concession snatched the initiative from his hands. In September he had agreed to the official reburial and rehabilitation of László Rajk. He had seen this less as a concession to Julia Rajk and her supporters than as a way to please the Yugoslavs. The execution had been Rákosi's contribution to the Soviet campaign against Tito; rehabilitation would win Yugoslav favour and dissociate Gerö from Rákosi. He did not reckon with the emotion which the reburial released and which engulfed the nation.

Julia Rajk planned her husband's reburial just as carefully as Erzsébet Nagy planned her father's thirty-three years later. She chose 6 October for the occasion, the anniversary of the day on which the thirteen generals of Arad were executed by the Austrians in 1849. She arranged for the remains, recovered from an unmarked pit beside a country road, to rest all day under the mausoleum of Kossuth, the greatest of Hungarian heroes. Like Nagy's, they were watched by a guard of honour, flanked by candelabra. The reburial was to take place in the line of graves of heroes of the Workers' Movement, superimposed on Kerepesi cemetery when the Communists came to power.

Julia Rajk, a gaunt figure, her face lined by suffering, went to the grave with her eight-year-old son, born just before her own arrest and taken from her before her husband's execution. The ceremony was the culmination of a long campaign to honour her husband's memory. She had turned down an offer of compensation. She wanted revenge. 'Murderers should not be criticized,' she had said, 'they should be punished.'[1]

Gerö was still in Moscow when the reburial took place. Kádár, Rajk's friend and betrayer, was on his way back from Peking. Two perdurable Communists, Münnich and Apro, represented the official world. Neither was the sort of man who could appeal to the emotions of those who had suffered so much under Rákosi. Münnich did his best, speaking of Rajk's murderers as 'sadistic criminals who had crawled into the sunlight from the stinking swamps of the "cult of the personality" '[2].

The invited guests were mostly Communists and comrades-in-arms of the victims, motivated by respect for their memory and hatred for their murderers. There was also shame for the part many of those present had played in their condemnation. As the poet Benjamin put it: 'It is my crime to have believed in yours.'[3] Nagy and his wife were quiet and withdrawn figures by the graveside. He was content to leave the speeches to Münnich and Apro and the attention to Julia Rajk. At the end of the ceremony she turned and momentarily embraced him: the only moment of tenderness in her bitter day of triumph. And as the official party dispersed, the ordinary people poured past the new graves.

The reburial was followed by a quickening of events. On 13 October a second reburial took place, this time of military victims of the purges of 1949. On the following day the newspapers carried the Political Committee's decision to readmit Nagy to the Party. Later his Chair at the university and his membership of the Academy of Sciences were restored to him. There was no word of Party or government office.

Demands for reform continued to spread. Local and specialist Petöfi Clubs inspired by the Budapest Petöfi Circle debates of the early summer were established. The country was ablaze with debating societies, discussion groups and local 'parliaments'. But the Communist leadership seemed unaware of the turmoil around them. On 14 October Gerö and Hegedüs left on an eight-day visit to Tito in Belgrade. They stayed there while in Budapest demands for reform proliferated. They did not even cut the visit short when Khrushchev flew to Warsaw on 19 October for a showdown with Gomulka and then, backing away from confrontation, accepted the Polish reform programme. It was as if they believed that to recover Tito's favour was enough to still the storm that was gathering at home.

In his own way, Nagy seemed as complacent. He had admittedly no formal responsibility in government or Party. But events were shaping as he had said they would, and the nation faced crisis. He was close to power. The British Minister in Budapest reported on 18 October that 'Nagy's star appears firmly in the ascendant and I am reliably informed that it is only a question of time before he obtains high office.'[4]

Yet on 20 October Nagy set off for Balaton. There he remained till the morning of 23 October. He stayed with the owner of a small vineyard, visiting a wine festival and soaking up the autumn sunshine. Photographs show us a portly middle-aged man relaxing on holiday without a care in the world. One might conclude that Nagy was woefully out of touch in these last days of peace. Perhaps to a degree he was; but in that complex and ambivalent personality there was also iron self-discipline and a remarkable capacity to wait upon events.

Elsewhere there was tumult. In Budapest, Miskolc, Szeged, Pécs and Sopron students were calling for marches and demonstrations. The Petöfi Circle demanded a special meeting of the Party leadership, with Nagy included. But until a minute before midnight Nagy persisted in his policy of seeking neither to control nor openly to encourage unrest. When his friends urged him to cut short his holiday and return to Budapest he refused. As the storm broke he still believed that he need only wait for power to fall into his lap.

The news of the Polish success in the showdown with

Khrushchev on 19 October had intoxicated the Hungarians. Poland was not just a friend but a precedent. The
reformers believed that what had been ceded to her must
surely be ceded to Hungary. And the fact that Khrushchev
had backed away from confrontation in Warsaw undermined the Hungarian authorities' self-confidence as much
as it encouraged the reformers. Excited mass meetings on
21 and 22 October began by passing resolutions of support
for Poland and ended by formulating demands for reform
in Hungary.

While Nagy remained quietly at Lake Balaton, his
friends were actively involved at these meetings. The most
significant was that at the Technical University on 22
October which formulated the reformers' demands most
clearly. Word of them was relayed to Nagy by telephone.

To a Reform Communist like Nagy, these demands were
reasonable and impossible at the same time. The students
said they wanted a new Central Committee; Nagy as prime
minister; friendship on a basis of equality with the Soviet
Union and Yugoslavia; elections; a new economic policy;
lower industrial norms and workers' autonomy; a new deal
in agriculture; an amnesty and a review of past trials;
specific concessions to patriotic feelings; and freedom of the
press. All these would have been sensible things to ask for
in a new and better Hungary. They reflected many of the
changes Nagy had started to make in 1953. But at a time of
crisis they seemed dangerously out of touch with political
reality.

Nagy may have hesitated because of the content of these
demands. He was even more doubtful about the way they
were put forward. They were publicized as widely as
carbon paper and duplicator would spread them. They
were thrown down as a clear challenge to the Party.
Demonstrations to back them were threatened for the
following day. Within days the course of events validated
this approach, but on 22 October it was shocking to a
Communist for whom loyalty was a central tenet and who
believed that the Party's job was to lead, not follow. Nagy

disagreed with his associates who wanted him to commit himself to support the reformers. He still put his faith in private argument within the Party leadership.

He may too have feared a counter-stroke by Gerö. Some time earlier he had been warned that Gerö hoped to provoke him into action and then destroy his influence for good. We do not know whether there was anything in this rumour: but it is a fact that in the week of 15 October many Hungarian army units were temporarily deprived of all except their small arms, in a way that suggests that the authorities may have decided to provoke trouble.

On 22 October Nagy again rebuffed friends who urged him to come back to Budapest and put himself at the head of the students. He would return as planned on the following day. On 23 October he set off for Budapest by car. On the way he passed through Székesfehérvár, one of the main Soviet bases in Hungary, where troops were already preparing to move to Budapest if required.

Nagy arrived in Budapest in the morning of 23 October and went straight into a meeting with his associates. We have seen that since his fall from power a group of Reform Communists had gradually gathered around him. All were young men, most in their thirties, generally more radical than Nagy in their approach to the problems with which Party and country were faced. Most had learned their radicalism in prison under Rákosi. The most prominent was Géza Losonczy, who eventually died in prison while the Nagy trial was being prepared. At forty-six, Ferenc Donáth, sentenced to twelve years imprisonment at the trial, bridged the gap between Nagy and the others. József Szilágyi became Nagy's secretary during the Revolution and was executed afterwards. Miklós Gimes, who died with Nagy, was a journalist who had been close to him for some years. So was Miklós Vásárhelyi, who became his press spokesman during the Revolution, went to prison with him and eventually formed the Committee for Historical Justice which, thirty years later, secured Nagy's rehabilitation. Other members of the group were Nagy's son-in-law, Ferenc Jánosi, and Szilárd Ujhelyi.

The group was far from being a band of brothers. Nagy as we shall see was about to cut himself off from them for three crucial days. There were personal tensions and differences about policy between them. Nevertheless, when he would let them Nagy's friends gave him invaluable service. During the Revolution they formed the nucleus of his political staff. They helped him in his dealings with representatives of all the other forces who crowded in on him in those days. And as we have seen most of them went into exile and prison with him.

Now they brought him up to date on developments in Budapest that morning. The university students were committed to a mass demonstration that afternoon, starting in Pest at the statue of Petöfi, the Hungarian hero of 1848, and moving on to that of Bem, the Polish hero of the same era, in Buda. The march would manifest sympathy for Poland; it would stake a claim for the same liberties for Hungary.

At Party headquarters, Nagy's friends reported, the atmosphere was tense, the leaders aggressive yet indecisive. Gerö had returned from Belgrade only that morning. He seemed by turns frightened of the malcontents and sardonically satisfied that they had exposed themselves to retribution. But he was probably uncertain on the key point: did Moscow want him to accommodate dissent or to crush it? Meanwhile the Minister of the Interior had been sending contradictory messages to the student leaders all morning.

Nagy's meeting with his associates on the afternoon of 23 October was acrimonious. They saw an opportunity for Nagy to exploit unrest, perhaps put himself at its head; he saw danger from the leadership and demonstrators alike. They had been convinced by the passion of Nagy's essays; he continued to distinguish between private persuasion within the Party and public demands for change. He wanted to wait for the Party to call him back to office. When it did he intended to pick up his programme where he had been interrupted in 1955. His friends reminded him in vain of the urgent radicalism of the essays he had written when Rákosi drove him into the political wilderness.

Losonczy in particular pressed Nagy to commit himself. Nagy rebuffed him. Eventually the meeting broke up. No one was satisfied. The group dispersed, to the university, Party headquarters, newspaper offices. Jánosi stayed with Nagy in the villa in Buda, a good three miles from the centre of the city.

Through the afternoon and early evening of 23 October, Nagy and Jánosi could follow a fast-developing situation only at second hand. They did not hear the speeches and poems at the Petöfi statue. They missed the heady sensation of national unity that accompanied the march across the centre of the city. They were far away· when workers, coming off the day shift in Ujpest, decided to see what was happening in the city centre, encountered the demonstrators there and joined them. They heard only belatedly that the crowds had moved on from the Bem statue to gather outside parliament and the radio building and at the Stalin statue.

At eight in the evening, Gerö broadcast to the nation. The broadcast was as ill-judged as everything else he did in the course of the crisis. With the nation demanding instant action, he vaguely offered a review of grievances and eventual redress. And he called the demonstrators' motives in question, succeeding only in provoking them to insist that the radio should broadcast a statement of their demands. At the time it was thought that he had deliberately set out to provoke an outbreak which he could crush. Knowing what we do of Soviet hesitancy it seems unlikely that he would have taken such a risk. Misjudgement and lack of political imagination seems a more likely explanation of a broadcast which led directly to the first bloodshed of the Revolution.

But even if Gerö had shown greater understanding, it is

unlikely that he could have brought the situation under control. The people wanted more than his grey, discredited kind of Communism. For some time, the crowds in Kossuth Square in front of parliament had been demanding that Nagy should speak to them. Losonczy came to his house, finally persuaded him to go to parliament. They piled into a little car and drove down into the city and across the river to parliament. Nagy expressed amazement when he saw that the Communist symbol had been cut out of the national flag. Like Gerö, he had been left behind by the day's events.

Inside parliament there was fear and confusion. Nagy was received coldly by Communists who wanted him to calm the demonstrators and yet feared that he had come to take command of them. Finally he allowed himself to be pushed out onto a balcony to address the crowd. It was nine on a dark October evening. For a while he was not noticed. Then someone saw him and called for silence. Slowly he got the crowd's attention.

Nagy started to speak to the crowd. He spoke without proper preparation, without any real understanding of the emotions of the last few hours. He tried to calm the demonstrators, ask them to disperse. The microphone was poor and few could hear him. Those who could responded badly. Quite misjudging their mood, he called them 'comrades'. 'There are no comrades here,' they shouted back. He asked them to go home, promised a Party review of their grievances. Few paid attention. He scrambled back into the building.

It was an unheroic, inadequate start to Nagy's last great adventure. Gerö could have done as much. But a journalist who was beside Nagy, relaying his words to the radio as he spoke, believes that this was the decisive moment in his political development, that on the evening of 23 October he cast off Communism for ever and became a simple and stubborn patriot.[5] This view surely misjudges and over-simplifies Nagy's development in the last days of his active political life. But it is clear that this rejection by the crowd shook Nagy. He may then have understood that his waiting game had exacted a price, and realized that he could no longer satisfy demands for reform merely by resuming the policies of the New Course.

From the parliament building Nagy went to Party head-quarters in a side street three hundred yards away. At the door he dismissed his companions, some say brusquely. It was a crucial, almost fatal moment. Only his son-in-law went inside with him. Nagy seemed to be going to join his enemies.

The situation at Party headquarters was as chaotic as in parliament. Gerö and Hegedüs were huddled with a small group of confidants, still resisting those who urged them to turn to Nagy for help. Eventually the Central Committee went into formal session. Nagy was not a member. He and Jánosi were kept waiting in an ante-room.

Meanwhile, away from Party headquarters the situation was fast deteriorating. The Stalin statue had been cut off at the knees, leaving only his great metal boots: the fallen statue became a source of souvenirs, like the Berlin Wall thirty-three years later. At the radio building, tempers had risen when the demonstrators tried to get their demands broad-cast. The security police had opened fire. Army units had given their arms to the demonstrators, who were firing back. Demonstration was turning into insurrection, and Hungar-ian forces – army, security police and ordinary police – were proving themselves too weak and divided to contain it.

The frightened members of the Central Committee turned to the question of Soviet military support. Some time in the late evening of 23 October they decided, or acquiesced in a decision taken elsewhere, to bring Soviet troops into Budapest.

The first Soviet armoured forces arrived in the city between one and two in the morning of 24 October. The Soviet objective was probably no more than to display potentially overwhelming strength, with no thought yet of engaging the insurgents. Certain Soviet military prepara-tions had been noted as early as 20 October, but they do not prove that any political decisions had been taken then. They were probably no more than precautionary moves at a time of rising tension. Similarly a Soviet decision to move forces towards Budapest was probably taken before noon on 23 October. But the order actually committing them to the streets could have been issued in response to the Central Committee invitation only an hour or so before they appeared.

Nagy himself was not present when the Central Committee endorsed the Soviet intervention. But at some point in the early hours of 24 October the Committee acknowledged that the Party needed him if it were to have any chance of controlling the situation. At 8.13 am on 24 October Budapest Radio announced the formation earlier that day of a new Political Committee; and the appointment of Nagy as Prime Minister. At 8.45 am it carried a declaration of martial law. And at 9 am it announced that the government had asked for Soviet help.

On the morning of 24 October, the leaders gathered in Party Headquarters were divided on how to respond to the insurgency which had grown out of the previous day's demonstrations. There were two options: to crush the insurrection by force, promising redress of grievance when order was restored, or to seek to appease the demonstrators, using force only in response to insurgent force. Gerö instinctively advocated the former course, Nagy the latter. The word from Moscow supported Nagy. It made it clear that the commitment of Soviet forces to the streets of Budapest did not mean that the Kremlin had decided that repression was the right answer to Hungary's problem.

But if appeasement was the chosen course, the question of how far to take it remained open. On the previous day Gerö had talked of concessions in the most perfunctory of ways. As we have seen, Nagy had rejected his friends' advocacy of far-reaching change. Now, appointed prime minister, he started to talk in terms which envisaged a return to the New Course. Mikoyan and Suslov returned to Budapest on 25 October and seem to have accepted Nagy's belief that this would be enough to get the people off the streets. With their backing, Nagy set out to restore the government's authority, his essential concession to the demonstrators being no more than the promise that this time, as in 1953, Communism would not forget man.

As Nagy, Mikoyan and Suslov sought a political solution, however, events on the streets were multiplying their problems. On the night of 23-24 October the people had found unity outside parliament, triumphed at Stalin's statue, and fought it out at the radio building with the security police. But fighting between insurgents and security police continued on 24 October. The presence of Soviet forces further angered the insurgents. It gradually became clear that no effective Hungarian force was available to the government: the army and the ordinary police stood by or helped the insurgents, the security police were running scared.

It was manifest that only the all-out use of Soviet force would break the insurgents, but this the Russians still wanted to avoid. Mikoyan and Suslov decided on a further move. Gerö and Hegedüs must follow Rákosi into exile. Nagy would be left to come to terms with the insurgents in his own way, though within a Communist-dominated frame of reference. Kádár, appointed First Secretary in Gerö's place, would set about restoring the Party's reputation. At noon on 25 October the radio announced these changes. Nagy and Kádár would broadcast that afternoon.

Within hours came the massacre in Kossuth Square in front of parliament, where Nagy had made his inadequate speech two nights before. Soviet tanks confronted a vast crowd of demonstrators. The situation was tense but peaceful. Then Hungarian security police fired into the square. The tanks returned the fire. Many died. It was uncertain how the shooting started, but it was clear that in the absence of Russians and security police there would have been no massacre.

Immediately the political changes of the morning seemed valueless. Just as the killings at the radio building on 23

October had devalued Nagy's appointment as prime
minister a few hours later, so the killings outside parliament
drained away any political value which Gerö's resignation
might otherwise have had. 'Nagy to power' had been a good
slogan on 23 October. Now the demonstrators blamed their
grief on the security police and the Russians. Once the
Russians were gone the security police would be impotent.
On 25 October the slogan to unite the nation was 'Russians
go home'.

In face of these difficulties, Mikoyan, Suslov, Nagy and
Kádár set about scratching together a new policy. Nagy
would be allowed to go further in coming to terms with the
insurgents. He could promise redress of grievances within a
continuing socialist system and the withdrawal of Soviet
troops to their barracks as soon as the fighting stopped.

To Nagy this meant a significant military concession to
the insurgents now, to be followed once order had been
restored by the New Course programme in which he put so
much faith. To Kádár it promised a reformed Party with a
continuing monopoly of power. To the Russians it offered
adequate stability in Hungary and the prospect of getting
their forces out of the fighting. But it fell far short of what
the revolutionaries now wanted. Embittered by the events
of the last forty-eight hours, they looked for the end of
Communism and the immediate expulsion of the Russians.
They were already beginning to formulate demands for a
Soviet withdrawal from Hungary, not just Budapest; and
for free elections which would inevitably destroy the
Communist Party.

In retrospect there is a tragic inevitability about the events
of the Hungarian Revolution, insurgents' demands always
in advance of authority's response. Yet few detected it at
the time, and until the last terrible days there is no sense of
fatalism to be identified in Nagy's efforts to master the
situation. There is no doubt that he started badly, that on
23 October he misread the balance of forces, and that he

was slow thereafter to adjust to an unimagined new situation. But by 26 October he seemed to have found his feet. That day he moved out of his isolation in Party headquarters and into the prime minister's office in parliament. The move reunited him with his old associates and gave him a chance to make a new start. He received a stream of visitors: Reform Communists, non-Communists, insurgents. They gave him the opportunity to start building bridges to new centres of power in what was a changed Hungary.

The meetings also gave him and his associates the chance to try to clear him of responsibility for the more unpopular of the government's actions since 23 October. Much was made of this issue at the time and immediately after the Revolution, primarily for political and propagandist reasons. There is a danger of the argument distracting us from what really happened in October 1956. But it is worth pursuing even now, if only for its place in Imre Nagy's record.

Essentially, Nagy's apologists at the time suggested that he was a prisoner of the Party from the time he went to Party headquarters on 23 October until he moved to parliament three days later. Specifically, they rightly denied that he was involved in the decision to bring in Soviet troops on 23 October. They tried, less justly, to dissociate him from the declaration of martial law on the following day. They contrasted the human tone of his radio broadcasts with the harshness of others, particularly Gerö. To justify the inadequacy of the policies Nagy put to the nation they suggested that he broadcast at the time more or less with a gun at his head. They claimed that Gerö and Hegedüs had consciously devised a plot to saddle Nagy with responsibility for repressive measures, undermine his position and prepare the way for reaction.

The United Nations special committee on the Problem of Hungary attempted to get to grips with this argument in their report: 'The evidence establishes that Mr Nagy was in no sense in a position to act in accordance with his own judgement from 24 October to 28 October. But it would doubtless be equally mistaken to conclude that Mr Nagy was prevented from identifying himself with the uprising from the start solely by the pressures to which he was subjected. There is little reason to believe that, at the outset, Mr Nagy was aware of the manner in which the situation would develop or that he foresaw that he was destined to become a leading figure. He was restored to the office of prime minister not as a result of any personal initiative on his part, but because his appointment suited the immediate purposes of Mr Gerö, aware as he was that, in the tense circumstances of the morning of 24 October, the Communist regime needed to be adorned with the façade of a leader acceptable to popular opinion. From that moment, Mr Nagy tended to become, seemingly against his expectation, the symbol for the Hungarian people of their unity. Nevertheless, in the days immediately after 24 October, he appeared to be hesitating between loyalty to his Marxist training, backed by an apparatus of force, on the one hand, and association with the cause of his countrymen, on the other. His predicament between 24 and 28 October is by no means wholly explained by *force majeure*. From his Marxist and Communist anchorage, he was carried along by events beyond his control, gradually aware of the intensity of the passions which the uprising had evoked and the reality of the grievances which it expressed, and gradually convinced that he must accept the responsibilities thrust upon him by circumstances.'[6]

In retrospect this analysis reads like a rather shrewd attempt by the committee to cobble together evidence from émigré sources intended to exculpate Nagy with their own more objective assessment of the pressures upon him. They note the evidence that Nagy was cut off from his friends and from forces outside the Party in the days he spent at Party headquarters, but play down suggestions that he was prevented by physical pressure from doing what he would otherwise have done. They rightly imply that he was a prisoner of his own Communist preconceptions and sense of Party loyalty. And they are right in suggesting that in these early days of the Revolution Nagy could not imagine a need to go outside the assumptions of his Party to find common ground with the people fighting in the streets.

In short, in these first days of the Revolution Nagy showed himself lacking in political imagination. We have seen that he was not party to the decision to call in the Russians; but we may surmise that he would have supported it if he had been admitted to the Central Committee by the time it was taken. He was responsible for the declaration of martial law. He was slow to see that even his kind of Communism was no longer adequate to the situation. He voluntarily put to the people in his broadcasts policies which they found inadequate. One of his associates at the time summarizes the position well: 'Imre Nagy was not a prisoner of the secret police in those days. He was a prisoner of himself.'[7]

But events did not stand still as Nagy and his apologists tried to put the record straight. Nagy had eight more days of freedom. The use he made of them did more than explanations to restore trust between him and the people. In those days he faced a headlong rush of events. Advised by one government after another, he did his best to steer a course between hazards. In these eight days, his political convictions moved further than they had moved in forty years.

On 26 October, Nagy went to parliament committed to the restoration of order and the re-establishment of Communist authority through a predominantly Communist government. When he left it for the Yugoslav Embassy on 4 November he was at the head of a truly representative coalition government. He was committed to free elections within months, which would inevitably have destroyed his Party. He had declared neutrality, withdrawn from the Warsaw Pact, denounced Soviet aggression and called for the protection of the United Nations and the four Great Powers. He was driven by events. He had no great master plan. But although he learned as he went along, there was a constancy and conviction that flowed from the beliefs formed in Moscow and Budapest, advanced as theories in the essays, and now put to work in practice.

In these days Nagy for once in his life made quick decisions. He had to: the situation on the streets was changing hourly. In the past he had dealt with carefully calculating and self-disciplined Party members and with a cowed population. Now he was dealing with a free Hungary. He came face to face with a passionate and resurgent patriotism, suspicious of Communism, critical of talk of reaching an accommodation with the Russians, snapping up each concession and asking for more. Retrospect is coloured by the tragedy that ended it all, but these were good, free days for Hungary. For Nagy they were the culmination of his political career.

On 27 October he announced the formation of a new government. It was still dominated by Communists, many of them unreformed. From outside the Party, Tildy and Kovács were included. Eight years before they had been Smallholder figures of stature. In the next week Tildy was to show great strength. But now, to the insurgents, he seemed old and weak. He had served as President of the Republic while Rákosi destroyed democracy: he was a suspect fellow-traveller. Kovács had spent years in Soviet captivity: he took office reluctantly. The composition of the new government did nothing to persuade the insurgents that those in power understood the new realities. It suggested that Nagy had still not caught up with events.

Having announced his new government, Nagy spent the rest of 27 October coming to terms with realities. He could deal with the insurgents' high expectations by the use of Soviet force or by concession. He wanted to avoid force. So did the Russians, with an eagerness that was forgotten when, later, they changed course. They now agreed to back Nagy in making concessions going wider than the reform under clear Communist leadership which he had sought so far. Very early on 28 October, he went to the Soviet Embassy. Through the Ambassador he consulted Moscow.

He came away convinced that the Kremlin was behind him and endorsed the concessions he was preparing to make.

On 27 October, while Nagy was still considering how far he could go, the government had announced that negotiations would start at once for the withdrawal of Soviet forces from Budapest. But on the following day, perhaps at the Soviet Embassy, Nagy learned of a plan to attack one of the main insurgent positions, that in the Corvin Cinema. The plan had been concocted by a group of Hungarian hardliners, probably encouraged by Soviet contacts. It offered the chance both to destroy the rebels and compromise Nagy. He and his Russian supporters put a stop to it, Nagy threatening resignation if it went ahead.

In the afternoon of that day, 28 October, Nagy made the most significant of his broadcasts so far. He announced a ceasefire; immediate Soviet withdrawal from Budapest; negotiations about Soviet withdrawal from Hungary; and the abolition of the security police as soon as order was restored. On 29 October he went further and disbanded the security police with immediate effect. With these commitments he at last won attention, closed the gap between leadership and insurgents. He sensed his success: visitors noted his new confidence that he was succeeding in bringing people, colleagues and Russians together.

The following day, 30 October, was a good one, with the following day the best of the Revolution. The ceasefire became fully effective. Soviet forces started to withdraw from Budapest. Nagy's allies established a revolutionary council at army headquarters, giving him the beginnings of a unified armed force at his command. He took another step which bound the insurgents closer to him, announcing the end of the one-party system and the formation of yet another new government. The Smallholders and Peasants now had full rather than token representation. A seat was reserved for the Social Democrats. Nagy also announced that negotiations were starting at once for the withdrawal of Soviet troops from Hungary entirely. He was as convinced as ever that he had Soviet agreement.

The news from Moscow confirmed this. On 30 October Mikoyan and Suslov came to Budapest again, bringing with them the text of the Kremlin's declaration on relations with the socialist states. It was by any standards a remarkable document which, had it been allowed to stand, might have provided an enduring basis for friendship between the Soviet Union and its Eastern European allies. Essentially it called for exactly the kind of relationship which Nagy had envisaged in his essay nine months earlier, one of equality based on independence, sovereignty and non-interference. It confirmed that orders had been given to withdraw Soviet forces from Budapest and that Moscow was ready for negotiations about their presence elsewhere in Hungary.[8]

To Nagy and to the world the declaration looked like a Soviet vote of confidence in his ability to master the situation. There were worrying passages: one recorded that reaction had exploited the Hungarian people's legitimate discontent, another prejudged the Hungarians' wishes by saying that it was up to them to guard their own socialist gains. But taken as a whole the declaration was straightforward, even generous, and enormously encouraging. It was a clear vote of confidence in Nagy and a confirmation of the success of his cooperation with Mikoyan and Suslov.

There were shadows that day too, however. A distant one was the British and French ultimatum to Israel and Egypt. It demanded that the combatants withdraw and threatened military intervention to keep the two armies apart and safeguard the Suez Canal. Nearer home was the massacre in Republic Square, where insurgents attacked the security police garrison in the Budapest Party headquarters and, when they surrendered, lynched them and a party activist named Imre Mező who had been close to Nagy. The ultimatum might provide a distraction if Soviet policy were to go into reverse and abandon the declaration on relations with the socialist countries; the massacre a pretext for renewing Soviet intervention in Hungary.

But there was no clear sign of these dangers in Nagy's

talks with Mikoyan and Suslov, with whom he spent much of 30 October. He had moved a long way in response to insurgent pressure in the last four days, but he believed that the Kremlin still trusted him. The Soviet declaration, despite its ambiguities, seemed to bear this out. So did his discussions with the Soviet emissaries. They seem to have rebuffed those Hungarian Stalinists who were still clamouring for Soviet military intervention and to have convinced Nagy that he still had their support.

Nagy and his Soviet partners were playing for high stakes, and they were agreeing on propositions unthinkable within the Soviet bloc only days before. They must have feared that they were opening a Pandora's box and there were clearly anxieties on both sides. Sándor Kopácsi, the Budapest police chief who rallied to Nagy and was tried with him, claims that as Mikoyan and Suslov left Nagy for the last time, Mikoyan said: 'Comrade Nagy, save what can be saved.' According to Kopácsi his eyes were filled with tears. This was a man who knew how near to the brink they were. Yet Nagy still believed that he had Mikoyan's backing. So did Kádár. When he returned from seeing Mikoyan and Suslov out, Kopácsi reports, Kádár said to Nagy: 'Imre, have we done it?' and Nagy replied, 'We've done it, János.'[9]

There is room in all this for dissimulation by the Soviet emissaries, for wishful thinking, for misreporting by Kopácsi. But the balance of the evidence suggests that when they left Budapest, Mikoyan and Suslov remained committed to support for Nagy's government and its decision to concede a multi-party system. It also suggests that Nagy and Kádár rejoiced in that confidence in their policy, believing that if they held to it they would be able to unite the country. It is not clear whether they yet realized that a multi-party system and free elections would sweep their own party aside.

So Nagy came successfully through the period from 26 to 30 October. He had brought the country from bloodshed to a precarious kind of order. The freedom fighters were forming peacefully into disciplined National Guards. There had been atrocities, some of them perpetrated by individual groups of insurgents, but there was no White Terror. Different groups were advocating different policies, and the pace of events had been bewildering, but there was no triumph of reaction. On 30 and 31 October the nation was united and at peace.

Nagy had been faced with pressures which he had no military power to resist: as he told a visitor, his power stopped at his desk.[10] His victories were moral ones, won by argument and example. As we have seen, he yielded ground in these days. But it is clear that he found many of the pressures with which he was faced intellectually irresistible. He gradually awoke to the fact that the insurgents were mostly socialists like him. They wanted socialism voluntarily arrived at, just as he did. Like him they wanted socialism without Stalinist distortion. Their arguments were essentially those he had used in his essays a year before.

With the Soviet Declaration of 30 October putting an end to the last vestiges of Stalinism, there was no longer any need for the successful Revolution to oppose the Soviet Union. Moscow now seemed prepared to allow the Hungarians to chart their own future. If Nagy and the revolutionaries wanted to steer towards socialism, they must do as Nagy had argued and carry the people with them. The best way to do that, to seek organic rather than arbitrary socialism, was free elections. The revolutionaries' demands might be dangerous in diplomatic terms. Militarily they risked provoking a Soviet return. But in political terms, Nagy agreed with them. Between 27 and 30 October, he gradually built a national agreement on what the Revolution was about. By 31 October the nation was united and the Revolution apparently successful.

Nagy with his grand–daughter in his garden in Buda, summer 1956. (Erich
Lessing/Magnum)

'The day I met my father'.
Imre Nagy with his wife
and daughter at
Schönbrunn in 1929.
(Erzébet Nagy)

In the bowler hat in which
he went to prison in 1927.
(Erzébet Nagy)

Imre, Mária and Erzébet
Nagy in Moscow, 1940.
(Erzébet Nagy)

Budapest in ruins, 1945. (Magyar Nemzeti Museum)

The land reform, 1945–47. Nagy distributes land certificates to poor peasants. (Magyar Nemzeti Museum)

The Hungarian parliament marks Stalin's death, 8 March 1953. Nagy is at the centre of the horseshoe, in the front row. (Magyar Nemzeti Museum)

Imre Nagy announces the New Course in parliament, 4 July 1953. Rákosi, who spent the next year and a half frustrating his reforms, is immediately behind him. (Magyar Nemzeti Museum)

With his opponents, Mátyás Rákosi and Ernö Gerö (standing) at the Party Congress, May 1954. (Camera Press)

Dancing the csárdás at the launch of the Patriotic People's Front, October 1954. (Camera Press)

With his wife at László Rajk's reburial, October 1956. (Hungarian Ministry of Foreign Affairs)

Comforting Julia Rajk. (Magyar Nemzeti Museum)

At home and at ease, three weeks before the Revolution. (Erich Lessing/Magnum)

The students' march which unleashed the uprising, 23 October 1956. (Hungarian Embassy)

Demonstrators call for support for Poland and for Imre Nagy. (Hungarian Embassy)

At the statue of General Bem, the Polish general who fought for Hungary in 1848–49. (Hungarian Embassy)

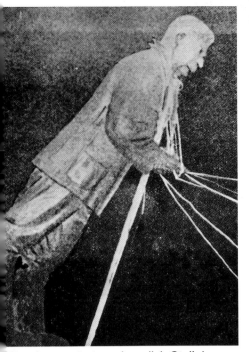

The demonstrators demolish Stalin's giant statue late on 23 October. (Magyar Nemzeti Museum)

Soviet tanks in the streets of Budapest. (Hulton–Deutsch)

Freedom fighters. (Topham)

Hungarian tanks guard a revolutionary strong–point at the Corvin cinema. (David Hurn/Magnum)

Teenage revolutionaries. (Erich Lessing/Magnum)

Imre Nagy declares
Hungary's neutrality.
(Associated Press)

The men who murdered
Nagy: János Kádár with
Nikita Khruschev in
Budapest, April 1958
(Hulton–Deutsch)

Friends, allies and fellow victims

Pál Maléter
(Hulton–Deutsch)

Miklós Gimes
(Hungarian Ministry of
Foreign Affairs)

Géza Losonczy
(Hungarian Ministry of
Foreign Affairs)

József Szilágyi
(Hungarian Ministry of
Foreign Affairs)

June 1989: the crowds in Heroes Square honour Imre Nagy's memory. (Magyar Nemzeti, Museum)

The reburial at Rákoskeresztür of Imre Nagy and his associates. (Hungarian Embassy)

Another way to remember Imre Nagy. (Franco Zecchin/Magnum)

Hungary opens its frontier with Austria and destroys Communism in Eastern Europe. (Udo Schreiber/SIBA–Press)

Chapter 10

WAR

The Soviet Union attacked Hungary in the early hours of 4 November. Its leaders probably committed themselves to that attack on the night of 30-31 October. It was carried to a militarily successful conclusion by 11 November. At the time and afterwards, the Soviet leaders had every interest in representing the operation as assistance to the more deserving side in a civil war. Kádár did his best to contribute to the thesis. But there was no fighting in Hungary between 31 October and 2 November. The Soviet invasion which started on 1 November, the armed attack on 4 November, the crushing of opposition between 4 and 11 November, these were military actions by one sovereign state against another. No Hungarian forces supported the Soviet attack. This was the only war between sovereign states in Europe in the last forty-five years.

1956 was a traumatic year for the Soviet leadership. Throughout it Soviet policy was hammered out in bitter argument among the leaders in the Kremlin. Many of them were opposed to Khrushchev's condemnation of Stalinism in the 'secret speech'. There was disagreement over policy towards the West and towards the satellites. Most of the leaders were convinced that a hostile capitalist world was poised to take advantage of Communist weakness. The appearance of monolithic unanimity which the leadership

153

presented was even more skin deep in 1956 than in easier years.

For most of the year, Soviet policy towards Hungary reflected the views of the reformers in the Kremlin. Their influence can be seen in Soviet contacts with Nagy in the spring and early summer. They triumphed in the decision to remove Rákosi from Hungary once and for all. They held Gerö back from decisive action against the Petöfi Circle in the summer. It was they who encouraged him to rebury László Rajk and readmit Nagy to the Party. As we have seen Mikoyan supported Nagy consistently through the difficult and dangerous last week of October. And in the Moscow Declaration of 30 October the views of the reformers on relationships with the socialist countries seemed to prevail.

At any time things could have turned out otherwise; and finally, with the decision to attack Hungary, they did. We know that when Khrushchev went to Warsaw in October he was determined to force the Poles to submit. It was only the unity of the Polish leadership and their readiness to use the army to resist Moscow if necessary which persuaded him to back down.

But Moscow viewed dissent by Communists anywhere, and in Eastern Europe in particular, as a treacherous affront. 'The Russians', Micunovic, the Yugoslav Ambassador, noted shortly after he arrived in Moscow in the spring of 1956, 'regard Eastern Europe as their own internal affair and . . . they will not need anybody's approval . . . for any solutions they may decide on.'[1] To a Soviet leadership which thought about Eastern Europe in this way, events in Hungary must have seemed at times a heaven-sent opportunity to reassert Moscow's authority after the Warsaw rebuff. The fact that when the troops went in on 24 October a whiff of grapeshot was not enough to blow trouble away could only add to the Kremlin's anger.

But there were arguments for caution too, and Mikoyan's reports from Budapest recommended accommodation. So for seven days from 23 October, disagreement raged in the Kremlin. The leaders were in constant touch with their Ambassador in Budapest, Yuri Andropov. Mikoyan and Suslov shuttled back and forth. The Chinese and the satellite leaders contributed some reassurance and more alarm. The events on the streets of Budapest were reported, misrepresented, analysed. Still the liberals prevailed in the Kremlin. Finally, Moscow's position was codified in the 30 October Declaration.

There were those at the time who suggested that the Declaration was mere deception, while Moscow prepared the blow that finally destroyed the Revolution. It is hard to accept this. The Declaration ranged much wider than such a deception would have required, dealing with abstract and general questions of relations with all the satellites, not just with the immediate problem of Hungary. In it Moscow gave hostages to fortune – so much so that when the Reform Communist leadership in Hungary thirty years later started to argue for greater foreign policy independence their spokesman, Mátyás Szürös, quoted the Declaration tongue-in-cheek as if it had never been superseded by tanks. It gave the West gratuitous propaganda material which it used to the full when Moscow changed course. No, the 30 October Declaration was seriously intended. For a day after its publication the view prevailed in the Kremlin that the right way forward was the creation of a Communist Commonwealth of Nations in Central and Eastern Europe.

On the night of 30-31 October, that view was reversed. It was decided that the Hungarian Revolution must be destroyed by force. It may have been assumed that Nagy could be detached from the revolutionary leaders and perhaps even put in charge of an administration obedient to Soviet orders. If not he would be swept aside. Mikoyan and Suslov were not present. Even if they had been it is unlikely that their expertise would have prevailed. When the weight of opinion on a major issue in any government starts to shift, detailed pros and cons go out of the window. The stampede to join the majority is even greater when the government is an absolute one, facing a crisis and working against the clock.

The Russians changed course essentially for domestic reasons. The army was resentful of the less than effective role it had been required to play in Budapest. According to Khrushchev, it was the main factor in the decision to intervene. Others exploited the situation. The Stalinists were able to point to the situation in Hungary as the latest disaster to flow from Khrushchev's reforms. Outside pressures were strong also. Moscow needed to reassert itself after yielding to the Poles. Khrushchev records that the Soviet leadership spent a whole night discussing with a Chinese delegation how to deal with what he repeatedly and revealingly calls the Hungarian 'mutiny'.[2] As the Russians talked, the balance of opinion repeatedly shifted; each time the Chinese consulted Mao by telephone; each time he agreed with Soviet inclinations. But the weight of Chinese influence clearly favoured intervention. So did the satellite leaders: heresy had to be dealt with before it spread and undermined their own positions. Even Tito let Moscow know of his anxiety.

To the Communist leaders it was of course profoundly shocking that a people should rise up against Communist rule. Nothing in their theory or practice provided for such an event. The Hungarian people had been liberated by Communism and the Red Army from their oppressors. They could not in logic rebel against the people's power. Class enemies, fascist elements and Western agents must be involved, engaged in counter-revolution. Khrushchev's memoirs graphically illustrate the Soviet leadership's assumptions. Even though they were written with the benefit of hindsight, there is little attempt at objectivity. The passages on Eastern European dissenters amount to nothing more than bad-tempered, generalized and frequently contradictory assertions. They leave the impression that Khrushchev, and no doubt his colleagues, was angered, baffled and frightened by events.

In these circumstances, the Russians probably looked to

events to illustrate the propositions which they wanted to see adopted as policy. The killings in Republic Square on 30 October, for example, could be represented as evidence that White Terror was taking charge and that 'honest Communists' were at risk throughout the country. The failure to get relief to Budapest Party headquarters before that massacre took place has been interpreted since, and may have been interpreted at the time, as proof that Nagy was aligning himself with reaction. The Franco-British Suez ultimatum in fact gave Moscow valuable distraction from events in Hungary, but it may have been represented in the Kremlin as evidence of capitalism's aggressive intentions. The argument from contagion had force: if events in Poland could so quickly infect Hungary, how quickly could unchecked violence in Hungary affect the rest of the satellites? The Red Army could not be seen to be defeated by a fascist rabble.

How did the Kremlin protagonists see the role of Imre Nagy in the events of the last seven days of the Revolution? His long-term reputation in Moscow must have been that of a reliable, somewhat unimaginative functionary, with a troublesome streak of stubbornness when it came to questions of agricultural theory and national standing. For twenty months he had done what Moscow needed during the New Course, deftly reconciling Moscow's requirements with Hungarian hopes. He had shown himself dangerously headstrong at the last meeting in the Kremlin in January 1955; but out of office, he had opposed Rákosi in a disciplined way, without taking the issue to the people. His essays, for those in Moscow who saw them, must have been evidence of doggedness and a certain impracticality. From first to last Rákosi certainly did his best to traduce him in the eyes of the Kremlin. But to the Russians Nagy had still seemed able and reliable enough to justify Mikoyan's decision to advance and back him during the first week of the Revolution.

During the week 23-30 October, he kept moving his ground as he tried to come to terms with the insurgents. He did his best to carry the Russians with him at every stage, but even as Mikoyan and Suslov approved of what he did, suspicions in the Kremlin were increasing. The admission of other parties to his government looked dangerous. So did talk of eventual elections. It was improvident but perhaps unavoidable to call for Soviet withdrawal from Budapest and to disband the security police. Talk of Soviet withdrawal from Hungary as a whole was even more alarming; but the Soviet Declaration, just as much as Imre Nagy, envisaged such a withdrawal. Nothing Imre Nagy did between 23 and 30 October provides a reason for Moscow to abandon him. His argument that every step he took had been agreed by Moscow or its representatives is well founded. And as we shall see, the assertion that he sealed his fate by withdrawing Hungary from the Warsaw Pact reverses cause and effect.

Yet events in Hungary could not fail to strengthen the hand of the hard men in the Kremlin. And when Mikoyan and Suslov got back to Moscow, they found that the balance of opinion among the Soviet leadership had shifted. Policy on Eastern Europe must be reversed and the 30 October Declaration abandoned. They accepted the decision. Preparations for the attack on Hungary were beginning. They were both political and military.

It was necessary to tell the allies in general terms what had been decided. According to Khrushchev, the Chinese delegation had got as far as Moscow airport on their way back to Peking when the Russians told them that they had after all decided to strike Hungary down. They acquiesced. On 1 November, Khrushchev, Malenkov and Molotov flew to Brest-Litovsk to brief Gomulka; the Poles, fresh from their own successful showdown with the Russians, did not press their objections to the point of rupture. Khrushchev and Malenkov flew on to Bucharest to meet the Rumanians and Czechs, then to Sofia to talk to the Bulgarians. All three accepted the decision to attack. Khrushchev and Malenkov set off for the most sensitive meeting of all, that with Tito.

Tito was at his retreat on the island of Brioni. Exhausted, frightened by a nightmare flight and an appalling sea crossing to Brioni, the Soviet emissaries spent ten hours with him through the night of 2-3 November. Khrushchev said they wanted to 'consult or rather inform' the Yugoslavs about events in Hungary. He stressed the urgency and secrecy of the visit. No notes were taken. 'It was as though', wrote Micunovic in his diary, 'we were all trying to make sure that no trace should remain of the summit meeting between Yugoslavia and the Soviet Union.' He was clearly haunted by the cynicism of the occasion. 'It is all very strange,' he noted, '. . . there is in fact a war going on . . . and it is being waged by the armed forces of the "first and biggest country of socialism" against the people of a "fraternal socialist country" and a member of the "socialist camp".'[3]

Khrushchev told the Yugoslavs of the Soviet contacts with the other East Europeans. They, like the Chinese, had agreed that counter-revolution stalked in Budapest. Nagy might or might not be an imperialist agent, but the restoration of capitalism was the likely outcome of his actions. 'If we let things take their course the West would say we are either stupid or weak, and that's one and the same thing,' Khrushchev said. 'We cannot possibly permit it, either as Communists and internationalists or as the Soviet state. We would have capitalists on the frontiers of the Soviet Union.'[4]

Soviet troops, Khrushchev said, would take a further day or two to get into position. He also told the Yugoslavs that Kádár and Münnich had defected to the Russians. There was no question but that Hungary was doomed. The Yugoslavs raised no effective objections. The talk turned to who should take Nagy's place and, warily and vaguely, to what Yugoslavia could do to smooth the coming transition of power in Budapest. Weary but successful, Khrushchev and Malenkov flew back to Moscow.

★

Meanwhile, the military preparations were going ahead. The first intervention in Budapest had been carried out by units stationed in Hungary, reinforced from southern Russia and Rumania. Most of these troops were being withdrawn from Hungary. New troops were moving in, mostly across the Soviet-Hungarian border at Zahony. The aim was to replace mauled and tainted units with fresh ones and assemble overwhelming force in Hungary. Completion of the preparations took four days.

These preparatory moves could not be concealed from the Hungarians. Our focus switches back to Moscow's political preparation for the onslaught, this time in Budapest. The Russians needed as far as they could to lull the Hungarian government and the insurgents into a false sense of security. They needed also to use the days before the army struck to make contact with Hungarian Communists loyal to Moscow and ready when the time came to take the legitimate government's place.

By the morning of 1 November, Nagy and the government were convinced that the Soviet Union was preparing an attack on Hungary. The physical evidence for this was already overwhelming. But until late on 3 November they went on hoping that the worst could be averted. Andropov played effectively on these last hopes with hollow repetition of Soviet good intentions. The interaction between hopes and fears, between private negotiation and public statement, between argument with Andropov and reassurance to the insurgents, give an impression of confusion and ineffectuality, even duplicity. Eye witnesses talk of Nagy's irritability under pressure at times, but the general sense is that he remained a commanding figure until the end. He was attempting the impossible; though some stayed loyal, others betrayed him; staff-work was poor; but Nagy was an effective prime minister in those three days.

Nagy spent 1 November locked in argument with Yuri Andropov. He summoned him first at 9 am, to protest that Soviet troop movements breached both the Warsaw Pact and the agreement that Soviet troops should start to withdraw from Hungary. Two hours later, Andropov came back, to assure the Hungarians that the troops entering Hungary were merely reliefs and would be withdrawn in due course. At noon he telephoned to report that Moscow still stood by the 30 October Declaration.

But telephone reports from all over Hungary reported the Soviet advance. Tanks and troops were pouring across the frontier at Zahony. In western Hungary the Russians were screening off the Austrian border. They were seizing Hungarian air bases. Already, individual officers were begging for orders to fire. At 2 pm Nagy telephoned Andropov. He threatened that if the Soviet advance was not stopped he would announce Hungary's withdrawal from the Warsaw Pact. At 4 the Cabinet endorsed this threat. At 5 Andropov appeared, and was confronted by the entire cabinet. Nagy told him that Hungary was no longer bound by the Warsaw Pact. He proposed to protest to the United Nations. Others, notably Kádár with his threat to fight Soviet tanks with his bare hands, supported him. Andropov could only repeat his promise that Soviet troops would be withdrawn and beg the Hungarians not to take the matter to the United Nations.

Just before 8 pm, Nagy broadcast to the nation. He announced that Hungary was withdrawing from the Warsaw Pact. Even now he did not tell the public why. Communications to the United Nations and to embassies in Budapest were more explicit. But Nagy still seems to have been looking for a way to induce the Russians to draw back. To arouse the country against them, to authorize the army to resist, would be to abandon hope.

Andropov played on this hope. Late on 1 November, he came yet again to parliament, urging Nagy to cancel his appeal to the United Nations. He still promised a Soviet withdrawal. The appeal was not cancelled, though it initially went almost unnoticed in a United Nations preoccupied with Suez. In a last effort to appease the Russians, however, the government issued a specific order to Hungarian troops not to engage the invaders.

It has been argued that it was denouncing the Warsaw Pact which sealed Hungary's fate, that Andropov was telling the truth when he repeatedly asserted that the Soviet troop movements were part of the withdrawal process, and that the Kremlin decided to attack only when Nagy refused to rescind his appeal to the United Nations. It is a hollow argument that stands chronology on its head and challenges all the evidence to the contrary. But as it lays the blame for the disaster that befell his country directly at Nagy's door it deserves analysis here.

Khrushchev himself makes it clear that the Soviet decision to attack Hungary was taken before the Chinese had left Moscow and that Marshal Konev then said that he would need three days to get his forces into position.[5] By 1 November Khrushchev and Malenkov were in Brest-Litovsk telling the Poles what Moscow had in mind. Yet Nagy only announced withdrawal from the Warsaw Pact on the afternoon of 1 November, by which time the Russian delegation was on the way to its next rendezvous in Bucharest. Of course Moscow very likely had earlier warning of Hungarian intentions from human or technical sources in the government offices in parliament. But the balance of diplomatic evidence suggests that the Soviet decision to attack was taken well before Nagy's decision to withdraw from the Warsaw Pact.

The military evidence is equally suggestive. By 3 November the Soviet Union had 2,500 tanks in Hungary. By dawn on 4 November it had deployed decisive force in the capital. The introduction of such massive forces took several days. It cannot be convincingly portrayed as having originally been intended merely to cover a peaceful withdrawal, which was abandoned only after Nagy's announcement. The worst that can be said about Nagy's denunciation of the Warsaw Pact is that it made Soviet attack even more certain; that it was ineffectual; and that it did nothing to save Hungary.

After his broadcast on 1 November, Nagy went on doing

what he could to avert the inevitable. He was to spend two more days locked in negotiation with Andropov, in discussion with his colleagues, and in efforts to ensure that nothing was done that could add to Moscow's determination to go through with the attack.

Kádár drew different conclusions. He had supported withdrawal from the Warsaw Pact. He had threatened to fight Soviet tanks with his bare hands. On the morning of 1 November he recorded a radio broadcast describing his new Communist Party. It was transmitted that evening. Kádár accepted manfully that the Party would be one among many, with past faults to live down and no assurance of power. His audience assumed that he remained committed to the Nagy government. But on the evening of 1 November Kádár disappeared. Like Nagy, he knew that a Soviet attack was inevitable. He may even have concluded that it was to be welcomed: without Soviet tanks there was no future for his Party or his ideas. Russian friends almost certainly established contact with him. With Münnich he left parliament. Münnich seems to have persuaded him to go to the Soviet Embassy.[6] From the Soviet Embassy they were flown together to Uzhgorod in the Ukraine. They had split an already beleaguered Communist Party.

Nagy and his colleagues struggled on. Andropov came to parliament again on the morning of 2 November. He reported that the Soviet government took note of Hungary's abrogation of the Warsaw Pact. The implication was that they accepted Hungary's decision, for they proposed political and military talks. It was clear that these might be no more than distractions. But for the Hungarians in their desperation the proposal represented hope regained, however tenuous. They responded in three diplomatic notes. They agreed to the proposal for political talks on the assumption that the Soviet Union would recognize the principles of equality, sovereignty and non-interference. They named Maléter to represent them in the military talks. And they protested yet again at Soviet troop movements into Hungary.

Still the Soviet advance continued. The discovery that Kádár and his allies had disappeared gradually added to the certainty that the trap was closing. Yet on 3 November, the last day of freedom, Andropov visited Nagy again. He said once again that the Soviet Union was willing to discuss the withdrawal of Soviet forces and proposed military talks. At noon General Malinin, the Soviet army commander, arrived in parliament. He and Maléter started the discussions. At three it was announced that they were going well. Malinin had promised that no new forces would move into Hungary.

Nagy announced his last government, with balanced representation from Communists, Smallholders, Social Democrats and National Peasants. Kádár had been gone for thirty-six hours but his name was included in the list. Maléter was promoted to Minister of Defence. The Social Democrats took the seats reserved for them at the last reshuffle. It was as much a game of shadows as Nagy's political activities in the twenties, but there was little else to do while the soldiers negotiated and the tanks advanced. At some point during the day Nagy dashed off a note to the Rumanian leader, Gheorghiu-Dej, a move which Khrushchev later described to Micunovic as 'proof of the isolation and despair of a man whom events had brought to the top and then overtaken, and who now didn't know what to do and was begging Dej for help, almost for salvation.'[7]

Kádár and Münnich had by now returned to Hungary. They based themselves under Soviet protection in a barracks in Szolnok, sixty miles from Budapest. Others, most of them old Rákosists, joined them. In the evening they went out to talk to Communist activists in the local Party secretariat. Like Nagy, they were waiting on events.

In New York, the attention of the United Nations was focussed on the Suez crisis. The Israeli attack on Egypt had started on 29 October, at the time that Nagy had first begun to get abreast of events in Hungary. The Anglo-French ultimatum had been issued on 30 October, as order started to return to the streets of Budapest. The Allies started to bomb Egypt on 31 October, in preparation for the first landings, planned for 4 November. Preoccupied with their need to destroy Nasser, the British and French were set on providing a distraction, what some would see as a justification, for Soviet action in Hungary.

The Third World cared about Egypt as it did not about Hungary. Eisenhower, on the eve of the presidential election, preferred to confront allies whom he could confound rather than enemies he could not. The Security Council record shows how little attention the United Nations gave to Hungary. At 4 pm on 30 October it convened to discuss the Middle East situation. The United States tabled a resolution. Britain and France vetoed it. On 1 November Nagy made his first appeal to the United Nations. But the next Security Council meeting, on 2 November, was again exclusively concerned with the Suez crisis. An American resolution was carried in the General Assembly by sixty-four votes to five (Britain, France, Israel, Australia and New Zealand), with six abstentions.

Only on 4 November did the Security Council turn its attention to Hungary, with nine votes in favour of a resolution condemning the Soviet attack, with the Soviet Union alone voting against and Yugoslavia abstaining. By that time Soviet tanks were prowling the streets of Budapest and the remains of the legitimate government of Hungary had taken refuge in the Yugoslav Embassy. So Nagy miscalculated if he believed on 1 November that the United Nations could do anything to save Hungary.

At home there was a glimmer of hope almost to the end. Maléter's talks with Malinin in parliament on 3 November about a Soviet withdrawal from Hungary seemed to go well. The Russians suggested that they should be resumed at ten in the evening, this time at Soviet headquarters at Tököl, on Csepel Island in the Danube ten miles south of Budapest. Suspicious, but determined to the end not to provoke the Russians, the Hungarians agreed.

The talks at Tököl started well enough. Two hours were spent discussing things like protection for Soviet war memorials after Soviet troops had left. For three days Maléter had been receiving reports of a Soviet advance; at best he can have hoped for a miraculous change of heart. Like Maléter, Malinin played out his role in the farce until the end. At midnight Serov, the Soviet security chief, burst into the conference room and announced that he had orders to arrest the Hungarian delegation. Malinin reacted with perhaps feigned surprise and indignation; but he took his own delegation from the room and left Maléter in Serov's hands.

So by midnight on 3 November, Hungary had no Minister of Defence. Nagy had been anxious from the start about Maléter's safety. When his telephoned reports from Tököl ceased the Hungarians sent out patrols. They also failed to report back. Reports of the Soviet advance continued to come in. Individual commanders asked for permission to engage the invaders. Nagy forbade them to do so. According to witnesses to the United Nations committee, he received with 'astonishment and even disbelief' a report that Kádár had established a renegade government at Szolnok.[8] It was manifest that the Soviet attack on Hungary, which for three days Nagy had continually tried to avert, was beginning.

Nagy called a meeting of those few members of his cabinet who were immediately available in parliament. At this eleventh hour they authorized the army to resist the invaders and decided to tell the nation and the world what was happening.

At 5.20 am on 4 November Nagy made a five-sentence broadcast on Radio Free Kossuth: 'This is Imre Nagy speaking, the President of the Council of Ministers of the Hungarian People's Republic. Today at daybreak Soviet troops attacked our capital with the obvious intention of overthrowing the legal Hungarian democratic government. Our troops are in combat. The government is at its post. I notify the people of our country and the entire world of this fact.'[9]

Half an hour later, Nagy broadcast again, calling on
Maléter and his delegation to return. It was a pointless
gesture; the delegation had been out of contact with the
government for six hours, and Nagy must have assumed
that they were prisoners; and if, as he may have feared, they
had gone over to the Russians as Kádár had done, no appeal
would have wooed them back to the national cause as it
went down into defeat. So the five-sentence broadcast
stands as Nagy's last statement to the nation and the world
as a free man.

At the time, and on many anniversaries afterwards, the
statement had a chilling political and psychological effect.
In phrasing it, Nagy rejected the national taste for drama
and hyperbole. He made it crystal clear that this was an
attack by a foreign power on a sovereign state and its legal
government. He omitted all reference to politics, ideology
and Communism. There was nothing in the statement on
which the Russians or Kádár could hang the propositions
with which they later made so much play: that reaction
stalked the streets of Budapest, that honest Hungarians had
sought Soviet intervention. But like so much of what Nagy
said and did in his stormy lifetime, the statement is
inadequate and incomplete. People who were with Nagy
stress how quickly he formulated what he wanted to say, as
if to excuse its inadequacy to the occasion.

Besides one great truth, the five sentences contain two
damagingly misleading statements. Nagy recorded that the
Hungarian army was in action; but the army had no chance
to fight except in small units isolated from one another. He
said that the government was at its post; but within hours
he and his Communist colleagues had accepted an
invitation to take sanctuary in the Yugoslav embassy. He
knew that Kádár claimed to have founded a rival
government; he may even have heard Kádár's open letter to
the nation, which had been broadcast fifteen minutes before
he spoke; but he made no attempt to denounce or discredit
this treachery. He must have known that the world was
listening, but he had no message for it beyond the bleak

notification of a foreign attack on the legal government of a sovereign state.

The United Nations report carries the text of a further statement which a witness alleged that Nagy dictated immediately after his broadcast. It is an angry, incoherent condemnation of the Russian attack. It talks of the Russians 'kidnapping the prime minister of a country which is a member of the United Nations'. It ends histrionically with a warning that 'today it is Hungary and tomorrow, or the day after tomorrow, it will be the turn of other countries because the imperialism of Moscow does not know borders . . .'[10]

This text has all the marks of a fabrication. An angry émigré giving evidence to the committee may have put some of his own emotion into Nagy's mouth. Or he may have felt that Nagy's reputation required something stronger than his last broadcast. The statement's call for a memorandum has a touch of Nagy. But in all his adult lifetime, Nagy never called his Soviet comrades Russians. It would have taken second sight to talk of kidnapping on 4 November. And the angry hopelessness of the last sentence is completely at odds with Nagy's style. The United Nations committee could not omit what would, if genuine, be a key document of the Hungarian Revolution, but there is no need for us, with hindsight, to take it seriously.

Every account suggests that circumstances in parliament in the early hours of 4 November were chaotic. Members of the government, political and literary figures, Cardinal Mindszenty, individual officers seeking instructions or bringing information, drifted in and out. Firing could be heard from the suburbs. The Cardinal wandered off with a secretary to the United States legation. The government organized the broadcasting of an appeal to the advancing Soviet troops. At 8 am Gyula Háy broadcast an appeal to the world from the Hungarian Writers' Union. In English, German and Russian it begged for help for Hungary. Then, at seven minutes past eight in the morning, Radio Free Kossuth went off the air.

*

By this time, Nagy and most of his Communist colleagues had left parliament. Several of them, with their families, responded to an invitation to take refuge in the Yugoslav embassy. Tildy, Szabo and Bibo, representatives of the other parties in Nagy's last government, remained in parliament. Soviet tanks arrived and ringed the building, Soviet officers moved through the corridors. What little centralized authority had been exercised from government headquarters ceased. Bibo, an unsung hero of the Revolution, sat undisturbed in his office composing a memorandum on the political future of Hungary.

Elsewhere in the city, freedom fighters and army units engaged the Russians. This time there were no military hesitations while Soviet delegates wrestled with the intricacies of Hungarian politics. Soviet tanks ranged the boulevards, destroying any building from which a shot was fired. The old units which, in the complications of the first intervention, had found themselves talking with insurgents, half-persuaded by them, were gone. The new ones had come to make war, some of them allegedly believing that the Danube was the Suez Canal and the men who fought them imperialists. The Russians posted artillery on the Gellért Hill in Buda to dominate the centre of the city. Later they used aircraft against the industrial suburbs. The war that came to Budapest in November 1956 was as real as the one that laid the city waste in the winter of 1944-45.

Behind the Russians came Hungarian Stalinists and political policemen. But on 4 November Hungary was essentially united against the invaders. No Hungarian units fought in support of the Russians. And in the early days of the invasion it was Russians who made the arrests as well as doing the fighting. Here too restraint was cast aside. Prisoners were shot out of hand. Deportations to the Soviet Union started. Kádár himself did not return to Budapest until 7 November, three full days after the onslaught began. Even then he came in a Soviet armoured car, to take control of a nation united in continuing resistance to the Russians.

It was an uneven battle. On the one hand the Russians deployed tanks, aircraft, artillery and armoured troop carriers. They used them without inhibition. On the other, small groups of Hungarian troops and freedom fighters fought tenaciously where they stood. The outcome was certain. Some groups were quickly overwhelmed or dispersed. Others held on for days. The Russians claimed that they were fighting capitalists and fascists, but it was the old Communist strongholds of Csepel and Sztálinváros that fought the longest. 'Iron worker, do not give in,' had rallied strikers against the employers in the old days. Now it rallied freedom fighters against the Russians. But by 11 November resistance had been overcome. The Soviet-Hungarian war of 1956 was over.

Chapter 11

MURDER

As Soviet forces moved into Budapest, the Yugoslav Ambassador invited Nagy to take refuge in the embassy. Similar invitations were extended to his Communist colleagues in the government, other prominent Communists, and their families. Nagy drove to the embassy as Soviet tanks were closing in on the parliament building. Others made their way there, or were collected by members of the Yugoslav Embassy. By midday on 4 November forty-two people, men, women and children, had taken refuge under Yugoslav protection.

It was a bold step to offer Nagy and his colleagues asylum in this way. The decision to do so must have been made at the top in Belgrade. Within days it involved Tito in a dangerous clash with Moscow, resolved eventually in a way that brutally discredited the Yugoslavs. It worsened the Hungarian crisis. Yet the Yugoslavs must have embarked on this dangerous course convinced that it would limit the damage done to Communism, Hungary and Soviet-Yugoslav relations by the Soviet attack.

They saw the offer as a natural consequence of Tito's meeting with Khrushchev and Malenkov in Brioni. They had then discussed damage limitation as allies, almost accomplices. The Russians had sought Yugoslav views, welcomed their suggestions. They asked Tito's opinion of individual Hungarian leaders. There was clearly agreement that Yugoslavia had a role to play in the Hungarian tragedy. The Yugoslavs believed that the Russians had endorsed the idea of taking Nagy out of circulation by giving him diplomatic asylum.

These were the circumstances in which the Communist leaders loyal to Nagy gathered in the Yugoslav embassy on the morning of 4 November. The late arrivals described the fighting, the Soviet tanks patrolling the boulevards and by now ringing parliament. Soon a tight ring of Soviet tanks and troops was established round the embassy also. Nagy asked about his non-Communist colleagues left behind in the parliament building, but the Yugoslavs would not allow him telephone contact with the outside world. He called his colleagues together in the first meeting of what came to be called the executive committee. Nagy still saw himself as the Prime Minister of Hungary, operating temporarily from friendly asylum.

But the Soviet attitude was changing fast. Writing his diary as he flew back to Moscow on 6 November, Micunovic sensed the change. Khrushchev and Malenkov had come to Brioni as friends. 'They behaved in an extremely cordial manner, as never before.' Later he wrote that 'Whatever we proposed in good faith in an effort to ease their difficulties, so as at least to reduce the bloodshed in Hungary, in the interests of both Russians and Hungarians and ultimately of all of us, Khrushchev and Malenkov accepted at once.' But now it was not difficult to foresee that 'the Russians and the newly formed Hungarian government will . . . start accusing Imre Nagy of things for which he is not to blame . . . And Imre Nagy himself, whom they are accusing of counter-revolution, is now enjoying the protection of the Yugoslav Embassy in Budapest. It is not far to go from making such accusations against Imre Nagy to extending them to those who have taken him under their wing.'[1]

Within twenty-four hours of his return to Moscow, Micunovic heard these accusations from Khrushchev himself. By now the clash of wills between Russians and

Yugoslavs was in the open. Soviet gratitude was a thing of the past. On 6 November a Yugoslav diplomat in the embassy in Budapest was killed by a bullet from a Soviet tank stationed outside. When on 7 November Micunovic went to protest to the Soviet Foreign Minister, Shepilov blustered, claiming that the tank gunner was responding to attack. When Micunovic saw Khrushchev later that day, Khrushchev went on the offensive, complaining at the Yugoslavs' failure to hand over Nagy and his companions. It could be interpreted, he said menacingly, as evidence that they had been acting throughout on Yugoslav instructions. Micunovic responded that the offer of asylum flowed from the line of action agreed at Brioni. He does not record how Khrushchev responded to a retort that was very near the bone.[2]

Challenged by this change in the Soviet attitude, the Yugoslavs had few cards. The Russians controlled access to the crowded Yugoslav embassy in Budapest. They had already shown their ruthlessness. The Yugoslav diplomat killed by Soviet fire bore a strong facial resemblance to Nagy; it was believed inside the embassy that he had been killed by aimed fire, in mistake for Nagy.[3] And the Russians were rapidly establishing their authority on the streets. Kádár was clay in their hands. They made it clear that they were prepared to escalate the quarrel until the Yugoslavs gave way. The Yugoslavs could only threaten to expose to the world the cynical understanding reached at Brioni, and how far the Russians had departed from it. But that revelation would discredit the Yugoslavs only marginally less than the Russians.

The Yugoslavs cast around for a solution which would save Nagy and their own reputation. They urged Nagy to come to terms with Kádár. At that time it did not seem impossible that Nagy would join Kádár in saving what could be saved from the tragedy. Kádár was doing his best to fudge issues and talking of reconciliation. On 11 November he told the nation that his government needed the help of other parties and viewpoints. Nagy and his group had not supported counter-revolution. They had nothing to fear from his government or the Soviet forces if they left asylum. The way was open for them to help the new government or find asylum in another socialist country.

But Nagy saw himself as the legitimate Prime Minister of Hungary, who had successfully reconciled Hungarian demands with Soviet wishes until Moscow and Kádár betrayed him. It is said that when he heard of the formation of Kádár's government he exclaimed, 'These people will kill me.'[4] But he may have imagined that even now Moscow would do business with him. More probably he thought that defiance, martyrdom even, could save the national unity achieved in the few days of quiet before the Soviet attack. He was as stubborn, and perhaps as unrealistic, as he had ever been.

On the same day as Kádár's conciliatory broadcast, 11 November, Tito tried to square the circle. In a speech at Pula he set out Yugoslav views on the Hungarian crisis. He condemned the first Soviet intervention of 24 October as 'absolutely mistaken'. But in a muddled, contradictory, almost incoherent passage he argued that, given a choice between 'chaos, civil war, counter-revolution, and another world war' and the intervention of Soviet troops, the second intervention was 'necessary'.[5]

The Pula speech enraged the Soviet leaders. They seized on references to Stalinism as an attack on the Soviet Union and added this to their list of grievances against Yugoslavia. It equally incensed the Hungarian refugees in the embassy. Tito had endorsed the Soviet attack and implied that Nagy, unchecked, would have permitted chaos and counter-revolution. The refugees concluded that they were no longer welcome in the embassy. They paid closer attention now to suggestions for getting them safely out of asylum there.

Tito despatched a deputy foreign minister, Dobrivoje Vidic, to Budapest. In a long talk with Kádár, a solution was thrashed out. In a formal note to the Yugoslav government, Kádár promised the refugees safe conduct to their homes and immunity from prosecution. The refugees feared treachery, but the Yugoslavs urged them to accept Kádár's word. Finally, at 6.30 in the evening on 22 November, the little party emerged from the embassy and piled anxiously into the bus that was supposed to take them to their homes.

Until very recently the world knew little about this bus ride beyond its place in the annals of betrayal. The United Nations report recorded the essentials. Because of the refugees' anxieties, the Yugoslav Ambassador sent two of his officials to see them safely to their homes. But the bus was stopped by Soviet vehicles, the Yugoslavs were forced off, and the bus driven away not to the passengers' homes but to a Soviet military establishment on the outskirts of Pest.

At the Soviet base the party was closely guarded by Soviet soldiers. Münnich appeared and spoke separately with each of the men, pressing them to sign an already drafted document. We do not know what language Nagy used when confronted with this betrayal of a friendship which went back to the Russian Civil War, by a man whose sick wife the Nagys had taken into their Moscow home when Münnich went off to fight in Spain. But all the group refused to sign Münnich's document, Szilágyi allegedly with contumely.

The following day the Workers' Councils of Budapest called a silent demonstration of protest. For an hour all traffic stopped and people stayed in their homes. The Russians took advantage of the demonstration. They drove their prisoners through the deserted streets in heavily curtained buses to the Mátyásföld military air station, where three Soviet aircraft were waiting. The survivors remember that the Soviet guards were nervous, that once again Szilágyi refused to do as he was told and was bundled onto one of the aircraft by force.[6] A pilot refused to tell them where they were going, but admitted that it would be a two-hour flight.

When the aircraft landed at a snow-covered airfield the prisoners assumed they were in the Soviet Union. Gradually it dawned on them that they were in Rumania. A convoy of cars and buses, the Nagys in a car, took them to Snagov, a holiday resort outside Bucharest. Most of the party were housed in a Party rest home, with the Nagys apart, in a house on the far side of a little lake.

There they lived for what was left of the fateful year of 1956. The members of the party read in turn the few books available. They made what they could of Christmas, organizing treats for the children. Conditions were comfortable, the food adequate. An obsequious waiter, later revealed to be a Hungarian-speaking secret policeman, brought them meals. They were prisoners, but they were treated as guests. Moscow still had all its options open.[7]

The world asked what had become of Nagy and his companions. On 23 November, Budapest Radio announced that two weeks earlier they had sought permission to leave Hungary to live in another Communist country. Rumania had agreed to receive them. The Yugoslavs, infuriated by the damage the kidnapping had done to their own credibility, refuted the story that they had gone to Rumania of their own accord: they made it clear that when they were in the embassy, Nagy and his colleagues had rejected the idea of seeking asylum there. On 3 December the Rumanian representative at the United Nations asserted that his country had agreed to a Hungarian request that it should give them political asylum so as to guarantee their personal security and to contribute to the restoration of order in Hungary. Their stay would be temporary; the rules of hospitality were being respected; they were displaying understanding and good temper.

In Budapest Kádár was moving from his efforts to woo the country to an attempt to crush it. On 5 December Miklós Gimes, who was to die with Nagy, was arrested; he had attempted to continue an open resistance to Kádár. On 9

December the Budapest Workers' Council, with which
Kádár had tried or had pretended to try to come to terms,
was outlawed. A general strike was called. Two of the
Council's leaders were arrested. The strike paralysed
Budapest on 11-12 December. On 11 December summary
jurisdiction was introduced. The press reported sporadic
'counter-revolutionary provocations'.

The situation continued to deteriorate in the New Year.
On 1 January, Khrushchev and Malenkov came to
Budapest for a three-day meeting with the Party leaders of
Hungary, Bulgaria, Czechoslovakia and Rumania. On 5
January Kádár spoke in public, not in the moderate and
ambiguous language he had cultivated hitherto but in harsh
and repressive terms. On the same day the United Nations
discussed Hungary and set up the committee which was to
produce the United Nations report. Ten days later Chou En
Lai came to Budapest and gave his backing to Kádár's
harsh words. The Writers' Association was suspended, a
number of writers arrested. On 19 January two of the best
known freedom fighters were executed. On the same day
two thousand people were arrested, amid talk of a renewal
of the Uprising. In the early months of 1957 a decision to
execute Nagy and some of his companions would have
horrified the world. But it might have served a purpose in
cowing a still restive country and made some kind of
political sense.

During the months in Snagov, Nagy started to write an
outline of his life. He called it *A Stormy Age*. Like the files
about his imprisonment and trial, the manuscript was kept
locked away in the Ministry of the Interior from his
execution to his rehabilitation. In 1989 it was returned to
his daughter, who intends to work on it and, perhaps,
prepare it for publication.

But from the manuscript returned to Erzsébet Nagy,
some eighty pages are missing. Nagy's old associates believe
that these pages concern Nagy's dealings with the Russians:
perhaps his dealings with Mikoyan and Suslov during the
Revolution and with Soviet envoys who visited him in

Snagov. If so, there may somewhere, perhaps in Moscow, be a first-hand account of the threats and promises which Khrushchev directed at him during this period in limbo in Rumania.

It is clear that Nagy's response to this barrage of persuasion was uncompromising. At a Kremlin reception on 3 December, Khrushchev talked to Micunovic about Nagy's conversations with Russian visitors in Rumania. In his diary Micunovic noted that Khrushchev seemed to be realizing that the Russians had got themselves into an unfavourable situation over Nagy. 'It looks to me as though, under interrogation, Nagy is not replying to questions as they would like.' But Khrushchev rejected a suggestion that it would have been better if Nagy had stayed at home in Hungary. 'The Russians obviously believe that Nagy's presence in Hungary would be a permanent threat to the process of pacification as the Russians conceive it.'[8]

In the early months of 1957, conditions for the little group of exiles in Rumania started to deteriorate. The pretence that they were honoured guests evaporated. Hospitality became house arrest. And in April security policemen came from Budapest and arrested the men in the group. They were manhandled, taken to a prison in Bucharest, fitted with welders' goggles which effectively blindfolded them, and bundled onto an aircraft for the flight back to Budapest. The goggles were removed only when they were inside the courtyard of the Fö Utca prison there. The days of ambiguity were over. Nagy and his companions were political prisoners, in danger of their lives.

Another fourteen months were to pass before Nagy's execution. There is little consistency about what was said in these months about Nagy by the Soviet and Hungarian leaders. Many forces were at work, none of them relevant to the issue of Nagy's guilt or innocence. Khrushchev was locked in a power struggle with Stalinists and other rivals in the Kremlin. In July 1957, he frustrated an attempt to overthrow him led by Malenkov and Molotov; but it was months before he was able to get rid of Bulganin who had been associated with it. In this power struggle Khrushchev's conduct of affairs, not least in Hungary, was a major issue. Linked with this was the question of relations with Yugoslavia, laboriously repaired in 1956 but grievously strained by the Soviet attack on Hungary and the kidnapping of Nagy. Nagy's life or death was a weapon in Moscow's hands, to be used as circumstances dictated to woo or punish Tito.

Circumstances in Hungary also came into the picture. Just before Nagy and his associates were brought back to Budapest, fears or expectations of a renewal of the Uprising reached fever pitch. In the light of what Soviet forces had done to Hungarian resistance only five months earlier, the idea of resuming the fighting must have been fanciful. But a whispering campaign began: 'We shall start again in March.' There were particular fears of trouble on 15 March, the anniversary of the 1848 Uprising against the Austrians.

Nothing came of these fears. At the end of March Kádár visited Moscow and clearly discussed the Nagy question with the Russians. Immediately afterwards Bulganin told Micunovic that it had been 'confirmed beyond question' that Nagy had long been in the service of a foreign power. Micunovic concluded that Nagy's situation was extremely serious.[9] At about the same time, Kopácsi's lawyer hinted to him in the Fö Utca prison that plans to put him and Maléter on trial on their own had been aborted; they were to go on trial with a larger group of defendants around Nagy.[10] Yet on 4 April Kádár told Western journalists that Nagy would not be put on trial although his position was delicate. We still cannot interpret with certainty what all these contradictory signals meant. But there seems to have been a real risk of a Nagy trial in the spring of 1957.

But if there was a crisis in April, it seemed to have blown over by May. On May Day Kádár addressed a big crowd on Heroes' Square. He said afterwards that it was then that he first sensed that the worst was over,[11] and photographs of the event seem to capture a real rapport between him and many of his audience. But Kádár still faced a threat from the Stalinists, who thought him dangerously lenient. It was only at the end of June that he overcame them in a trial of strength.

In July Khrushchev and Tito once again patched up their differences, so badly damaged by the Nagy kidnapping. They met at Snagov, where Nagy had been taken. The place had other memories. It was in Snagov that Stalin's instruction that Yugoslavia should be expelled from the Cominform was carried out and the great attack on Tito's heresy begun. It would have been an appropriate place to demonstrate the reconciliation by agreeing that Nagy should be released into retirement.

But for whatever reason, Khrushchev was not ready for magnanimous gestures, and in November 1957 relations between the Soviet Union and Yugoslavia deteriorated once again. Tito refused to sign a declaration of international Communist solidarity on the occasion of the fortieth anniversary of the October Revolution. At once, criticisms of Nagy resurfaced: from his old friend Münnich, who accused him of encouraging the West to intervene in 1956, and in a tendentious Hungarian government White Book about the Revolution. His life was clearly at risk once again.

In January 1958 Münnich replaced Kádár as Prime Minister. To mark the occasion he held a press conference, at which American correspondents asked him about Nagy. He replied that Nagy was guilty of grave crimes. He had to respond to them. He was not therefore in a position to give them the press interviews for which they asked. The world assumed rightly that a trial was in the offing. We now know that on 28 January charges were laid against Nagy and his associates. On 6 February, the first, secret and abortive trial began.

Sándor Kopácsi was tried with Nagy and later wrote in exile a highly coloured account of the occasion. His experience suggests that the prisoners were subjected to great psychological pressures but not to physical torture, and that they were prepared for their trial in long interrogations. He describes how when the day for the February trial came the prisoners were collected from their cells in the Fö Utca prison, where they had been held in solitary confinement since their return from Rumania.

Losonczy was missing from the group. According to Kopácsi he had been murdered in his cell because his mind had failed him and he would not make a satisfactory exhibit in a show trial. It seems more probable that he died in the course of a botched attempt to feed him by force. Nagy was the last member of the group to be brought from his cell, with the deference which his personality had extracted from his captors in Rumania, when they housed him and his wife apart from the rest of the party: 'He came out of the cell as if he were coming out of a meeting room, his face preoccupied. I found him a bit thinner, but the build was the same: the peasant or the sixty-year-old blacksmith, the village strongman in the most commanding period of his life. The legendary pince-nez straddled his nose as before.'[12]

The first trial collapsed. The circumstances are still obscure, but the judge seems to have proved himself too weak to bring the trial to a satisfactory conclusion. He suffered a heart attack, real or diplomatic. Perhaps the setback caused the Russians to change their minds once again about how they might use the case against Nagy in their quarrel with Tito. The prisoners were taken back to their cells.

A few weeks later, Jozsef Szilágyi was put on trial alone, in Kopácsi's view because Khrushchev demanded at least one victim quickly and Szilágyi had enraged his captors by his outspokenness. Kopácsi was a witness at the trial, which was a prearranged farce. The sentence imposed on 22 April was inevitable, and Szilágyi was hanged two days later.[13] Two of Nagy's closest associates in the Revolution were gone.

Still the Russians dithered. At the end of March Kádár

visited Tito. Inevitably the Nagy affair was a central issue between them. The man who had promised Nagy safe conduct, and who may by now have been fighting, diffidently, apologetically, to save him from Russian vengeance, faced the man who had offered asylum and been humiliated by his kidnapping. Tito pressed Kádár for Nagy's life. Finally, Kádár assured him that Nagy would not be tried for the time being.

A few days later Khrushchev came to Budapest. Kádár took him to Csepel, the steelworkers' bastion which had fought so long against the Russians in 1956. Khrushchev's speech was typically unconstrained: he unburdened himself of violent criticism of both Rákosi and Nagy. But still the signals about Nagy's fate were confused: the criticisms of him did not appear in the official version of the speech.

The Yugoslavs continued to arouse Soviet anger, which the satellites dutifully mimicked. Late in April the Yugoslavs held their Party Congress at Ljubljana. Moscow and the satellites were represented only by their ambassadors. In May *Pravda* carried a major attack on Yugoslavia, and Voroshilov cancelled a visit to Belgrade at the last moment. In May the Hungarian Party newspaper, *Népszabadság*, published a criticism of the Yugoslav Congress containing several references to Nagy's revisionism and his links with Yugoslavia.

Khrushchev was more categorical. In a speech in Sofia on 3 June he used vitriolic language about Yugoslav involvement in Nagy's criminal actions in 1956. The temperature was rising, but it had risen before. The whole thing was like a feud between schoolgirls, tempers high, malice sharp; but on this feud hung the choice between life and judicial murder.

The decision was taken that as an object lesson to the Yugoslavs, Nagy must be destroyed. It was certainly taken in Moscow. Kádár may have argued against it. Kopácsi believes that his own life was saved by Kádár's pleading. It may be so, and Kádár may have pleaded for Nagy, Maléter and the others also. But he did not take his arguments to the lengths of threatening resignation, and throughout his long life Kádár never admitted that the decision was taken in Moscow, never sheltered behind the argument that he was powerless to resist the Russians. On the day Nagy was reburied in 1989 he was still taking on himself the responsibility for withholding clemency. But it remains a fact that in the circumstances of the fifties it was always the political will of Moscow that was decisive, and it was Moscow that decided that Nagy and his companions must die. If he tried, Kádár failed to shift the Soviet leaders; and for thirty-one years afterwards he loyally covered up for them.

Kopácsi describes the defendants' journey from their cells to the predetermined verdict that awaited them in the Fö Utca courtroom. 'At the head of the procession, Nagy climbed the first of the flights of stairs . . . as he climbed the steps, he seemed to get bigger before my eyes. Here was someone who had passed from words to acts, who had written, with his pen and his life, a chapter of history. He knew he was going to die. But . . . nobody could ever tear the pages signed Imre Nagy from the book of history.'[14]

The procession reached the courtroom, bright with lighting for the cinema photographers who recorded the occasion. Kopácsi alleges that the prisoners knew for certain that Kádár and his associates were in the adjoining room, sweating through a trial in which many of them, former associates of Nagy, could easily have been defendants. Other surviving defendants attribute the story to Kopácsi's search for colourful detail.

It is clear that the trial was a charade, whose outcome had been decided in advance. The charges were manifestly ill-founded, ignoring the fact that in November 1956 Nagy was the legitimate Prime Minister of Hungary and Maléter his duly-appointed Minister of Defence. The only logic which makes sense of the prosecution is the idea that all resistance to Soviet wishes is by definition treason against a socialist state lying within Moscow's orbit. For those who do not accept that proposition, the death sentences which the court imposed were judicial murder.

The prisoners were spared a few horrors which Rajk and Mindszenty earlier were not. It was not a show trial and there was no need for preliminary torture to ensure that they spoke their lines correctly. Kopácsi records that he was promised his life in return for a plea of guilty; he also claims that it was manifest in Nagy's behaviour that he forgave this minor betrayal. Within the horror of the predetermined verdict and the illegality of the trial's premises, the court was conducted with procedural decency.

Nagy pleaded not guilty. He described himself as Prime Minister of Hungary, rejecting the accusation that he should describe himself as 'former prime minister': as far as he was aware, the office which had been legally conferred on him had not been legally taken away. He argued his case firmly, with dignified calm.

To some, this is the calm of a man who knew that the Russians, not his Hungarian judges, would make the final decision and who believed that they would save him. To others it is the dignity of a man who had reconciled himself to death for a cause in which he believed. Being human, he may have been tempted to try to save himself by the surrender he had refused in Rumania and during the preparation of the trial. But at this eleventh hour surrender would have given his opponents victory. He did not surrender, and seems to have argued his case to the end.

The judge imposed the sentences. Nagy's was inevitably death. Like the others, he was permitted to make a final statement to the court. Like the rest of the proceedings it was filmed and shown on Hungarian television at the time of the reburial. Thirty-one years after the secret trial, Hungary saw Nagy's upright peasant figure, respectable in a dark suit, white shirt, and tie, much leaner after nineteen months' confinement but still very much the man who, speaking in his calm and deliberate way in parliament five years earlier, gave hope back to his country. He said that he considered his sentence unjust. 'My sole solace in this situation is my conviction that sooner or later the Hungarian people and the international working class will exonerate me of the grave accusations, as a consequence of which I must sacrifice my life.'[15] The time would come when justice would be served. He did not seek clemency.

After eighteen months' indecision, the regime moved with guilty haste. At the time of Nagy's reburial, only weeks before his own death, Kádár was still telling his cronies that he had made a formal decision not to exercise clemency. The Minister of the Interior, the judge and the prosecutor had all advised him that the legal case was overwhelming, that there was no case for mercy. With his profound respect for the law, Kádár had felt that he could not overthrow a verdict so justified.[16]

By 1989, Kádár may have believed all this, but it cannot reflect any kind of reality. Moscow wanted Nagy's neck. There was nothing Kádár could do to save him, unless he had taken the supreme risk of a resignation that might not have saved Nagy, might have risked his own neck, and might have damaged Hungary. If Kádár reviewed the sentences at all it was as a formality. He let them stand.

Early in the morning of 16 June 1958, the death sentences were carried out in the courtyard of the Central Prison, to which the condemned men had been transferred immediately after the trial closed on the previous day. There is a story, perhaps based on nothing more than macabre imagination, that Nagy was forced to watch as his companions were hanged. It is said that he and they spoke defiantly on the scaffold. It is a fact that on that June morning Gimes, Maléter and Nagy paid the price that Szilágyi and Losonczy had already paid, and gave their lives for their beliefs and for their country.

Chapter 12

CONTRIBUTION

When a man dies, we ask what he has achieved. In Nagy's case it seemed at the time to be very little. Although his execution aroused a global storm of indignation, attention focussed on the lessons of the murder rather than the achievements of his life. His abduction, imprisonment, trial and execution were seen to demonstrate once again a great negative truth: that at the heart of Communism there was nothing more than a moral vacuum. There was recognition of Nagy's courage and of the magnitude of his tragedy. But there was little appreciation of the relevance of his life to the problems of the age.

As we have seen, his essays, published a year earlier, had disappointed most readers. They wanted something further-reaching than an insight into Nagy's crabbed and pedantic mind and into the cynicism of the system he attacked. They did not find it. They found glimpses, but nothing more than glimpses, of something more grandiose. The essays had been written for a readership of the Communist initiated. They were written in code, by a man shaped by a lifetime in the bosom of an all-consuming Party. He wrote them a year before the events which so fundamentally altered his beliefs: the popular Uprising, the failure of the Party in face of it, and the attack by which Moscow restored the order of the graveyard.

In the first days of the Revolution, too, Nagy had

disappointed the world. He had seemed slow to grasp what was happening, hidebound in his reactions. When he finally recognized reality, he repeatedly failed to put himself at its head. The agronomist, the Party theoretician, still seemed to dominate Nagy's personality, inadequate qualifications for a prime minister in the eye of a hurricane.

Belatedly, Nagy had come to terms with the Revolution; and in its final days tried to save it from the Russians. By now his heroism was beyond question. But he failed to impose himself, perhaps could not have hoped to impose himself, on events or on the people with whom he had to deal: the Revolutionaries; his comrades in the shattered Party; the bourgeois politicians emerging from prison or exile or the shadows; and the Russians above all. Perhaps no one could have saved Hungary in those dreadful days of early November 1956. Nagy, for all his courage and goodness, was manifestly inadequate to the task.

So he went down the long road to his execution, twenty last months in the shadows. The world knew nothing of that road except what Moscow and Budapest chose to tell, hearing nothing at all from Nagy, his colleagues and sympathizers. From the regime's White Book it learned something, by reading between the lines and the lies. It could deduce that Nagy did not surrender, did not even bargain, maintained his dignity as the legitimate Prime Minister of his country. But the execution seemed at the time to draw a line under a tragic and wasted life in the service of a system which had once again consumed a faithful son.

But time brings perspective, and as the events of Nagy's life and death receded a little into the past it became possible to see his achievement more clearly. Three things emerged to stand to his credit in the book of history.

The first was the service he did to himself and his reputation when he stood firm against the forces which came to reimpose alien authority upon his country. After a lifetime in the shadow of Communism, compromising uneasily between Marxist ideals and their brutal implementation, Nagy in the end established his dignity as a man. As we have seen, he did so later in the Revolution than his apologists suggest. But from 1 November he stood like adamant. When the Russians came, he defied them. When they crushed Hungary he resisted Kádár's blandishments. He faced execution rather than buy his life at the price of his integrity.

The second thing which the world identified as it pondered on Nagy's life was the service he gave to the Communist world. His execution seemed at first to demonstrate that Communists had failed to learn the lesson which he had tried to teach them: that Communism could only wither if it ruled by terror, in isolation from the people it set out to serve; and that it could only flourish if it deposed dogma and remembered man. But gradually the execution came to seem an aberration of Communist policy, a last assertion of Stalinism.

Communism under Khrushchev and Kádár remained an evil system, but it did not again plumb the depths that it reached under Stalin and Rákosi. Moscow destroyed the Prague Spring but it did not murder Dubcek. Once they had done away with Nagy, the Communist leaders seemed to listen, however tentatively, to his words. 'Whatever has become of Communist morality, human respect, and honour,' he had asked, 'if there are Communist leaders according to whom the unjustly executed Comrade László Rajk was a coward because he admitted to false charges in order to deceive the Party leaders, leaders who act as if it were not they themselves who contrived the mendacious charges and the means for getting the confession?'[1] They continued to pursue a barren and futile faith, but they did not again stoop to the evil which had framed Rajk and betrayed Nagy.

Throughout his life, Nagy argued for building Communism without resort to terrorism, that 'most impossible of all impossible propositions.'[2] In the Revolution he was faced with the choice between Communism and humanity, not as a question of theory or of emphasis but as a stark choice between two incompatible goods. In accepting the multi-party system and leaving the Warsaw Pact, he chose to deprive Communism in Hungary of the machinery of state terrorism it would need if it were to survive. Harder-headed men swept him aside and destroyed him. But he had shown Communism a way out of the wilderness into which Stalinism had taken it. After his murder it never fully relapsed into the moral vacuum of Stalinism.

But Nagy's greatest service was not to himself or to his Party but to his country. He did not make the Hungarian Revolution. But he did make it possible. For most of the young reformers whose discontent with the old system prepared the way for the Uprising, Nagy was, in the words of the American scholar, Charles Gati, 'both a genuine father figure and the last hope for socialism with a human face'. When the Revolution came, Nagy tried to steer it: 'he became the last hope for freedom and independence for all Hungarians.' Nagy gave the Revolution its essential character. It was his belated but vital commitment which made it what it was: coherent, positive and representative of the whole nation. '. . . Before it was all over he had realized the dream of ten million Hungarians by withdrawing Hungary from the Warsaw Pact and reconstituting the postwar, multiparty coalition government.'[3] Nagy and the Revolution went down to defeat, but they gave Hungary back its self-respect.

Any small nation cares that the world should think well of it. Before 1956 outsiders did not think well of Hungary. They remembered the chauvinism and frivolous injustice of the old order, the alliance with Hitler and the halfhearted efforts to save Hungary's Jews. The peculiar brutality of Hungarian Communism under Rákosi was a reminder of the enmities and lack of love which mar the charm and brilliance of the Hungarian personality. 1956 changed all this, as it changed Hungarians' attitudes towards themselves. When foreigners thought about Hungary after 1956, they recalled first the courage and unity of Hungarians in revolt against odds, and the dignity and unity of Hungarians in defeat. Courage and dignity they had always had, but at the moment when they needed it most it was Nagy who gave them national unity.

So Nagy's life, ended so brutally on 16 June 1958, was not the wasted and tragic thing it seemed. But it is the sequel, his posthumous influence, which make him a figure of interest even today, more than thirty years after his death and getting on for a hundred years since he was born.

'Stone dead has no fellow' tells only part of a truth. An execution can create a legend, as it did with St Joan. After his execution Nagy had his own legend, despite all of Kádár's efforts to expunge him from the historical record. And when Kádár discovered that he would have to use Nagy's methods if he was to reconcile Soviet interests and the Hungarian people, it became certain that Nagy would wield a posthumous influence quite as great as any he had enjoyed in life.

All this became apparent relatively soon after his execution. In 1963, five years after the execution, David Holden wrote in the *Guardian*: 'Imre Nagy, the man who died, should be smiling in heaven over the living – for behind the watch-towers on the Danube he is winning his battle after all.'[4] Nagy went on winning that battle for another twenty-five years. Kádár the living had the policemen and the levers of power. Nagy the ghost had the legend and the policies to reconcile Communism and man. So Kádár, the man who let Nagy die, went on articulating his ideas and using his policies.

In the end, not even Nagy's version of Communism could save it. As Kádár aged he became more inflexible. In the eighties his caution, which had served his country well since the Revolution, denied him the courage to make the big changes that alone could save the situation. Suddenly, Communism, even Reform Communism, found itself overtaken by the demands of Hungarian patriotism. Hungarians demanded the right to be free men, not Communists; Magyars, not satellites; Europeans, not members of the socialist camp. They wanted the right to the truth about the past, not just a sanitized version which saved the Party's and Moscow's face. They demanded democracy, not People's Democracy. They asked, in short, for the things towards which Nagy had groped and which, for a few days in the Revolution, Hungary seemed to achieve. This, just as much as a relatively decent Communism, was part of Nagy's legacy.

So the influence Nagy exercised after his death was quite as useful as any that he wielded in his lifetime. It played as big a part as the influence of any living man or woman in bringing Hungary back to democracy and decency. That posthumous influence is the subject of the remainder of this book.

Chapter 13

REPRESSION

When Imre Nagy and his colleagues were reburied, over three hundred other political offenders interred in Rákoskeresztür were commemorated with them. Like Nagy, they had been executed in the Central Prison across Kozma Utca in the years after the Revolution.

They were not the only victims of the retribution which followed the Uprising. Western governments estimated that perhaps two thousand people were executed by the Russians and the Kádár regime in those years. They ranged from Nagy and members of his cabinet to conscripts who obeyed orders to engage the returning Soviet forces. The man who led the attack on Budapest Party headquarters and was held responsible for the only organized atrocity committed by the insurgents was among them. So was 'Uncle Szabo', who commanded the garrison of young people who held a major junction in Buda against Soviet tanks. The victims included the army officer who escorted Cardinal Mindszenty to Budapest when the insurgents released him from house arrest. There were young people detained until, on their eighteenth birthday, they were old enough for execution. Apart from soldiers, most seem to have been working men from Csepel and Ujpest.

As has been seen, there was no legal basis for the Nagy trial. The Russians demanded and Kádár carried out his judicial murder. The same is true of most of the executions which followed the Revolution. There were no doubt many among those executed who had taken life in the fighting, just as there were a few who had lynched security policemen. But Kádár himself had acknowledged, before he denied, the legitimacy of the Uprising. The vast majority of those condemned for their actions in October had taken part in a spontaneous uprising against oppression and were often responding to security policemen who fired first. There was no conspiracy, no incitement by Western agents. There was no wish to restore capitalism, no danger of a White Terror. As for those sentenced for their actions in November, the soldiers among them were legitimately engaging a foreign invader, the civilians resisting an illegal attack. Some were executed for resistance afterwards, particularly in the workers' councils. Almost all the victims were innocent men and women, who deserved the rehabilitation which Nagy's reburial began.

The dead were only a proportion of the victims of the terror of 1956-60. Immediately after the Revolution, many young people were seized and deported to the Soviet Union. Early in 1957, trials started. The sentences were savage. Kádár had his reasons. He believed that only ruthlessness could appease Moscow and restore order. He sometimes hinted at regrettable necessity. He did not resort to show trials. And although brutality and crude psychological pressure were used against prisoners awaiting trial and after it there was no reversion to the routine torture of the Rákosi years.

But these are small extenuations, more persuasive in thirty years' retrospect than at the time. Kádár's terror then was added to his treachery in the silent indictment which Hungarians compiled against him. Nevertheless, terror achieved its objective. It gradually persuaded Moscow that Kádár, initially a suspect figure, could be relied upon. And it cowed an embittered people.

It was accompanied by repression that went much wider than imprisonment and execution. In the late fifties and early sixties Hungary was not just a country cowed by authoritarian rule. It was effectively terrorized into putting its brief days of glory behind it. Informers everywhere served the secret police. The Workers' Guard demonstrated the Party's power. A heavy Soviet military presence watched over the army which had proved so unreliable in 1956. Soviet advisers controlled the security police and the ministries. In 1957 and early 1958 the Soviet and Hungarian leadership were still intensely nervous, if with little reason. After the Nagy executions they had even less reason for anxiety. But 1956 had taught them no end of a lesson. Repression tinged with terror was designed to ensure that there would be no repetition. Arrests and even executions continued into 1960.

At the same time, some pressure was reduced. In April 1959 came a limited amnesty, perhaps a first sign that the regime had gathered its confidence together. In December the Party held its Seventh Congress, and asserted that though it had to maintain vigilance on both fronts, it had in large part won the fight against the dogmatism which had characterized the Rákosi years as well as Nagy's revisionism. Shortly afterwards, the drive to get peasants back into the collectives was begun, often by arbitrary means. But agriculture apart, the Seventh Congress marked the end of post-Revolutionary retribution and a shift to the undramatic repression which characterized Hungarian life for another twenty-five years.

It was followed in 1960 by another amnesty to mark the anniversary of the liberation. This time several of Nagy's associates – Tildy, Donáth, Jánosi and Vásárhelyi – were released. But it fell well short of general amnesty. And the regime was as ready as ever to use secret terror to break opposition. Prisoners in Vác excluded from the amnesty went on hunger strike. According to Kopácsi they were dealt with ruthlessly, some of them taken back to the Fö Utca and threatened with execution.[1]

Gradually what hope had remained after the Revolution died. Hungarians reconciled themselves to the limited safety and prosperity which Kádár offered. The Party's confidence grew. In December 1961, Kádár formulated the theory of alliance, an implicit abandonment of class war. A few months later the Central Committee asserted that workers, peasants and intellectuals now formed a unified socialist society. In August it condemned the 'unlawful trials of the years of the cult of personality' and expelled Rákosi and Gerö from the Party. All law-abiding citizens, it asserted, 'can live and work in tranquillity in our socialist homeland.' University access for the middle classes was made easier. So was travel to the West. And Kádár's soothing phrase that 'those who are not against us are with us' was published in the newspapers.

In the autumn of 1962, the United Nations dropped the 'Problem of Hungary' from its agenda. Emigrés accused it, perhaps justly, of wearying in its well-doing. But the change made it possible for Kádár, with his pathological fear of appearing to yield to pressure, to continue to ease conditions in Hungary. On 22 March 1963 came the Bill of Oblivion. It amnestied those who had abused power under Rákosi and those who had fought in the Revolution. Almost all the men of 1956 still in prison were released, Bibo and Kopácsi among them. The Secretary General of the United Nations visited Budapest. Kádár claimed that there were no political prisoners in Hungary.

In the years in which retribution was giving way to routine repression in Hungary, the Party embarked upon and swiftly carried through the collectivization of agriculture. The episode lasted from the winter of 1958 to the spring of 1961. It ran counter to the hesitant relaxation of pressure in other fields in those years. How it was carried out, and with what results, is central to any analysis of Nagy's influence on his country in the thirty years after his death.

The debate started inside the Party in the autumn of 1958. The arguments were kept secret at the time, but Kádár summarized them in a speech twenty years later. He described the harsh view, which 'asserted that the middle peasants had to be divested of everything'. He described the soft view, which believed that 'the appropriate conditions for the reorganization were lacking'. But in his reconstruction, it was of course the middle view, the moderate line, which prevailed: '. . . finally a correct. decision was made' – a decision which Kádár recalled twenty years later as a decision to lead the peasants willingly into the cooperatives.[2] That would have been Nagy's policy. But in fact the events of 1958-60 were not like that. The peasants faced pressure, compulsion.

In the late fifties there were in fact both agricultural and political arguments for the drive to get the peasants back into the cooperatives. In retrospect, with the evidence of the relative success of Hungarian agriculture, they look stronger than they did then. At the time collectivization looked like just another turn of the screw against a prostrate people. The methods used were not those Rákosi had adopted; but they were far from the frank man-to-man persuasion propaganda suggested. The regime asserted itself harshly in the countryside in the winters of 1958-59 and 1959-60. It was safe enough to do so: there was no risk of rural insurgency. The process added rural fear to the terror which pervaded the cities. But it succeeded in its unstated purpose, of convincing Moscow that, however unreliable he may have seemed at the height of the Uprising, Kádár could be trusted to implement sound socialist policies.

Kádár later talked of collectivization as one of the three great formative steps in the history of people's Hungary. The first was the seizure of power, the third the economic reform introduced in the late sixties. So he created a continuity, between the Communist Party's first steps to power in Hungary, his own actions to establish himself ten years later, and the more mellow, acceptable face of a mature Communism. But this was rationalization, of a policy adopted to impress the Russians, perhaps to persuade them that it would be safe to ease the pressure in the cities which had made the Revolution.

Nagy, with his faith in scientific Marxism and his passion

for finding correct agricultural policies for his Party, would have despised such a pragmatic approach. In 1958 he would have judged that it was a decade too soon to embark on extensive collectivization. Yet ironically, Kádár's pragmatism succeeded. He combined pressure to join collectives with toleration, even encouragement, of private farming on small plots on the side. The peasants settled down to do a minimum in the cooperative fields and as much as they could on their own plots.

The authorities invested heavily in capital equipment. Within a decade Hungarian agriculture was a success story. By comparison with the West it was under-funded and unproductive. By comparison with agriculture elsewhere in Eastern Europe and with industry in Hungary, it did well. It brought agriculture back towards the levels of production achieved in the Hungary of the great estates, while lifting rural living standards well above those of the old days, and often above those of the urban proletariat. Looking down on events, Nagy might reasonably have concluded that despite his over-hastiness, Kádár's agricultural policies were succeeding; and that though they had been introduced too hastily, they owed their success to the fact that as far as content was concerned they were loyal to the Nagyist model.

With the completion of the collectivization drive, Hungary lost its last live political issue. From then on, letting sleeping dogs lie was the ruling principle. Of course, the tacit compromise between Moscow and the people must be maintained. Moscow must not be provoked. Nor must the Hungarian people. The Party's job was to give Moscow absolute loyalty on ideology and foreign policy and the people the security and prosperity which would distract them from their broken dreams. From the early sixties to the early eighties it succeeded, but when it had to it still resorted to authoritarian methods to enforce the compromise.

Repression did not vanish from Hungary in the sixties. After 1963 it no longer needed its cutting edge: any post-Revolutionary spirit that had survived was broken and the people were eager for a compromise, for self-censorship. But the acquiescence which permitted the Party to rule with a light touch was itself a product of repression, and it demanded, day-in, day-out, things which in themselves formed part of the repressive process.

For two decades Hungary was required to forget its past. It was forced to lie about its relationship with the Soviet Union. Hungarians had to subscribe also to a myth about their future. It maintained that their eager objective was 'building socialism'. This formula had no meaning; but like other formulas it devoured a generation. Post-Revolutionary Hungarians were consumed not by terror but by the tedium of forced hypocrisy.

A simple story illustrates the quality of this repression. On a summer's night in 1969, an American astronaut walked on the moon. On the same evening the Soviet Union put an unmanned satellite into orbit. A Hungarian journalist on a minor newspaper put the American news on the front page, the Soviet news inside. He was reprimanded, dismissed. For twenty years he found no other work in journalism.

Years later, in the early eighties, the ground was beginning to move under the Party's feet. A few dissidents were at work, writing essays, publishing mildly subversive magazines, remarking quietly that the Emperor's clothes were ragged. They were able to express themselves at all only because the Party refrained from crushing them. But the Party, for all its shows of openness, did not cease to harass them. The police, the courts, the informers were still deployed, but now they did no more than rebuke dissenters where once they had destroyed insurgents. Hungarian society in the eighties was infinitely gentler than in the fifties, but it was still subordinated to the same principles. The Party had a monopoly of wisdom, the regime of power. Dissent was unacceptable, the course of history preordained. Reform within the Communist Party did not unseat those principles. The slow erosion of the Communist Party's grip on events did.

Chapter 14

REFORM

For twenty years from the mid-sixties, the idea of reform was the central theme of Hungarian political and economic life. The aim was to carry further the post-Revolutionary compromise. Kádár reasoned that if he could build an efficient socialism which delivered prosperity, personal security, and a modicum of liberty outside the political arena, the people would continue to accept his Party's monopoly of power and subservience to the Kremlin. In the New Course Nagy had drawn the balance in rather different terms. But essentially Kádár was trying to do what Nagy had done between June 1953 and January 1955. He turned to the ideas that Nagy had pioneered, and to many of his instruments.

Reform was in large part organic, inexplicit. It had many elements. The first was a gradual return to normalcy as the repression which followed the Revolution was relaxed. Kádár resisted the dogmatists who wanted to recreate the idea of a society under siege. Slowly terror, exaggeration and hysteria were leached from Hungarian society. There were occasional relapses, particularly at major political events: as late as the fortieth anniversary of the liberation in 1985, for example, the public celebrations were still Stalinist in tone. But even on such exceptional occasions there was no hint of a cult of personality or of the other exaggerations which Rákosi had brought from Moscow to Hungary.

In everyday life, improvement was more consistent. Very cautiously, Hungarians recovered a sense of personal security under the law. The limits were clear: dissent was persecuted as much in the early eighties as in the sixties, if by much gentler methods. But all the way to the triumphant explosion of the late eighties, the vast majority kept well clear of dissent, of politics entirely. The return of legalism, the rejection of arbitrary methods brought this majority real benefits.

There was of course a price, paid by individuals at the time and by the whole society when change finally came. For forty years the people were deprived of political choice, political expression. Parliament miserably failed to express any view but the Party's. The people were deprived also of the conventional vehicles of civil society: social and interest groups, articulate churches, the good works of spontaneous charitable organizations. The Communist Party monopolized power. Kádár gave little real influence or representational capacity to the Patriotic People's Front, which Nagy had created and tried to build up as a link between people and Party. But things were infinitely better than they had been under Rákosi. The terrors of the post-Revolutionary period were a vivid reminder of the price of disorder. And the bleakness of conditions in Hungary's Communist neighbours dramatized her relative good fortune under Kádár's reforms.

This good fortune was most dramatically evident in the economic field. There was no return after the Revolution to the industrial exaggeration of Rákosi's Stalinism. Nagy's more moderate demands on the workers were continued. So was the attention he had given to consumer goods as well as industrialization, to the here and now as much as to future generations. After the arbitrary methods needed to get the peasants back into the cooperatives in the late fifties, agricultural policy too was moderate. Agriculture and industry began to deliver the modicum of prosperity which, so striking by comparison with the hardships of the rest of the Communist world, became the hallmark of 'goulash Communism'.

Even the Hungarians' sense of national identity was given its head a little. Nagy's appeals to nationhood had been part of the indictment that the Kremlin levelled against him when they rebuked him and let Rákosi drive him from office in 1955. His respect for it had led him astray again in 1956, and eventually to the gallows. But national identity was too powerful a force to defy or ignore for long. By the early sixties it was once again on the agenda. Kádár's declaration that 'he who is not against us is with us' recognized the potency of national unity and modulated the old harsh emphasis on class differences and interests.

National occasions were commemorated, national characteristics acknowledged. Hungary's sporting successes provided a safety valve for national emotion. Once again the limits were close and clear. There could be no expression of the nation's antipathy to the Soviet Union. Socialist internationalism rather than national interest dominated foreign and foreign trade policy. But within these limits a sense of nationhood, as deeply felt as the longing for prosperity and for personal liberty and security, was given room to express itself once again.

Most of these limited changes for the better emerged unannounced. Many of them flowed naturally from the gradual relaxation of the pressure with which Kádár had established himself in the early sixties. The exception was the Economic Reform, a carefully prepared and widely publicized programme introduced on 1 January 1968. Indeed, the Economic Reform seemed at the time the main lever of change in Hungary and the main feature which distinguished it from its unreformed and relatively less successful neighbours.

Like most of the better characteristics of Kádár's Hungary, the Economic Reform sprang from Nagyist roots. It sought to bring common sense, human aspirations and ordinary market forces back into Hungarian economic life. Its details, which have been exhaustively analysed elsewhere, are unimportant. Its means and aims are not.

The Reform's purpose was to satisfy Hungary's investment and consumption needs by making its economy efficient and internationally competitive. The chosen method was essentially to allow greater scope to individual judgements and desires, by distancing the management of individual enterprises from the central planning machinery and by replacing command by market forces. The Reform was the first and most sophisticated such experiment in the Communist world. It attracted more attention to Hungary than it had enjoyed since the terrible days of the Uprising.

Hungarian spokesmen always emphasized that this was purely an economic reform. There was no intention, they implied, of shifting the focus of politics or society. Hungary was a People's Republic, its people united in building socialism and wholeheartedly committed to their country's place in the socialist camp. The Economic Reform sought to alter and improve economic means, not to subvert agreed economic or political aims.

This emphasis was a necessary tribute to Moscow and to ideological orthodoxy. Eight months after the Economic Reform was launched, the Soviet Union sent troops into Czechoslovakia to destroy a bolder, more avowedly political attempt to meet popular aspirations. The invasion, in which the Hungarians were forced to participate, was a dramatic demonstration of the limits of Soviet tolerance. It emboldened domestic critics of the Hungarian reform. They represented a continuing threat to Kádár as he proceeded to introduce the Reform.

The desire to keep the Economic Reform economic probably reflected Kádár's own wishes as well as his fears of Party critics. But it ignored the infection which the ideas of reform would inevitably spread outside the economic sphere. A manager trusted to make economic decisions would, in time, want to make social, even political ones. An economy in which command from the centre no longer predominated would lead to questioning of central authority in politics. And a society once again putting its trust in market forces in the economy would expect to see them respected in other fields as well.

In the long run all these forces, unchecked, were likely to have a much more powerfully destructive effect on Party authority than the positive benefit it would gain from controlling an economically more effective and prosperous country. Nagy would have accepted that reality because he attached highest priority to understanding between Party and people. Kádár may at first have chosen not to recognize it. But gradually he and his associates came to understand that political danger lurked in economic reform and took steps to limit it.

To the habitual caution with which he approached any unorthodox or unfamiliar proposition, Kádár added a determination to erect a ring fence around Economic Reform. This created contradictions which prevented the Reform being pursued to its logical conclusion. The Reform was hobbled. Even in its heyday it could not deliver unequivocal success. As national and world economic conditions became more difficult, necessary changes were delayed or avoided altogether. In the end the Economic Reform, for all its achievement, was so restricted that when in the eighties the test came, economic weakness and inflexibility were prominent among the forces that destroyed the Communist Party's power to control events.

The problems which the Reform encountered were not solely ideological ones. Within five years of its launch it ran into the heavy economic seas of the seventies. These were good years in East-West political terms. But the storms that followed the first oil shock of 1973 threatened Eastern as much as Western Europe. The Eleventh Party Congress in 1975 brought the first overt political challenge to Kádár's economic policy. He sacrificed a prime minister but maintained his reform policies. Brezhnev endorsed them. Kádár had won a battle, but he knew that the dogmatists remained hostile. He wrapped his approach to the economy in yet more caution and ambiguity.

The consequence was that Hungarian economic policy failed to respond to the challenges that flowed from the first oil shock. Reform and international respectability had brought credit-worthiness. It seemed as if Hungary could borrow its way out of trouble. But by the time of the second oil shock in 1979, the Hungarian leadership was deeper in debt, unprepared to face more economic adversity, and deterred from drastic structural adjustment by fears of ideological criticism and ᴬ popular resentment. If the seventies had been good years for the Reform, the eighties promised only difficulty.

Kádaŕ was sixty-eight in 1980. He had nine more years to live, but already he was ageing, inflexible, putting more faith in his own sclerotic instincts than in the advice of his economists. He no longer faced criticism from the dogmatists within his own Party. But the leadership in Moscow were ageing with him; and suspicious. He had sacrificed the main architects of the Reform in 1975 and was surrounded by second-rate figures.

The Party Congress in March 1985 seemed to offer a last chance to take effective action. The chance was missed. Kádár was no longer capable of decision. His subordinates were jockeying for the succession. They were unwilling to advocate reform measures which might have set the ideologues against them; action against unprofitable plants which would have damaged the interests of old-fashioned loyalists in heavy industry; cut-backs in consumption to check the country's decline into debt. The Congress showed itself resolute for drift. It bought short-term popularity with concessions to the consumer which the country could not afford. Hard decisions were deferred to another day.

The focus of attention shifted away from the economy to fields where it might be easier to arouse enthusiasm, give a sense of direction to change. There was a new emphasis on parliament, with reforms requiring more than one candidate in every constituency. The result was an election in 1985 which, for the first time since the forties, aroused anything other than scepticism. The Communists enjoyed all the advantages of organization. But the vote was not rigged. It returned a number of members from outside the Party, some sense of individual accountability, and a willingness, hesitant at first, to express views at odds with Party orthodoxy.

But the Party retained a monopoly of power, and one old man authority within it. Increasingly he cut himself off from all but cronies. Younger men impatient for power saw Kádár's removal as a necessary first step to tackling the country's problems. The old arguments about reform – should it be faster, slower, cosmetic, thorough? – were overtaken. Economic Reform and associated reforms in other fields had had successes. They had made Hungary a more tolerable society than others in Eastern Europe. But they had failed to check decline into economic crisis and to give the Party manifest authority.

By 1986 the shrewder men in the Communist Party were beginning to recognize that the choice no longer lay between real and cosmetic reform under Communist leadership. The coming battle would be between Communists committed to thoroughgoing political and economic reform on the one hand and the dissenters, rapidly forming themselves into an effective opposition in waiting, on the other. To the Communist leaders, it must have looked like a safe battle in which to engage. Communism in Hungary had thirty years of relative success behind it. A whole generation knew nothing except the Party's rule. Reform Communists, rid of the inhibitions which prevented men like Kádár from acknowledging past sins and committing themselves to wholehearted reform, would be able to unite Party and nation as Nagy had done in 1953.

But before Reform Communism could engage the opposition in battle, Kádár had to be removed. In May 1988, Károly Grósz, a Communist who within months was to be swept aside by others more committed to Reform Communism than he, carried through the coup which removed him, protesting and broken, from the power he had monopolized for thirty-two years. Kádár's attempt to use Nagy's formula to reconcile Party and people, the

Kremlin and Hungary, ended in personal defeat. It was still an open question whether Reform Communism or multi-party democracy would replace it.

Chapter 15

EUROPE

Despite their sense of linguistic and ethnic isolation from all other Europeans except the Finns, the Hungarians see themselves as a European, and indeed a Central European, nation. In their eyes, fifty years of partnership in running the Empire until its fall make them joint heirs of the Habsburg legacy. They despise the Slovaks and the Czechs in different ways, view the Serbs and Poles and Croats with a wary regard, and hate the Rumanians. Beyond Austria, they look to Western Europe for cultural and national influences as pure as their own. Tell them that an Englishman finds it difficult to do business in Eastern Europe; they will counter with the certainty that things are very different here in Central Europe. For Hungarians, the heart of Europe is not very far from Budapest.

In their picture of Europe they feel a particular alienation from the Russians. Their attitude to their great neighbour is a mixture of dislike, contempt and fear. Russian intervention destroyed the Hungarian revolt against the Habsburgs in 1849. The Russian front consumed a generation in World War I. The collapse on the Don consumed the Second Army in 1943. Two years later the Red Army brought ravage, rape, Communism and alien authority. In 1956 Soviet intervention destroyed another generation's hopes. For nearly fifty years Hungary dutifully celebrated its liberation by the Red Army, but behind the formalities there was more hatred than gratitude to the liberators.

For two years after the war the Hungarians struggled for democracy at home and openness to Europe abroad. By 1948 they were quite cut off from the West. The regime's policies isolated Hungary from the parts of the continent with which it felt an affinity, corralling it with the alien Slavs and despised Rumanians. Hungary found itself at Moscow's mercy, condemned to subservience to its interests and a hypocritical respect for its wisdom.

The defeat of the Revolution increased still further Hungary's isolation from the West. In its immediate aftermath, the refugees escaped, but the Iron Curtain clanged down behind them. For the West, Kádár was a leper. It sought to isolate him, and ordinary Hungarians suffered in consequence. It pursued the 'Problem of Hungary' in order to punish an illegitimate puppet regime, but that pursuit, and the regime's counter-measures, doomed Hungary to separation from the West for six years. It was 1962 before the United Nations agreed to drop the Hungarian question, 1963 before the Secretary General visited Budapest and ended Hungary's international ostracism.

In those early years after the Revolution, the essentials of Hungarian foreign policy were simple: to reject criticism and support the Soviet Union. They were expressed through commitment to the Warsaw Pact and Comecon, to socialist internationalism and the struggle against imperialism. There was no room for any greater sophistication until the West could be brought to accept the Soviet occupation and the Kádár regime. When it did, and began to treat the country as a Soviet ally rather than a pure puppet, there was scope for Hungary to begin to play a minor part on the European stage once again.

But for twenty years the role was circumscribed, by a near-absolute subservience to Moscow. This subordination did not reflect Hungarian interests or aspirations. It flowed from Kádár's fear of offending Moscow, of arousing its suspicions and bringing down Soviet displeasure on little Hungary. Through these years, foreign policy, like reform and domestic security policy, was distorted by Kádár's need to prove his loyalty, to buy oblivion of the days in 1956 when he joined Nagy in defying the Russians before he defected to them.

The 1968 Czechoslovak crisis faced Kádár with a challenge to this policy. In May, Hungarian representatives went to Moscow to discuss events in Prague with the East Germans, Bulgarians, Poles and Russians. The possibility of intervention may already have been on the agenda. It was certainly in the air. Nevertheless, in June Kádár signed with Dubcek a treaty of friendship, cooperation and mutual assistance.

On 21 August, Soviet forces occupied Czechoslovakia. The satellites were required to join in. Kádár, haunted no doubt by memories of 1956, played for time. But haunted or not, he could not bring himself to resist Moscow's will. Despite the treaty of friendship, Hungarian troops marched into Slovakia, just as they had marched into Yugoslavia in 1941. Kádár did not take Teleki's way out. He let the world know that he had tried to warn Dubcek and argued that Czechoslovakia, just like Hungary, had been close to counter-revolution.

The West put the invasion behind it more quickly than it had come to terms with the rape of Hungary twelve years earlier. Hopes of détente still dominated Western policy, gradually made real by the East-West agreements reached in the early seventies. And its domestic reforms gradually won Hungary fame and popularity in the West.

It seemed to promise Nagy's kind of Communism, a kind which did not forget man. Hungarian Communism offered prosperity, security, a little freedom for the individual, a warm welcome for the Western visitor. Western commentators tended to ignore the constraints within which these good things were to be had. They noted how much better things were in Hungary than in its Communist neighbours, glossed over the pallor of Hungary's imitation of Western Standards. Hungarian representatives effectively encouraged these rose-tinted observations. Gradually Hungary was credited with a special status on the European scene.

Kádár's devotion to Moscow quietened the suspicions which Western favour aroused there. He rejected the idea that Hungary offered a model to others. National circumstances and experience were unique. Hungary wanted trade, cooperation and friendship with all its neighbours. The relationship with Moscow and with the Soviet world was however of a different and finer quality than that with the West. Hungary's commitment to socialist internationalism was complete.

Out of these contradictions and half truths, a recognizably different Hungarian position on European questions began to emerge. Gradually Hungary's position in the socialist camp came to be expressed in the sort of terms Nagy had used in his essays twenty years earlier, with their emphasis on national identity as well as socialist solidarity, on the importance of experience as well as ideology.

Until the very end of the decade, the seventies brought no political challenge to this attempt to be all things to all men. Europe, West and East, faced problems in the world outside, notably with the oil producers, and at the end of the decade regional issues produced a challenge of strength between the superpowers, into which their clients were drawn. But by and large the seventies were a period in which East-West relations in Europe seemed set fair.

Hungary benefited from this thaw, as from its own improving, if inflated, reputation. In 1976 Kádár visited Austria. Six months later he went to Rome and was received by Paul VI. He went to Bonn at the invitation of Helmut Schmidt. The French Prime Minister visited Budapest. So did Billy Graham. In January 1978 Cyrus Vance brought back to Hungary the crown and regalia of Saint Stephen, taken West at the end of the war and held in Fort Knox until Hungary was judged sufficiently free of outside tutelage to recover these symbols of its historical identity. At the end of the seventies it looked as if a solidly Communist Hungary, loyal to Moscow and its alliance, had recovered its status as a nation and as an actor, if a bit-part actor, on the European scene.

But the clouds were gathering. Moscow had seen the détente of the seventies in Europe as something separable from its search for advantage in the rest of the world. Despite détente it continued to build up its military strength in Europe. Slowly the West reacted and its attitudes hardened. In December 1979 it committed itself to deploy new medium-range nuclear forces in Europe if it could not persuade Moscow to withdraw its own. There followed the Soviet coup in Kabul, the seizure of the United States embassy in Teheran and the fast-spreading conviction in the United States that it still faced a global challenge from an evil empire that only power could contain. Hungary's bid for a small say in the affairs of Europe was entering a stormy decade.

Its economic need for détente remained. A central problem which its managers faced as they tried to make Hungarian industry and agriculture more competitive was the distortion to which Stalinism had subjected Hungarian trade. The first Five Year Plans had turned Hungary from an agricultural exporter into a relatively primitive industrial producer. They had locked it into bilateral exchanges with its economically more backward neighbours, especially the Soviet Union. These trading partners provided low quality products and markets for low quality goods. Trade within the bloc encouraged stagnation, removed the stimulus to seek world standards. Greater exposure to the West was an essential element in economic reform.

A gradual increase in trade with the West raised no political or ideological problems. Institutional change might; yet Hungary needed a developing relationship with Western economic institutions if it was to escape from the industrial and trading trap which Stalinism had created and twenty years of Kádárism had failed to spring. In the first instance it needed membership of the International Monetary Fund.

The decision to apply for membership was the first international issue of substance on which Hungary risked Soviet misgivings, even perhaps displeasure. At the time Hungarian spokesmen argued their case in determinedly non-confrontational terms. They implied that the Hungarian leadership took its own decision, with Soviet understanding but not necessarily consent. Later they put it about that Hungary had faced down Soviet unease and even disapproval. The fact is that Hungary risked Soviet displeasure, but on a matter which could be represented as more technical than political, in which a real but non-political Hungarian interest was at stake. In May 1982 Hungary became a member of the IMF.

In the same year Hungary began to seek a relationship with another Western institution, the European Community. The first moves were made cautiously, with very great discretion. As with the Reform and the application for IMF membership, the Hungarians stressed that this was an entirely economic initiative, devoid of political significance. They wanted an association with the Community which would bring balanced commercial benefits, redress the specific wrongs which some Community countries' restrictions did to Hungarian exports. This caution cost Hungary some Western sympathy. It was seen as refusing to pay a political price for commercial benefit. But it ensured Soviet acquiescence in a move which again pointed up Hungary's special position between East and West.

While Hungary cautiously pursued its economic negotiations with the Community, more dramatic political events monopolized attention. They centred on the battle of wills building in Europe between the two alliances over intermediate nuclear forces. The date for deployment of Cruise and Pershing missiles approached: a challenge not just to Moscow but to an articulate Western European opposition critical of any further twist in the nuclear spiral. Events in Poland increased East-West tensions, with the

West introducing sanctions against the Soviet Union and Poland. In November 1982 Andropov succeeded Brezhnev, but he showed no sign of backing away from the West's challenge to Moscow. Unimaginable as it may be in the nineties, there seemed in the early eighties a real possibility that the West, weakened by its own critics of deployment, might back down instead.

This rising tension threatened Hungary's attempts to play a wider, perhaps even useful, role on the European stage. It persisted nevertheless. In the late summer of 1983 the French Prime Minister, the American Vice President and the British Foreign Secretary visited Budapest in rapid succession. Just before Sir Geoffrey Howe arrived Soviet fighters shot down the Korean Airlines Flight 007 over the Soviet far east. The event seemed to exemplify the Soviet military menace and the danger of war by accident. A month later the United States invaded Grenada. In November NATO started to deploy Cruise missiles and the Soviet Union broke off the Geneva talks. The stage was set for Hungary's second, still tentative step towards a real role in European affairs.

Hungarian officials started to talk about the contribution which small states could make to East-West dialogue while remaining completely loyal to their allies. In January 1984 the Party's chief spokesman on international affairs wrote a tortured theoretical article about the interplay between international and national considerations in the development of socialism in Hungary. One practical point peeped through the thicket of theory: in its approach to international affairs each East European country had the right to take advantage of its own specific possibilities.

By the time the article appeared, Hungary was committed by events to such a challenging course. When the Soviet Union withdrew from the Geneva talks in November 1983, plans already existed for the heads of government of the three NATO countries due to receive American missiles – West Germany, Britain and Italy – to visit Budapest. At the end of 1983, each of the three proposed dates early in 1984. The West was taking literally Hungarian arguments that even small European states like Hungary had something to contribute to the European security debate.

It seemed at the time and it is manifest in retrospect that the Russians wanted the invitations to be cancelled. It was the duty of the East European allies to join Moscow's boycott of contacts with the West. Talks in Budapest would reduce the sense of crisis, undermine Soviet efforts to create pressures on Western governments to postpone deployment of the missiles.

The Hungarians, in their first defiance of Moscow on a political issue since 1956, quietly stuck to their guns. The visits were spaced out, those of Andreotti and Kohl postponed; but Mrs Thatcher's visit in late January 1984 took place as proposed. It delighted the Hungarian people and reinforced a dialogue between London and Budapest. But it had a wider significance. It kept contact between East and West open; it asserted the case for discussing political issues generally, not just arms and arms control; and it manifested a new, cautious Hungarian confidence in international affairs. For the first time in forty years, Hungary was starting to play a role of its own in European affairs.

But Kádár was not christened János for nothing. After this moment of assertiveness the old pattern of conformity on all major issues seemed to reassert itself. Hungary was at pains to show itself a good ally. Arguments for a national role in international affairs were deployed only in coded articles in theoretical magazines. Hungary's desire to play a European role was coyly demonstrated at the Budapest Cultural Forum, where political points could be made under the cloak of discussion of Europe's cultural destiny.

A year later, Gorbachev came to power in the Soviet Union. In retrospect, March 1985 can be seen as a milestone for the Soviet Union and its satellites as important as November

1917. It marks in a sense the true point of transition between this chapter, about Hungary's role in Europe and on the international stage in the Kádár years, and the next, about the fulfilment that came once Kádárism had been swept away. But Kádár had three more years of power, four of life, after Gorbachev's accession. There is a continuity between Gorbachev's European policy and his predecessors' and its impact on Hungary which can best be traced in this chapter.

By the time Gorbachev came to power, Communism in Hungary was running into an impasse. The economy was deteriorating rapidly, and with it Communist self-confidence. Kádár no longer had the authority to force through the measures necessary to restore economic health. His likely successors would not even advocate effective action for fear of the political price it might cost them.

We have seen that all this resolute irresolution reached its climax at the Party Congress of 1985. The economic austerity programme was abandoned, concessions to consumers introduced. Economic prospects deteriorated. By the time Kádár visited London in the autumn, he had one real message wrapped up in the words of wisdom about Europe and British-Hungarian relations. Hungary, in its economic need, wanted Western cooperation. It particularly needed investment, technology, industrial collaboration. For another year and a half, Kádár repeated this message, while failing to force through the changes that would have made such cooperation possible. His visit to London was no more than a last feather in an old man's cap. It did not bring the help needed to save his regime. Nor did contacts with other Western capitals.

In diplomatic matters, as in domestic and economic, Kádár had wanted to pursue Nagy's ideas for thirty years. They presupposed Hungarian sovereignty and the pursuit of Hungarian interests as well as socialist ones. But political, ideological and personal timidity prevented Kádár forcing these ideas through to success. Gradually he slipped into senility. The men around him competed for the succession. It looked at the time like a conflict between two different kinds of Communists: cautious heirs to Kádár and bolder men going back to the ideas which Nagy had propounded.

In fact, of course, a different conflict was in preparation, between two interpretations of Nagy's legacy, between Reform Communism and parliamentary democracy. It became possible to play out that conflict only when it became clear that Gorbachev was ready for, perhaps even hoped for, fundamental change in the relationship between the Soviet Union and what had been its East European empire.

Chapter 16

FULFILMENT

In a few short months in 1988 and 1989, Communist
authority in Hungary disintegrated. The Party entered
the period with almost 800,000 members. It ended it
broken. The political initiative passed from Communists
and ex-Communists to inexperienced groupings advocating
parliamentary democracy. On 23 October 1989, the
thirty-third anniversary of the Uprising, Hungary committed itself to a multi-party system. It expunged the cant
word 'People's' from its official designation and became the
Republic of Hungary. In March 1990, a general election
was held. Hungary had returned to the parliamentary
democracy which Nagy and his cabinet promised in the last
days before the Soviet invasion of November 1956.

In those miraculous months, Hungary moved close
behind Poland on its way to representative democracy. In
doing so it prepared the path that most of its other
neighbours in Eastern Europe were to follow. Developments inside the Party linked with pressures from outside,
concessions with ineffective efforts at repression, symbolic
changes with shifts of substance. Demands for historical
justice and Nagy's rehabilitation went forward together
with efforts to democratize Hungary. The initiative shifted
steadily within the Party towards the reformers, and moved
beyond them into the hands of the new opposition.

1988 started with a symbol, the formal abolition of exit

visas. By the spring, gesture was assuming substance: on 15 March the largest crowd since that of 23 October 1956 assembled at Petöfi's statue. Kádár clung to power but seemed incapable of using it. He summoned the first Party Conference (as distinct from the periodic congresses) to be held since 1957. Two weeks before it, Károly Grósz visited London. His press conference was seen as a bid for Western favour and a signal that he was preparing an attack on Kádár. It came at the Conference. Three out of four of Kádár's close associates launched a coup against him. He made a rambling, reluctant speech, clinging physically to the microphone. The conference ejected him into honorific obscurity; Grósz seemed to gather to himself Kádár's lost power and to offer the prospect of tough-minded and realistic leadership.

Grósz still believed he could control events. The first challenge to this conviction came on 16 June when people gathered to commemorate the execution of Imre Nagy. Three hundred people clashed with the police at plot 301 in Rákoskeresztür cemetery. A requiem mass in a Pest church for Nagy and the 324 other victims of Rákoskeresztür was halted after fifteen minutes. Motorcycle police broke up a demonstration in Nagy's memory in the centre of Budapest. But Grósz matched repression with appeasement, hinting that at least a partial rehabilitation was possible. A month later he held back the security police when a crowd of thousands marched to the Rumanian Embassy to protest at the treatment of the Magyar minority in Transylvania.

Events elsewhere were on the march. In June, Gorbachev held a special Party Conference of his own. There was dissension within it, to match the demonstrations against the KGB in Moscow and Leningrad and the Baltic states' first demands for partial independence. At a Warsaw Pact meeting, Grósz called for Soviet troop withdrawals from Hungary. During a visit to the United States in July he begged for Western understanding. But by rejecting the possibility of political rehabilitation for Nagy he alienated

Hungarian Americans who could have helped him. An amnesty in September for 1956 offenders still excluded those found guilty of treason.

Unlike Kádár, Grósz had no personal stake in holding Nagy's supporters at bay. But he understood, just as clearly as those who were agitating for rehabilitation, that such a move would undermine the Party with which Kádár had sought to obliterate Nagy's memory. Until the end of 1988 he still seemed to be holding together the kind of Party power, tolerant of moderate dissent but ultimately authoritarian, which Kádár had maintained for over thirty years. He still looked like Hungary's best hope of orderly reform.

But Grósz's authority lasted less than a year. The ground was shifting in the Soviet Union and elsewhere in Eastern Europe. The opposition were emboldened. Finally dissent within the Party undermined Grósz's position. Imre Pozsgay, the Reform Communist who over the years had used his position in the People's Patriotic Front to build a Nagyist profile and popularity, began to propound policies of his own. They were reformist and popular. They embraced concessions to the opposition and envisaged real democracy. Pozsgay effectively upstaged Grósz. Open disagreement between them undermined confidence. By the summer of 1989 the conflict had brought the old Hungarian Communist Party to ruin.

In the old days, even disagreement at the very top of the Party would not have so infected Hungarian politics. Rákosi and Nagy worked in bitter rivalry but in double harness for a year and a half, and as we have seen it was not Nagy's criticism of Rákosi's autarchy thereafter which eventually brought Revolution. In 1989, however, a whole range of circumstances reinforced the destructive effect of dissension among the leadership.

The most central was the Party's loss of self-confidence. It had ruled for thirty-three years, imposing order and acquiescence but failing, and knowing that it was failing, to elicit real support. Even in the early eighties, Party membership was falling. The majority of the nation lived unpolitical lives, viewing the Party with unexpressed contempt. Dissenters, gradually growing bolder, articulated a little of this contempt.

The Party could point to no manifest achievements. It had kept the peace between Moscow and people, delivered a little prosperity. But in the eighties the prosperity faded, debts accumulated, hard-won industry drifted into obsolescence. This Communist Party above all others had sought justification through economic success. As failure pressed upon it instead, its confidence evaporated.

It had been accustomed to look to Moscow for instruction and inspiration. In the mid-eighties it found neither there. Communism in the Soviet Union had failed even more dramatically than in Hungary to deliver economic well-being. It was the threat of economic collapse above everything else which had prodded Gorbachev into *perestroika*. And change in the Soviet Union deprived Hungarian Communists of the assurance of the old certainties. Kádár had hesitated to pursue reform with real vigour because he feared Moscow's suspicions. His successors feared to nip demands for much further-reaching reform in the bud because they had no assurance of Soviet backing if they did so. And for all that Gorbachev asserted that the East European Parties must work out their own salvation, it was manifest that he believed that salvation was to be found in reform within limits laid down by the Party.

In such uncertainty, different groups of Party members began to go their own ways. Many abandoned ship. Some took refuge in stand-pat conservatism. Some, and perhaps the most enterprising, turned to the radical solutions which Pozsgay offered. Steadily the Party shed its mantle of certainty, of unanimity. For years it had concealed an almost complete absence of ideological conviction. Now *sauve qui peut* replaced the pretence of certainty.

Imre Nagy's legacy once again became an issue. Kádár had built on his economic legacy, at first with some success.

He had tried also to imitate his decency, his concern for individuals. He had always drawn the line at any serious political experimentation. All the same, in Kádár's later years some modest political expectations had been aroused: through tolerance of dissent, parliamentary reforms, the encouragement of debate within the Party and in Pozsgay's Patriotic Front. With Kádár gone, such expectations rose.

They were expressed in many ways. One was the swelling demand for the truth about the past. Everyone in Hungary knew that October 1956 was the zenith of the country's twentieth-century experience. But for more than a generation the official record had misconstrued the Revolution: as a counter-revolution encouraged from outside, an incipient White Terror. In his man-of-the-people speeches Kádár fudged the point, when he talked of the tragedy of 1956; but the official record endured. So did the lies about Soviet intervention, about the abduction of Nagy, about the crimes for which he died. We have seen that to the very end Grósz, innocent of Kádár's crimes in 1956, could not bring himself to acknowledge the truth about Nagy's fate. It had too direct a relevance to the demands about the future that were growing in the early months of 1989.

In the end Pozsgay forced Grósz's hand. Grósz went to a conference in Switzerland: a conference of captains of Western commerce to be wooed. In his absence Pozsgay called 1956 a Revolution and hinted at Nagy's rehabilitation. There was a rumpus when Grósz returned, from which Pozsgay emerged with the tactical advantage. Nagy's family were promised a decent private reburial. The search for the bones in plot 301 at Rákoskeresztür began. At the same time negotiations began about the ceremony between family and friends on one side, Party and state on the other.

The outcome was the private occasion commanding the attention of all Hungarians described in Chapter 1. Party leaders were reduced to asking permission to attend the public cermony before the funeral. They were allowed to do so, but to represent the state, not the Party. They were excluded from the reburial altogether. Nagy's daughter, a quiet, private woman in her early sixties, out-manoeuvred the Party. June 16 1989, was a good day for the quiet, the private, the once-humiliated, in Hungary.

After the reburial came the accelerating rush of events which in six months swept away the post-war order in Central and Eastern Europe. The first of them was the last act in the Nagy legal process. On 6 July 1989, the Supreme Court in Budapest found that Nagy had not been guilty of the charges for which he had been condemned. He and his companions were formally exculpated. On the same day, at the same hour, came the news that János Kádár was dead. He died at the age of seventy-seven, broken, guilt-ridden, incapable at the last even of the repetitive apologia with which he had filled his dying weeks since the reburial. Kádár had had his thirty-one years of power after Nagy's execution; on 6 July Nagy had the last word in court.

A week after Nagy's final rehabilitation, George Bush arrived in Budapest. His hosts presented to him a symbolic strand of barbed wire from the frontier barrier, proclaiming the end of the Iron Curtain. Four by-elections quickly followed: the first free elections since 1947. The Communists did badly against tyro opponents. In September they lost another by-election. A few days later it was announced that Party and opposition had reached agreement on arrangements for a multi-party general election. No one believed that the Communists could hope to win it.

On 6 October came the final débâcle. The Communists held a Congress of the Hungarian Socialist Workers' Party. It was the fourteenth since Kádár had put the Party together in the chaos of 1956. It was also its last. By 1202 votes to 159 the delegates voted to wind up the Socialist Workers' Party. In its place they founded the Hungarian Socialist Party. It renounced the idea of the dictatorship of the proletariat, of the one-party state. 'The present concept of socialism, the Stalinist system, has exhausted all its social, economic, political and moral reserves, and has

proved unsuitable for keeping pace with global developments', announced a Party declaration. 'Thus the history of
the Hungarian Socialist Workers' Party has come to an
end.'[1]

The Party committed itself to handing over the bulk of
its assets to the state. It promised to surrender control of
the Workers' Guard, the Communists' stormtroopers since
1957, to the government. 'Workers of the world unite' was
removed from the masthead of the Party newspaper. The
Socialists faced a future as one party among many in a free
Hungary. The malcontents, Grósz among them, talked of
building a new Communist Party.

It was just over two weeks before 23 October, the
anniversary of the Uprising. In those days in 1956 Hungary
had moved from the Rajk reburial to a fight for freedom. In
1989 it moved from reconstituting the old Party to
reconstituting the state. On 23 October the acting
President, Mátyás Szürös, went out onto the balcony from
which Nagy had spoken on 23 October 1956. He
announced measures adopted by parliament on the
previous day. October 23 was to be a day of national
reconciliation. All the victims of the years between 1948
and 1962 were to be rehabilitated. After forty years the
Hungarian People's Republic had become the Republic of
Hungary.

Meanwhile, George Bush's symbolic strand of barbed
wire had had major consequences. Hungarians were already
free to travel. But the killing zone along Hungary's Western
frontiers was a poor advertisement of the country's new
freedoms. Its removal would graphically demonstrate the
change. Before long, East German holiday-makers on their
annual pilgrimage to Lake Balaton and Lake Fertöd
discovered that next to nothing stood between them and the
road through Austria to the Federal Republic. They
gathered at the frontier, packed into the Federal German
embassy in Budapest and the Red Cross camps opened to
house them.

Tension rose, among the refugees, between Budapest

and East Berlin. The Hungarian authorities argued that they were caught between the expectations of Bonn and the demands of East Berlin. They temporized as the autumn weather grew cooler. But they needed Bonn's goodwill more than Pankow's. Their people expected further liberalization. Finally the frontier to Austria was opened. Berlin complained bitterly that no fraternal government had ever betrayed another in this way. Budapest held to its decision: the holiday-makers vanished into Austria and West Germany. Already Hungary's relations with nearer neighbours were embittered: with Czechoslovakia over the Nagymaros Dam and with Rumania over Transylvania. A menacing Little Entente seemed to threaten Hungary.

But the opening of the frontier had started a process that East Germany found difficult to stop. It banned travel to Hungary but continued to allow it to Czechoslovakia. East Germans flooded the Federal embassy in Prague. Again tension rose. Repeatedly Prague and East Berlin gave way. Crowded trains, decrepit cars carried the pilgrims through Bohemia into Bavaria. Crowds mobbed the railway stations at Leipzig and Dresden.

The unimaginable was happening. The disciplined East German people snatched control of their destiny from their rulers. On 10 November the Berlin Wall was opened. The Czechs and Slovaks, as disciplined as the East Germans and still more cautious, finally asserted themselves. So did the Bulgars. And at the very end of the year of miracles, the wind of freedom, which had blown for the first time at Nagy's reburial, blew even through Rumania; it blew away what was left of the East European Empire that Stalin had created.

So in the course of 1988 and 1989, the Hungarians, inspired by memories of Nagy and the desire to fulfil his legacy, had done more than their share in bringing freedom to Central and Eastern Europe. It remained to complete the process through free elections at home. They were planned for the spring of 1990.

Fifty parties prepared to compete. Both wings of the old Communist Party said they would take part. So did representatives of the democratic parties – Smallholders, Social Democrats, Peasants – which Rákosi had destroyed forty years earlier. Spokesmen emerged for new groupings of every political colour.

The most effective of the new politicians grouped themselves in two organizations, the Democratic Forum and the Alliance of Free Democrats.

The names of these groups were new, but they stood for old forces in Hungarian politics. The Forum emphasized national and rural virtues, a traditionalist approach to politics. In terms of political alignment, it stood close to the Smallholders. But the Smallholders Party was being put together again after thirty years of silence by old men shaped by old memories. The Forum leaders shared their principles but sought to express them in more contemporary ways. They believed in the nation, in a search for old continuities, in rural and traditional values. Their opponents focussed on the reverse of this traditional medal and accused the Forum of nationalism, hostility to the cities, even anti-Semitism. The truth is that in English terms the Forum were advocating old-fashioned Tory values.

They faced the Alliance of Free Democrats, Victorian Liberals to their Tories. Like the Forum, the Free Democrats' beliefs were right-of-centre ones. Its leaders, many of whom had first come to prominence as dissenters in the early eighties, traced their ideas back to the pre-war 'Westerners', who had looked to international modernism for solutions to the problems of Hungary under Horthy. The Alliance was cosmopolitan in its approach, a party led by urban intellectuals, more impatient and radical than the Forum in its approach to political and economic problems.

A new electoral system was devised, based loosely on that of the Federal Republic of Germany. Hungarians boasted that it was the most complex in the world. It provided for 176 seats to be filled on a constituency basis, 152 more in proportion to votes polled in the counties, and a final 52 from a national list. The system was calculated to give a voice to all opinions while avoiding the weaknesses of pure proportional representation. Its critics claimed that it would encourage a proliferation of parties and ridiculed it as over-complicated. Its supporters claimed that it would be justified by results.

The first round of voting was held on 25 March 1990. On that day Hungarians went to the first meaningful nationwide polls since August 1947, the first truly free and fair election since November 1945. They voted under the shadow of unmanageable economic problems, with rising inflation and unemployment bringing home the human costs of reform. Pessimists claimed that the electorate were cynical, uninterested, unprepared for real democracy. They forecast a fiasco. But the voters went to the polls with a touching enthusiasm, and polling was ordered and decent.

The 25 March vote did produce the inconclusive result which the electoral system's critics had forecast. The two main parties ran nearly neck-and-neck, the Forum winning nearly twenty-five per cent of the votes, their opponents just over twenty-one per cent. But the near-extinction of the forces which had ruled Hungary since the 1948 was clear. The Smallholders won almost twelve per cent, the Young Democrats almost nine per cent, and the Christian Democrats six-and-a-half per cent of the votes. Against these three-quarters of the votes, Pozsgay's Socialists, the old Reform Communists and the last hope of the left, got just under eleven per cent of the vote. As for Grósz, his hardline Communists won less than the four per cent they needed for representation in the new parliament.

Two weeks later, on 8 April, came the second round. This time the results were clear. While the other main parties' share of the votes held roughly steady, that of the Forum increased as they gathered in votes which in the first round had gone to special interest groupings. With their centre-right allies, the Smallholders and the Christian Democrats, the Forum won 229 out of the 386 seats in parliament, sixty-two per cent of the votes, almost exactly the share that the Smallholders had won in 1945. The Alliance had nearly a hundred seats and the basis for effective opposition. But Pozsgay's Socialists were reduced to thirty-three seats in a parliament which their Communist predecessors had dominated for three decades. Just as Tocqueville's France was manifestly the same place after thirty years of Revolution, Consulate and Empire, so the dominant forces in Hungary were quite unchanged after four decades of Communism.

For another three weeks the men of the old government held the ring. The system in which they had grown up had been shattered. They faced marginalization in a parliament in which the Free Democrats would lead the opposition to a Forum-led government. They had been persons of consequence: Nyers, father of the Economic Reform, Pozsgay of the Patriotic People's Front, Szürös and Horn who had given Hungary a foreign policy of its own. Now their day was done. But in different circumstances, each in his different way, they had tried to create a decent Communist system. When it was swept aside, they played a not unworthy part in bringing Hungary back to pluralism.

On 2 May the new parliament assembled. Forum and Alliance had struck a deal. The prime objective was to make it possible for the new government to get necessary legislation through parliament quickly. As part of it an Alliance leader was elected President of the National Assembly and, therefore, interim President of the Republic. Mátyás Szürös, the Communist interim President who had proclaimed the new Republic five months before, retired to the back benches. Árpád Göncz, sixty-eight years of age, Free Democrat politician, 1956 freedom fighter, political prisoner for seven years thereafter, President of the Writers' Association, writer and translator who had taught himself English in prison, founder member of the Committee for Historical Justice which won Imre Nagy reburial and rehabilitation, became President of Hungary.

Now Göncz led the new Assembly in a declaration that reiterated the resolution adopted by its predecessor in October 1989. It formally recorded that the 1956 Uprising had been a revolutionary fight for freedom. It proclaimed 23 October a national holiday. And it declared that Hungary could see at last that the hopes of 1956 and its sacrifices had not been in vain. The process of legitimizing the Revolution was complete.

In the name of the Assembly, Göncz invited József Antall, fifty-six years of age, Forum leader, son of a Smallholder politician, historian and archivist, political activist in 1956, to form a government.

It faced enormous problems. Hungary must learn to operate a democratic system it had only once previously experienced. Society was embittered by forty years of authoritarian rule. Where the majority welcomed democracy some asserted old nationalist and racist doctrines. The economy was weak, the industrial environment a wasteland. The workforce was demoralized, de-skilled. Industry was only marginally competitive. Hungary had to reshape its economy and complete the process of realigning its foreign trade. But there were doubts whether it could compete, pay its way, reduce its massive debts. Reform of the economy was vitally necessary, but it would bring more pain, stretch a stressed society on the rack.

There was a welcome for Hungary's new democracy, but she nevertheless faced problems abroad. Moscow was threatening the Baltic states as it had once threatened the satellites. It was not completely fanciful to suppose that Hungary's great Eastern neighbour might disintegrate. The position of the Hungarian minority in Rumania was pitiable. The prospect of a united Germany recalled old memories. Yet the reach into Central Europe of the other Western powers was weak. Hungary had always looked to them for salvation and time after time they had failed to save her. It was going to take an immense effort for Hungary to find a place in the new Europe.

All the same, 2 May 1990, was a great day for the

Hungarian people. After more than forty years of tyranny, lightened only by the New Course, by the extinguished hopes of 1956 and by Kádár's attempts to build on the ruins of Nagy's achievement, representative government had returned to Hungary.

Epilogue

ASSESSMENT

Earlier chapters of this book have traced Imre Nagy's life and the legacy he left behind him. In this epilogue it remains to assess his achievement and answer the questions posed in the prologue. Did he die a Communist or a patriot? Would he stand today for Reform Communism or for democracy? How central was Nagy's legacy to Hungarian history since his execution? Does he deserve to be remembered as one of Hungary's heroes?

We have seen that Nagy's life was full of ambiguities. From his early manhood he was plagued by contradictions. On the one hand he was a simple Hungarian countryman with his way to make in the world, shaped by human loyalties and patriotism. On the other he was a convinced Bolshevik, loyal to Communist verities, convinced that scientific Marxism could bring human happiness.

The last thirty years of his life were taken up by efforts to resolve these contradictions. His position shifted, at first very slowly. In Moscow he closed his eyes to Stalin's terror, persuaded that Hungarian Communism would be different. Back in Hungary he pressed the agricultural policies he believed in, opposed the shift to forced collectivization. When he got power he tried to close the gap that yawned between his Party and his countrymen. In power and in opposition he attacked the excesses by which Communism imposed itself on Hungary. His attack on Party terrorism threatened its authority, just as his search for a more human Communism blurred its purposes. In his eyes these risks were justified. He believed that if he could establish confidence between Party and people he could build a Communism which ruled by consent and not by force.

In 1956 the catastrophe he feared, which gave such urgency to his essays, overtook the country. The Party lost power and the nation seized it. For thirteen days he fought to recover the initiative, not for the old Party but for a shifting coalition of forces which gathered around him. At the beginning he seemed to be fighting for a reformed Communism, exercising power with a wisdom and moderation which the Party had not hitherto displayed. He shifted to a sharing of power, and finally to competition for power in a multi-party democracy. By 1 November 1956, it looked as if Hungary would hold free elections within six months. Then the Russians came back, and the elections which would have swept Nagy's Party from office were delayed for thirty-four years.

Once the tanks came back, Nagy could have saved himself by recantation and cooperation. But the experience of the last thirteen days ruled that out: he had helped forge a heady national unity and faced Moscow's black betrayal. He was too stubborn to betray those lessons. So there remained for Nagy nothing more than imprisonment, trial and execution. After that came official oblivion on the one hand, and on the other a posthumous influence which over thirty years helped change Hungary into a country in which, had he lived, he might have been at ease.

What, at the time and looking back, did people say of Nagy? György Lukács, the Marxist intellectual, praised his integrity and intelligence but questioned his political ability.[1] Others saw him as an academic, committed to Party loyalty but remote from political cut and thrust. In Moscow in the thirties he taught a Russian student at the Institute who, half a century later, asked a visiting Hungarian whatever became of Imre Nagy. He could not believe that the bespectacled lecturer he remembered had turned into the man Moscow traduced as a dangerous counter-revolutionary politician.[2]

Writing in the forties Nagy's namesake, Ferenc Nagy, dismissed him as a politician of small calibre, who did what his Party told him. The best he could say of Imre Nagy was that he was the most Hungarian of the Communist leaders.[3] Paul Ignotus thought that in the salami years he was complacent, self-deluding. There are stories of his doing good by stealth, steering his daughter away from the Ministry of the Interior, for example, and urging an opposition MP to get out of politics while the going was good.[4] Many Hungarians were suspicious, thinking of him as a Muscovite employed to put an agreeable false face on his ruthless Party. Others remembered his wartime broadcasts and the land distribution, and valued his efforts to hold his Party back from policies that could only be carried through by force. Even in the late forties there was a sense that here was a decent man caught up in a criminal enterprise.

Looking back, one of Nagy's friends tries to explain this ambiguity with a historical analogy. He compares him with a man who, four hundred years earlier, discovered too late that he had committed himself to the wrong side in the Reformation. He believes that in the thirties, Nagy saw where Communism was taking Russia and realized the error of his own commitment to the faith. But he was ruled by Party discipline and the instinct of self-preservation. He kept his doubts to himself, cherishing the illusion that in Hungary things would be different. In Hungary he discovered that there was to be no difference: his leaders were nothing more than criminal servants of Moscow.[5]

There is general agreement that in 1953 Nagy brought new hope to Hungary. We have seen the effect of his speech in parliament on 4 July. People remember his voice, his simple words. They felt that at last they were listening to a Hungarian, not an apparatchik. No one questioned Nagy's Communist commitment, but they sensed that he was preaching a different kind of Communism that wanted to meet ordinary Hungarians half way. There was a sense of gratitude for small mercies. Nagy was not about to dismantle Communism. But New Course Communism might be the best an occupied Hungary could hope for. It was better by far than Rákosi's version.

People who remember Nagy's twenty months in office stress how lonely he seemed. They sensed his isolation from his comrades, while his Communism set him apart from ordinary Hungarians. We have seen that gradually this loneliness was reduced, as the writers and journalists rallied to him and Rákosi's Communist victims came out of prison. But there was still a distance between Nagy and those who put their faith in him.

This may in part have been due to his pedantic, schoolmasterly ways. In part it was due to Nagy's loyalty to his Party. He wanted to criticize the Party from within, not listen to less proper criticism from his friends. There is a testiness about some memories of Nagy. On the very day of the Revolution, for example, he parted angrily from his closest supporter, Losonczy, isolating himself from him and most of his other friends for the critical first few days of the Uprising.

Some contemporaries may have felt that Nagy ran with the hare and hunted with the hounds. Many ordinary Hungarians did not believe that there could be any such thing as a good Communist. Within the Party there was inevitably a coolness between a Muscovite who had criticized Rákosi but escaped prison and homegrown Communists like Kádár who had spent three terrible years in gaol. Those who had made sacrifices for the forced industrialization in which they believed felt that Nagy faltered and changed course precisely when it should have started to produce results. Someone who knew him in his first period as Prime Minister claims that he heard Nagy talk to Russian visitors about his compatriots as if they were scum.[6] More recent allegations of association with the KGB do not seem to have surfaced at that time. But in a country riven by hatred and suspicion, Nagy did not escape hostility.

But to others, Nagy's goodness shone through. For them, he was manifestly simple, straightforward, Hungarian. He might lack political skill. He could be unfuriatingly academic, doctrinaire. His Party loyalty seemed at times to stand in the way of common sense. But they saw him as essentially well-intentioned, a good man.

There were ambiguities again when the Revolution came. To the crowds outside parliament on 23 October Nagy seemed out of touch, just another Communist who did not understand that the Party had been overtaken by events. His friends were enraged when he seemed to abandon the radicalism of his essays and go back to the New Course doctrines he had preached three years earlier. He seemed to deliver himself into Gerö's hands, willing to provide a front for continued repression. Once he had escaped from the influences which surrounded him in Party headquarters, his friends had to work hard to clear him of responsibility for what happened in the first days of the Uprising.

Then came the days in which he came to terms with the insurgents, created national unity by identifying himself with popular demands and supported Kádár in the creation of a new and cleaner Communist Party. In this period any sense of ambiguity stems from the speed with which he had to adapt to the changing situation. He had to hold reactionaries at bay, construct alliances, convince the insurgents that he had embraced their policies, start to lay foundations for a new democracy – and all the while seek to carry Moscow with him.

There are varying assessments of Nagy's performance in these crucial days. Some talk of chaos in his offices in parliament, others of his untiring accessibility. Others point to his success at just that time in uniting the insurgents with police and army and creating the National Guard. One can hear that he was enduringly calm, even commanding; or that he vacillated endlessly, overwhelmed by the pace of events.

But the record of how those events were tackled tends to justify Nagy. He came to terms with the insurgents, wooed them into joining him. National unity was created. Order was restored. Nagy succeeded in creating a coalition government, working effectively with men like Tildy and Bibo. The new Communist Party was set up; and of its leaders only Kádár deserted and joined the old Stalinists in flight to the Soviet Union. Nagy even persuaded, or seemed to persuade, Mikoyan and Suslov to put their faith in him. In the appallingly difficult days from 27 October to 3 November Nagy proved himself master of the situation.

Whether he could have remained on top of events if the Russians had not attacked Hungary is a might-have-been of history. His enemies used to point to the massacre at Budapest Party headquarters in Republic Square and argue that the Revolution would inevitably have been overtaken by terror. Seven years after the Revolution Kádár recalled the beginning of the White Terror in 1919, when Horthy swept aside a well-meaning left-of-centre government that followed Béla Kun's. 'I presume that Imre Nagy was destined to play a similar role. He, too, would have been told after six days: get up and get out. And he would have taken his hat and coat and left.'[7] We cannot prove Kádár wrong. We can point to his interest in peddling this thesis, and the absence of any serious evidence to support it.

It is much more probable that if the Russians had withdrawn from Hungary the precarious order which Nagy had been able to establish would have been maintained. There would inevitably have been a reaction after the euphoria of the Uprising, a falling away from the standards which left donations for victims of the fighting piling up in unguarded collecting boxes. But the National Guard would have patrolled the streets. There is no evidence that the four-party coalition would not have held together and kept attacks from both extremes at bay. Elections in the spring of 1957 would in all probability have brought to power a bourgeois coalition led by the Smallholders. Kádár's new Communist Party would have faced an uphill struggle to re-establish itself, cleanse its reputation, recover in opposition the popular trust it had lost in power. Hungary might have seen in 1957 what it is seeing now in the nineties.

So if things had turned out otherwise, Nagy himself might have lived out the autumn of his days in respected opposition. He might even have achieved office. One can see him as a good Speaker of a parliament restored to the power it had lost when he first presided over it. Gratitude for his role in 1956 might even have made him a non-executive President of a decent little neutral Republic in the heart of Europe, intent on modest prosperity and good relations with its neighbours. But the Russians came back, Hungary was consumed by terror, and Nagy started his last pilgrimage in the Yugoslav embassy.

Memories of him there are warm. He was a calm and conscientious chairman of the executive committee. He showed no sign of the despair which Khrushchev claimed to detect in his message of 3 November to Gheorghiu-Dej.[8] He was courteous to the women, kindly and avuncular to the children among the refugees. Some of his companions believe that he still expected to come to terms with Kádár, others that his calm was that of a man who had lost all hope but was determined to play his role with dignity to the end. Clearly he was disillusioned by Moscow's betrayal of the deal he had done with Mikoyan. After the first week in the embassy he was angered also by Tito's Pula speech, recognizing that he was no longer welcome under a Yugoslav roof. But even then Nagy did not despair. He played a full part in the negotiations with the Yugoslavs, and through them with Kádár, about safe conduct.

Those who were in the embassy with Nagy recall how uncertain the prospects seemed if they trusted Kádár's word. But Géza Losonczy's widow remembers Nagy's calm assurance when she asked him if their enemies would let them go to their homes as was promised. 'Of course, Marika,' he answered. 'It's been agreed.'[9] But his nervousness and uncertainty showed. He led the little party back from the bus once, suspicions aroused. Then the Yugoslavs reassured him, and Nagy led them out to keep their appointment with treachery.

Even after the kidnapping, his companions remember that he radiated confidence, even optimism. He may have felt that he had to show a courage he did not feel. But Losonczy's widow remembers him saying on the flight to Rumania: 'They are taking us away from Hungary but they must talk to us.'[10] Micunovic records an impression that he looked anxious on arrival at Bucharest airport; but a companion remembers him almost lightheartedly answering the Rumanian who welcomed them with: 'Thank you, but we did not ask you to invite us.'[11]

In Rumania and later in prison in Budapest, Nagy's stubborn fatalism seems to have taken charge. He might have saved himself by abject recantation. He might even have been accepted into Kádár's government. But he had been twice betrayed, on 4 November and when he came out of the embassy, both by Moscow and by Kádár. He was sixty and had survived forty years of activity in a lethally vicious system. He had seen what his countrymen wanted and had discovered, tentatively in 1953 and at last in full measure during the Revolution, the satisfaction of leading a united country which he loved with Magyar passion. He was too old to spoil that by pleading with his enemies.

Hence the calm that shines through the patchy accounts of Nagy's last eighteen months. He seems to have been stubbornly sure of himself, impervious to temptation and threat alike, unaffected by the vagaries of Soviet policy towards Yugoslavia and his own fate. One of his friends believes that he may still have put his faith in friends in Moscow, but it seems unlikely. He may have hoped that his companions might be spared, as most of them were, but not himself.

He probably understood that younger men should want to save themselves: Kopácsi claims for example that Nagy showed understanding of his own compromise with the prosecution.[12] But Nagy, like his closest associates, was unbending. After Losonczy's death in prison and Szilágyi's execution, there was nothing except calm dignity at the trial, rejecting mis-statements and refusing to ask for leniency. The film of Nagy's last statement in court shows an upright, respectable figure. He spoke calmly, briefly, his personal dignity secure at the centre of a squalid farce committed to his judicial murder.

Did he die as a Communist or a Hungarian patriot? Losonczy's widow is sure that he kept his Party faith to the end. He accepted the discipline of a Bolshevik. His faith in Communism as a disciplined structure of belief had in the past shackled him in a posture of hesitation and indecisiveness. During the Revolution he threw off the shackles but remained a Communist. Her second husband, Szilárd Ujhelyi, another of Nagy's companions, qualifies this view. In 1953 he was the first man after Stalin's death to put into words the distinction between the old methods and the essential content of a Communist faith. In 1956 he went further and accepted that Communism had no historic right to rule. It had to subject itself to the test of genuine elections, which the Communists might lose.[13]

Nagy's daughter takes up Ujhelyi's point. She believes her father kept his faith in Communism. But the nation's confidence and Russian betrayal in 1956 sharpened his realization that the Communists and their doctrine were only a small part of Hungarian life. Between 1953 and 1956 he gradually came to place the interests of the country above those of any party. He remained profoundly convinced of the values of socialism. But they had to compete with other values for the nation's approval. In relationships with Moscow and its neighbours, Hungary must be independent, equal and neutral. All this came together in acceptance of a multi-party system.

Erzsébet Nagy's second husband develops the point. Despite his Calvinist birth and Marxist education, Nagy was at heart a humanist. In the Soviet Union after the First World War he was attracted to Communism as the obvious way of serving humanist ideals. But in Russia and Hungary he saw it promote these ideals by terror. Until November 1956 he had never thought of the Soviet Union as his country's enemy. Then it showed itself treacherous and implacable. All that was left was patriotism, and a belief that democracy came first in his country's service.[14]

Was Nagy all goodness, a heroic figure? We have seen that the truth is more complex than that. But there was a great goodness about him. Mrs Ujhelyi smiles like a young girl when she remembers him: 'I liked him very much. I did not know him deeply. But he was attractive, honest, decent.' Miklós Molnár was a journalist who saw Nagy at work during the revolution. He wrote of him afterwards: 'His was a character of fundamental goodness, integrity, and simplicity, with sound common sense, a love of books, and of the soil, and loyal to those close to him. When he took the helm during the storm of 1956, he was no strong and confident helmsman, yet he was a *man*.'[15]

There is agreement that Nagy went bravely to his death. Of all the defendants at the trial, only he, it is said, was quite uncowed. Even the regime's White Book reflects his intransigence; repeatedly it records that 'Imre Nagy had nothing to say'.[16] His was the courage of quiet hours in solitary confinement and of a secret trial, loyal to a hard-won conviction in rejecting approaches from those with whom he had once shared a faith.

When we come to Nagy's legacy, we return to ambiguity. For thirty years his name was scarcely mentioned in public in Hungary. Yet his memory haunted Kádár throughout. Immediately after the execution, Kádár was defensive when he tried to justify it to a group of Hungarian officials: 'Comrades, because we entered on this course on November 4, it was necessary to go to the very end.'[17] As we have seen, he was still haunted by the memory of his victim when the time came for Nagy's rehabilitation and for his own encounter with his Maker. If things had turned out otherwise, Kádár could easily have gone to the gallows with

Nagy. So could many of the members of Kádár's successive cabinets and Political Committees. It is not over-fanciful to think of Nagy as the brooding ghost at the cabinet table.

His memory certainly infected Kádár's policies. 'He who is not against us is with us' was Nagyism, putting national unity ahead of class doctrine. After the first forced recollectivization, Kádár's agricultural policy was Nagyist. So was the quiet impersonality of his style, the concern for people, the determination that the personality cult and political hysteria should not find their way back into Hungarian life. The Economic Reform was a more formal, crabbed, better-prepared New Course. Goulash Communism expressed the concern for ordinary people which Nagy had introduced into Communist practice. Cautious reassertion of the national identity built on Nagy's faith in patriotism. Kádár built a Hungary very like Nagy's ideal at the time of the New Course. He flinched from enacting the ideas in Nagy's essays. And he rejected the pluralism and the risk of losing power which Nagy embraced in his last days of liberty. In the end it was the failure to go all the way that Nagy had envisaged going which spelt the end of Kádárism.

The Communist leaders who succeeded Kádár found it difficult to agree on how to deal with pressure for Nagy's rehabilitation. Károly Grósz feared where it would lead, Imre Pozsgay saw it as a way to build up Reform Communism's credentials. In the end, on the eve of the reburial, the Communist government committed itself to an assessment, very different from what official Hungary had had to say about Nagy over the years since his execution: 'The ideals of Imre Nagy and his followers, their endeavours which had democratic, humanistic and national features, are important components of the policies of the present government . . . Imre Nagy was an outstanding statesman who recognized the need for changing the unviable policies that are alien to our traditions, and for asserting national characteristics and everlasting values . . .'[18]

*

Will Nagy's memory survive as one of his country's heroes? It should. He was the first statesman after Stalin's death to enunciate the ends and means of a humane Communism. He brought his countrymen back from a nightmare. He formulated the principles of a Communism which would not forget man. He united his country during the Revolution. He set out to give it freedom, independence and democracy. He accepted that this might sweep his own Party to the sidelines of political life. He defied the Russians and gave Hungary a legend. His influence guided Kádár's policy for thirty years. His rehabilitation set Hungary on the road to freedom and that freedom inspired the search for liberty throughout the Soviet world.

In 1957, a year before the execution, Hugh Seton Watson wrote of Nagy: 'He remains one of the few outstanding figures thrown up by the East European Communist system of the last decade. He has neither the heroic glamour of Marshal Tito nor the penetrating political vision of Milovan Djilas, and he has not been so fortunate as Wladyslaw Gomulka. But he has shown himself a brave and honest man and a true patriot, unusual qualities in a leading Communist. He will have his place in the history of his own country and of Europe.'[19]

A despatch from the British legation in Budapest four days after the executions reflects the same balance: 'As for the victims, though as Communists they were not previously granted much sympathy, they will now be honoured as Hungarians who paid with their lives for defending this country's independence against the Russians.'[20] Long afterwards, an American historian summed up: '. . . when he died . . . he did so without denying what he had done and without recanting what he had stood for. A genuine hero, he belongs on the pedestal where his compatriots have put him.'[21]

An old man in Hungary who fought in the Revolution puts Nagy's claims to immortality in grander and more emotional terms. Only very rarely, he said, could a man from a small country affect the course of history. Nagy was one such man. He did not lack honesty, but his ideological preconceptions made it hard for him to start on the path of truth. But he pursued his pilgrimage, and made two great contributions to the history of his own country and of the countries of the Communist world. In 1953 he turned Hungarian Communism away from evil, and fought a lonely fight against the criminals who wanted to turn it back. In 1956 he shook off his Communist shackles and put himself at the head of a united Hungary. Three decades later, those contributions came to fulfilment.[22]

The last word properly belongs to Miklós Vásárhelyi. He was at Nagy's side during the Revolution and went to Rumania, prison and trial with him. He is the closest of Nagy's associates still living in Hungary. It was he who established the Committee for Historical Justice to secure Nagy's rehabilitation and tell the true story of the events of 1956.

On the day of the reburial, Vásárhelyi spoke at the ceremony in Heroes' Square. He recalled Nagy's words to the nation during the Revolution and described what he had achieved. 'The weapons fell silent, the blood of brothers ceased to flow, order was restored, the process of reconciliation and democratic transformation got under way . . .'

The reputation of the Hungarian people, Vásárhelyi said, had never shone as brightly as it did in 1956. Then outside intervention destroyed the Revolution, but it could not extinguish memories of it, or of Imre Nagy. Now society was ready for reconciliation. Their search for it would show the respect that was due to Imre Nagy. But Hungarians would not forget what had happened in 1956. They were impatient, and they wanted now the freedom, legality and justice which the Revolutionaries had dreamt of.[23]

Thus Vásárhelyi linked past and present, old dreams and new promise, Nagy's work and Nagy's legacy. If the people of Hungary can complete the work which Imre Nagy started they will deserve the inheritance he left them. As for Nagy himself, to have introduced the concept of decency, honesty and humanity into the wasteland that Stalin made of half the world is an achievement by which any man might gladly be remembered. With an honoured grave in a free homeland in a free Europe thirty years afterwards he has a worthy memorial.

Bibliography

C. A. Macartney's massive study *October Fifteenth* (Edinburgh University Press, Edinburgh, 1956) provides a masterly and detailed account of events in Hungary from the late nineteenth century up to the end of the Second World War. His much slimmer *Hungary, a Short History*, (Edinburgh University Press, Edinburgh, 1962) takes the story back to the origins of Hungary, and up to the 1956 Revolution. In *Hungary and the Soviet Bloc* (Duke University Press, Durham, 1986) Charles Gati takes up the story in 1944 and carries it to the mid-eighties. Bennett Kovrig's *Communism in Hungary: from Kun to Kádár* (Hoover Institution Press, Stanford, 1979) covers the whole period from 1918 to 1979.

Gati's and Kovrig's analyses of events are reinforced by several books by émigrés, most of whom left Hungary after the Revolution. Ferenc Nagy, the smallholder prime minister who was driven out in the late forties, gives his own impressions in *The Struggle Behind the Iron Curtain* (Macmillan, New York, 1948). Paul Ignotus and George Páloczi-Horváth provide accounts of the Communist seizure of power and the terror in *Political Prisoner* (Routledge and Kegan Paul, London, 1959) and *The Undefeated* (Secker and Warburg, London, 1959) respectively. Other émigrés such as Tibor Méray in *Thirteen Days that Shook the Kremlin* (Thames and Hudson, London, 1959), Tamás Aczél and Méray in *The Revolt of the Mind* (Thames and Hudson, London, 1960) and Miklós Molnár

244

in *Budapest 1956* (George Allen and Unwin, London, 1971) concentrate on the events leading up to the Revolution and the dramatic days of the Revolution itself. Gyula Hay's *1900* (Hutchinson, London, 1974) is a more discursive autobiography which throws some interesting sidelights on the circumstances of Nagy's life. In his book *In the Name of the Working Class* (Lester & Orpen Dennys, Toronto, 1986) Sándor Kopácsi, who was tried with Nagy, deals with the Revolution and trial. But of all the émigrés Ferenc Váli provides the fullest and most scholarly account of events in *Rift and Revolt in Hungary* (Harvard University Press, Cambridge, Massachusetts, 1961). Veljko Micunovic's *Moscow Diary* (Doubleday, Garden City, New York, 1980) stands apart from all these books: his contemporary diaries give a fascinating insight into Soviet-Yugoslav relations during the Revolution and afterwards from the Yugoslav Embassy in Moscow.

All these books touch on Nagy's own contribution but none provides a full life of Nagy. His own essays, published in English as *Imre Nagy on Communism* (Thames and Hudson, London, 1957) and in French as *Un Communisme qui n'oublie pas l'Homme* (Tribune Libre, Plon, Paris, 1957), are heavy going but yield a good deal of information to close analysis. Forewords, by Hugh Seton-Watson and François Fejtö respectively, cast further light on his role. So does *Imre Nagy, Réformateur ou Revolutionnaire?* (Droz/Minard, Geneva/Paris, 1959) by Miklós Molnár and László Nagy. Finally, Milovan Djilas' *The New Class* (Thames and Hudson, London, 1957) and *The Unperfect Society* (Methuen, London, 1969), though not directly relevant to Hungary, vividly illuminate the distortions of Communist society which so exercised Nagy himself.

The United Nations *Report of the Special Committee on the Problem of Hungary* (United Nations, New York, 1957) is in a class of its own on the Revolution, as is *La Vérité sur l'Affaire Nagy* (Tribune Libre, Plon, Paris, 1958) on Nagy's execution.

For thirty years after his execution, the story of Nagy was

expunged from the official record in Hungary. But János Kádár's *Selected Speeches and Interviews* (Akademia, Budapest, 1985) has some relevance. So does János Berecz's book *1956: Counter-Revolution in Hungary: Words and Weapons* (Akademia, Budapest, 1986). And with Nagy's rehabilitation three useful books appeared in Hungary, none of them yet available in translation. They are Aron Tóbiás's *In Memoriam Nagy Imre* (Szabad Ter, Budapest, 1989), Judit Ember's *Menedékjog* (Szabad Ter, Budapest, 1989), and *A Nagy Imre Vonal* (Reform, Budapest/ Debrecen, 1989) by Ferenc Dér and Lajos Péter Kovács.

NOTES

Prologue: Obsession
1 Z. Mlynár: *Night Frost in Prague*, London, 1980; p. 157.
2 Ferenc Fehér and Agnes Heller: *Hungary 1956 Revisited*, London, 1983; p. 158.
3 Conversation with György Aczél.

Chapter 1: Reburial
1 Conversation with György Aczél.

Chapter 2: Youth
1 C.A. Macartney: *Hungary, a Short History*, Edinburgh, 1962; p. 182.
2 C.A. Macartney: *October Fifteenth*, Edinburgh, 1956; vol. I, p. 10.
3 Gyula Illyés: *People of the Puszta*, Budapest, 1967; p. 73.
4 Harold Nicolson: *Lord Carnock*, London, 1930; p. 78.
5 Quoted in E.H. Carr: *The Bolshevik Revolution*, London, 1953; vol. III, p. 71.
6 Carr, *op. cit.*; vol. III, p. 74.
7 Imre Nagy: *On Communism*, London, 1957; p. 241.
8 Macartney: *Short History, op. cit.*; p. 220.

Chapter 3: Exile
1 Conversation with Erzsébet Nagy.
2 'The Master of Hypocrisy', *Népszabadság*, Budapest, 9 May, 1957.

3 György Lukács: *Record of a Life*, London, 1983; p. 127.
4 Conversation with Erzsébet Nagy.
5 Winston Churchill: *The Grand Alliance*, London, 1950; p. 148.
6 Macartney: *October Fifteenth, op. cit.*; vol. I, pp. 489-490.

Chapter 4: Office
1 All Party Parliamentary Delegation: 'Unanimous Report on Hungary', mimeograph, London, 1946.
2 Ferenc Nagy: *The Struggle Behind the Iron Curtain*, New York, 1948; p. 160.
3 Imre Nagy: *Egy Évtized*, Budapest, 1954; p. 90.
4 George Páloczi-Horváth: *The Undefeated*, London, 1959; pp. 122-3.
5 Ferenc Nagy, *op. cit.*; p. 160.
6 *ibid.*; p. 180.
7 Conversation with Erzsébet Nagy.
8 Ferenc Váli: *Rift and Revolt in Hungary*, Cambridge, Mass., 1961; p. 35.
9 Ferenc Nagy, *op. cit.*; p. 190.
10 'Unanimous Report', *op. cit.*
11 Bennett Kovrig: *Communism in Hungary: from Kun to Kádár*, Stanford, 1979; p. 203.
12 Paul Ignotus: *Political Prisoner*, London, 1959; p. 49.

Chapter 5: Terror
1 Imre Nagy: *On Communism, op. cit.*; p. 145.
2 *ibid.*; p. 146.
3 *ibid.*; p. 146.
4 Imre Nagy: *Egy Évtized*, Budapest, 1954; p. 146.
5 *Népszabadság*, Budapest, 9 May, 1957.
6 Mária Hollán: *A Few Pages from my Life*, private publication; p. 61.
7 *ibid.*; p. 41.
8 *Irodalmi Ujság*, Budapest, 2 November, 1956, translation

Hungarian Literary Gazette Anthology, London, 23 October, 1957.
9 Imre Nagy: *On Communism, op. cit.*; p. 144.

Chapter 6: Power
1 *Ibid.*; p. 107.
2 Tibor Méray: *Thirteen Days that Shook the Kremlin*, London, 1959; p. 7.
3 Imre Nagy: *On Communism, op. cit.*; p. 153.
4 *Szabada Nép*, Budapest, 5 July, 1953.
5 Hollán, *op. cit.*; p. 49.
6 Páloczi-Horváth, *op. cit.*; p. 221.
7 Váli, *op. cit.*; p. 33.
8 *Szabad Nép*, Budapest, 12 July, 1953.
9 Imre Nagy: *On Communism, op. cit.*; p. 271.
10 *ibid.*; p. 271.
11 *ibid.*; p. 143.
12 Imre Nagy, speech in Parliament, 28 January, 1954.
13 Imre Nagy: *On Communism; op. cit.*; p. 282.
14 *ibid.*, p. 296.
15 *ibid.*, p. 296.
16 *ibid.*, p. 179.
17 Vali, *op. cit.*; p. 137.
18 Imre Nagy: *On Communism, op. cit.*; p. xxxiii.
19 Tamás Aczél and Tibor Méray: *The Revolt of the Mind*, London, 1960; p. 294.
20 *ibid.*; p. 316.
21 *ibid.*; p. 319

Chapter 7: Opposition
1 Méray, *op. cit.*; pp. 22-8.
2 Conversation with Áron Tobiás.
3 Charles Gati: *Hungary and the Soviet Bloc*, Durham, USA, 1986; p. 137.
4 Imre Nagy: *On Communism, op. cit.*; p. xxix.
5 *ibid.*; p. 44.
6 *ibid.*; pp. 50–1.
7 *ibid.*; p. 56.

8 *ibid.*; p. 62.
9 *ibid.*; p. 49.
10 Páloczi-Horváth, *op. cit.*; p. 252.

Chapter 8: Cross-Currents
1 Aczél and Méray, *op. cit.*; p. x.
2 C.L.S. Cope to E.F. Given, 27 January, 1956.
3 Aczél and Méray, *op. cit.*; p. 324.
4 Veljko Micunovic, *Moscow Diary*, New York, 1980;
    p. 44.
5 *ibid.*; p. 88.
6 János Berecz: *Counter-Revolution, Words & Weapons*,
    Budapest, 1986; p. 88.
7 Conversation with András B. Hegedüs.
8 Sándor Kopácsi: *In the Name of the Working Class*,
    Toronto, 1986; p. 92.
9 Micunovic, *op. cit.*; pp. 76-7.

Chapter 9: Revolution
1 Aczél and Méray, *op. cit.*; p. 402.
2 *ibid.*; p. 438.
3 *ibid.*; p. 268.
4 L.A.C. Fry to Secretary of State for Foreign Affairs, 18
    October, 1956.
5 Conversation with Áron Tobiás.
6 'Report of the Special Committee on the Problem of
    Hungary', New York, 1957; para. 258.
7 Conversation with Sándor Fekete.
8 Published in *Pravda*, Moscow, 31 October, 1956.
9 Kopácsi, *op. cit.*; p. 152.
10 Conversation with Mihály Simai.

Chapter 10: War
1 Micunovic, *op. cit.*; p. 32.
2 N.S. Khrushchev: *Khrushchev Remembers*, Boston,
    1970; p. 418.
3 Micunovic, *op. cit.*; p. 132.
4 *ibid.*; p. 133.

5 Khrushchev, *op. cit.*; p. 418.

6 William Shawcross: *Crime and Compromise*, London, 1974; p. 85.

7 Micunovic, *op. cit.*; p. 152.

8 'Report of the Special Committee', *op. cit.*; para. 287.

9 *ibid.*; para. 291.

10 *ibid.*; para. 291.

Chapter 11: Murder

1 Micunovic, *op. cit.*; pp. 144, 146.

2 *ibid.*; pp. 148–52.

3 Conversation with Miklós Vásárhelyi.

4 Conversation with Áron Tobiás.

5 The text is printed in Micunovic, *op. cit.*; pp. 447-8.

6 Conversation with Szilárd Ujhelyi.

7 Conversation with Szilárd Ujhelyi.

8 Micunovic, *op. cit.*; p. 177.

9 *ibid.*; p. 223.

10 Kopácsi, *op. cit.*; p. 235.

11 Conversation with János Kádár.

12 Kopácsi, *op. cit.*; p. 248.

13 *ibid.*; pp. 258-60.

14 *ibid.*; p. 272.

15 Budapest Radio on 15 June, 1989, summarized in BBC monitoring report of 22 June, 1989.

16 Conversation with György Aczél.

Chapter 12: Contribution

1 Imre Nagy, *op. cit.*; p. 56.

2 Páloczi-Horváth, *op. cit*; p. 252.

3 Gati, *op. cit.*; pp. 127-8.

4 *Guardian*, Manchester, 21 October, 1963.

Chapter 13: Repression

1 Kopácsi, *op. cit.*; p. 291.

2 János Kádár: *Selected Speeches and Interviews*, Budapest, 1985; p. 423.

Chapter 16: Fulfilment
1 Quoted in the *Independent*, London, 9 October, 1989.

Epilogue: Assessment
1 György Lukács, *op. cit.*; p. 127.
2 Conversation with Áron Tobiás.
3 Ferenc Nagy, *op. cit.*; p. 180.
4 Conversation with Erzsébet Nagy.
5 Conversation with Péter Földes.
6 Conversation with Mihály Simai.
7 Kádár, *op. cit.*; p. 227.
8 Micunovic, *op. cit.*; p. 152.
9 Conversation with Mária Ujhelyi.
10 Conversation with Mária Ujhelyi.
11 Conversation with Mária Ujhelyi.
12 Kopácsi, *op. cit.*; p. 273.
13 Conversation with Szilárd and Mária Ujhelyi.
14 Conversation with Erzsébet Nagy and her husband.
15 Miklós Molnár: *Budapest, 1956*, London, 1971; p. 27.
16 *The Criminal Conspiracy of Imre Nagy and his Accomplices*, Budapest, 1958.
17 Shawcross, *op. cit.*; p. 247.
18 Quoted in the *Independent*, London, 15 June, 1989.
19 Foreword, Imre Nagy: *On Communism*, p. xxviii.
20 J.E.D. Street to Secretary of State for Foreign Affairs, 20 June, 1958.
21 Gati, *op. cit.*; p. 128.
22 Conversation with Péter Földes.
23 Budapest Radio, 16 June, 1989, summarized in BBC monitoring report of 20 June, 1989.

INDEX